FROM COLONIALISM TO COMMUNISM

HOANG VAN CHI

with an introduction by
P. J. HONEY

From Colonialism
to Communism

A Case History
of North Vietnam

FREDERICK A. PRAEGER, *Publisher*
NEW YORK · LONDON

FREDERICK A. PRAEGER, *Publisher*
64 University Place, New York 3, NY, USA;
77-79 Charlotte Street, London, W1, England

Published in the United States of America in 1964
by Frederick A. Praeger, Inc., Publisher

Published in the United Kingdom in 1964 by
The Pall Mall Press, Ltd., London and Dunmow

© Hoang Van Chi, 1964

Library of Congress Catalog Card Number: 63-10721

This book is Number 136 in the series of
*Praeger Publications in Russian History and
World Communism*

Printed in the United Kingdom

CONTENTS

	Introduction by P. J. Honey	vii
	Author's Foreword	xi
	Maps	xiii
PART I	GRANDEUR AND SERVITUDE OF A SMALL AND WEAK NATION	
	One Vietnam in the Past	3
	Two Vietnam in Modern History	9
PART II	INDEPENDENCE FOR THE NTH TIME	
	Three Ho Chi Minh, the National Hero	29
	Four Emergence of Communism	41
	Five The Final Triumph	57
PART III	FIRST STEPS TOWARDS A TOTALITARIAN REGIME	
	Six Economic Levelling	75
	Seven The First Wave of Terror	90
	Eight The List of Traitors	101
PART IV	THOUGHT REFORM	
	Nine Ideological Operations	109
	Ten Control-discussion	118
	Eleven Correctional Training	124
	Twelve The Five Lessons	139
PART V	LAND REFORM	
	Thirteen General Outlines of the Land Reform	163
	Fourteen The Land Rent Reduction Campaign	169
	Fifteen The Land Reform Campaign Proper	192
	Sixteen Rectification of Errors	209
	Seventeen Revolts and Repressions	221
	Eighteen Resumption of Collectivisation	240
	Recommended Further Reading	246
	Index	247

Introduction

Before the Second World War, little was known in the world about Vietnam or the Vietnamese people. The country itself was an integral part of French Indochina and was always referred to as Annam. Few in the West, with the exception of the French, were familiar with its name, and fewer still had ever visited it. The outside world, therefore, evinced some surprise when it learned from the pages of the press in 1945 that the Democratic Republic of Vietnam had declared its independence of France. But so much else was happening as a result of the ending of the war against Japan that Vietnam was quickly forgotten. With the outbreak of war between Vietnam and France at the end of 1946, events there again caught the notice of the press, but it was generally assumed that untrained and badly armed Vietnamese troops stood little chance of survival against the French Expeditionary Corps and that the uprising would soon be quelled.

In the event, France proved unable to suppress the Viet Minh, as the Vietnamese resistance movement was then known, and the war in Indochina increased in scale dramatically. To many in the West, and in particular to those Americans who interested themselves in Asian affairs, it appeared to be an independence war fought by Vietnamese nationalists seeking to throw off the yoke of foreign domination and to establish their country's independence. American sympathies, in so far as they existed at all, tended to be on the side of the Viet Minh, but for some time the United

States was not directly involved. Only as the 'cold war' developed and the West became aware of the expansionist aims of communism did the United States pay serious heed to French claims that the Viet Minh was a communist, not a nationalist, movement, and the object of the fighting was the imposition of communism on this part of Asia. Subsequently, American aid was channelled, in ever greater quantities, to French forces in Indochina and to the newly-formed Vietnamese National Army fighting beside them. But, in spite of this, the Viet Minh emerged victorious. Hostilities came to an end with the battle of Dien Bien Phu and peace was restored by the international conference meeting at Geneva in the spring of 1954.

Under the terms of the Geneva armistice agreements, Vietnam was divided into two halves at the 17th parallel, the North being placed under Vietnamese communist control and the South under that of the nationalists. For the first time, a communist state came into being in South-east Asia, and the importance of this fact cannot be overestimated. Moreover, North Vietnam is the traditional gateway from the Far East into South-east Asia: it was through this territory that the Japanese had come as recently as 1941 to accomplish their lightning seizure of that area. There can be little doubt that the Democratic Republic of Vietnam was regarded by the communist bloc as the point from which communist domination would spread out over the region. The United States immediately came to the help of the neighbouring countries with military, economic and technical aid, but already American troops have been obliged to withdraw from Laos and the struggle is continuing in South Vietnam. This could well be only the beginning of the communist push.

To combat such aggression effectively, it is first essential to understand the methods and the thinking of the Vietnamese communists. Only when this has been done can their next moves be anticipated and satisfactory counter-measures be prepared in advance. However, the task is not as formidable as it might at first appear, because the Vietnamese have never evolved any original military or political techniques of their own but have preferred to copy them from others, and frequently repeat tactics which have once proved successful. It would appear that this lack of orginality is a Vietnamese national characteristic, and not a newly-developed one either.

Speaking about the Vietnamese early in the nineteenth century, the Frenchman Chaigneau, who had spent the greater part of his adult life serving the Emperor Gia-Long and held the post of a senior mandarin at the court of Hué, said: 'Do not expect invention from them, but be assured that their talent for imitation will never be at fault.' A century and a half later, in 1962 to be precise, the prominent Vietnamese intellectual, Dr Nguyen Ngoc Bich, wrote of the Vietnamese communists: 'Every happening and every action have to be made the objects of a critical reflection from which a lesson must be drawn. The purpose of this reflection is to avoid the repetition of past mistakes rather than to provide a sure guide for future actions. However, the practice not infrequently results in a certain lack of imagination in the planning of future action, for its devotees are more readily inclined to repeat past actions whenever these are considered to have been successful instead of confronting a new situation with completely open mind and devising a set of plans for that specific situation. This is why the Vietnamese communists have so frequently been reproached, albeit sometimes unjustly, for being naturally more inclined to imitate or to repeat than to create something new for themselves.'

The full details of the steps by which the communists gained control of North Vietnam, how these steps were planned, and the discussions which took place between the communist leaders are, of course, known only to these leaders themselves. Nevertheless, it was possible for observant and intelligent members of the resistance movement to note what was happening around them, to analyse orders, directives, and exhortations emanating from the leadership, and thus to assess the progress of events with a high degree of accuracy.

The author of this book, Mr Hoang Van Chi, joined the Vietnamese resistance movement at the outset because he wished to fight for his country's independence. He was not a communist but, even when he became aware that the communists had secured full control of the movement, he continued to support it. For the non-communist nationalists to have acted differently would have risked splitting the whole movement, thereby permitting France to maintain her domination over Vietnam. After the defeat of France, however, he ranged himself on the side of the Vietnamese nationalists in their struggle against communism.

During his years in the resistance movement he had ample opportunity to study the techniques of the communists and to find out how their minds work. He witnessed the imposition by the Chinese of Mao Tse-tung's teachings and was present when the agrarian reform was carried out. He has attended the notorious people's courts in North Vietnam which were responsible for the deaths of so many innocent victims.

Much of what is written in this book was observed at first hand by Mr Hoang. The remainder is based upon the very considerable research carried out by him. The whole book describes how the Vietnamese communists first seized control of the patriotic anti-colonial movement and then imposed a communist régime upon North Vietnam. This alone makes the book an important study of modern communist techniques in action, but since these same techniques, with only minor variations, are being employed today in South Vietnam and are likely to be attempted in other countries of South-east Asia in the future, Mr Hoang's work will become a textbook for all who have to deal with communist attempts to dominate Asia.

Mr Hoang Van Chi has, by his past writings, contributed greatly to the outside world's knowledge of the Vietnamese communists, and his recently published article 'Collectivisation and Rice Production' (China Quarterly, No. 2, 1962) has explained the reasons for the failure of communist agriculture, not only in Vietnam, but in China and North Korea too. This present book is his most ambitious undertaking to date, and it is my opinion that it will become one of the standard works on Asian communism.

P. J. Honey

London

Author's Foreword

This book is devoted to the study of the last phase of the Vietnamese revolution, and pays particular attention to a technique which has come to be known by the name of 'Land Reform'; this was the means used by the Vietnamese communist leaders to transform an anti-colonialist struggle into one directed towards the establishment of a communist régime. It is an elaborate process which exploits mass psychology to the full and must be accounted the greatest contribution of Mao Tse-tung to Marxism-Leninism, at least in the field of practical application. In the opinion of the author it is probably the most important innovation of our epoch.

Deriving directly from Mao's major theoretical contribution—the employment of the peasantry as the main force for a communist revolution—this process was first applied, albeit in a somewhat crude and undeveloped form, in Hunan during the Peasants' Movement of 1926. The collapse of this movement and the subsequent retreat of the Chinese communists to Yenan for more than a decade provided Mao with the opportunity to develop his political thinking and to perfect his new technique. This enabled him in 1949, when he assumed power in China, to eliminate all potential resistance to his régime, and to provide it with a solidity which was capable of withstanding the shock of 'great leaps' either forwards or backwards.

The technique was specifically devised for China—being adapted more or less to Chinese social conditions and mentality—

and was carried out throughout China immediately following the founding of the People's Republic. A few years later the process was implemented in Vietnam under the supervision of a group of Chinese agents. Living in a village deep inside the communist controlled zone, and participating in the resistance movement, I had ample opportunity to observe the implementation of Mao's process in the Vietnamese villages: a process which filled me with both wonder and fear.

In the following pages I have attempted a description of what I have seen—and, in some instances, participated in—in the hope of making a modest contribution towards the advancement of social science, and, at the same time, of providing information not hitherto available to foreign authors writing about Vietnam or Asian communism.

A single book cannot cover the whole ground. My intention has been to provide an objective survey of the Vietnamese problem in a form which indicates the principal factors in the problem to the general reader. For those who wish to make a further investigation of the subject, I provide a list of writings in this field.

I must add that it has not been my intention to oppose or vindicate any of the existing ideologies or political systems. I consider all these to be equally outdated. My hope is simply that accurate information about Vietnam's past and recent experiences will contribute to the formulation of an entirely new philosophy which will be in better agreement with modern discoveries in science and technology.

I am deeply indebted to the Congress for Cultural Freedom for a generous grant which permitted me to spend a year in research and writing. My special thanks are due to J. P. Narayan whose kind guidance was most helpful, to P. J. Honey who introduces me to the reader, and to Mrs Honey who kindly revised the manuscript. It owes much to her keen sense of style and proportion. Finally, I thank all my Vietnamese friends who provided me with invaluable information.

Hoang Van Chi

Paris

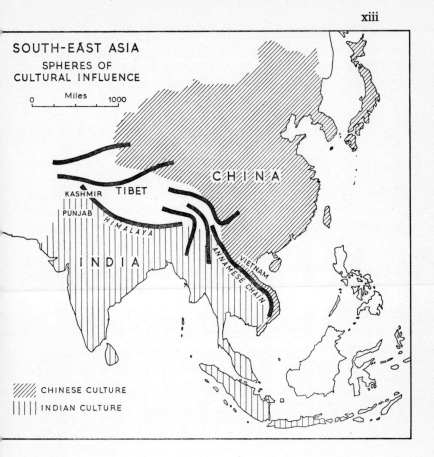

SOUTH-EAST ASIA
SPHERES OF
CULTURAL INFLUENCE

0   Miles   1000

CHINA

KASHMIR   TIBET
PUNJAB
HIMALAYA
INDIA
ANNAMESE CHAIN
VIETNAM

///// CHINESE CULTURE
||||| INDIAN CULTURE

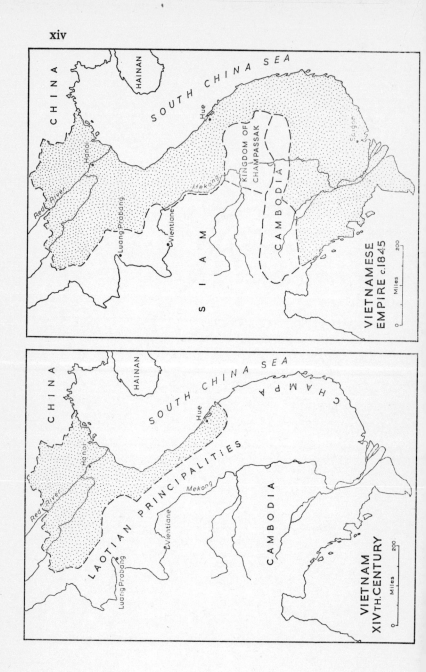

VIETNAMESE EMPIRE c.1845

VIETNAM XIVTH CENTURY

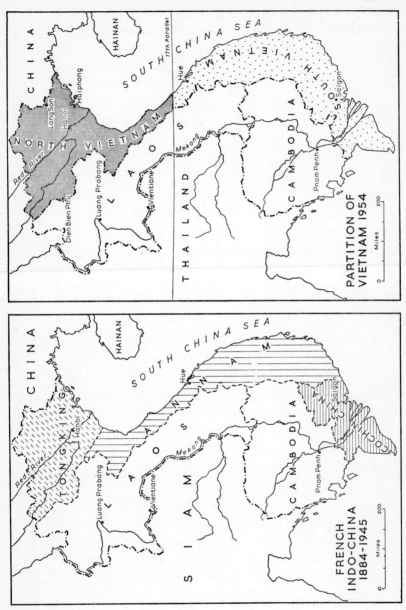

PARTITION OF VIETNAM 1954

FRENCH INDO-CHINA 1884–1945

PART I

GRANDEUR AND SERVITUDE OF
A SMALL AND WEAK NATION

'The very existence of Vietnam as a
separate country, and the survival of the
Vietnamese as a distinct people, must be
regarded as a miracle, for which scores of
historians have so far tried vainly to find
a satisfactory explanation.'

Joseph Buttinger (*The Smaller Dragon*)

ONE

Vietnam in the Past

Vietnam is in Asia, and her destiny and the role she has played throughout history are largely determined by her geographical position on the Asian continent.

In contrast to Asia, the continent of Europe constitutes a single geographical unity. Its natural barriers are not so great as to prevent constant interchanges between races and cultures. The Asian continent, however, is divided by the Himalayan range and its eastward extension, the Annamese Chain, into two separate geocultural unities, the one subject to the influences of Chinese civilisation, and the other to Indian cultural influences.

This geographical division of the continent has brought with it advantages as well as disadvantages. The Himalayan range, while not preventing the peaceful spread of certain religious and philosophical concepts from the south to the north, or the slow migration of a few tribes from north to south, has effectively impeded any major military invasion from either region of the other region. Thus India and the other countries in southern Asia were enabled to conserve their own form of civilisation free from any admixture of Han culture, and to develop their social and political institutions undisturbed by the intermittent expansionist movements of the Celestial Empire. Even today, this mountain barrier has a most important function. Should an agreement eventually be reached between India and China on a frontier which follows, more or less, the MacMahon Line, and should the United States succeed in defending South Vietnam and in preserving at least an impartial neutrality for Laos, then the whole range, running from Kashmir in the west to Vietnam in the east, will demarcate a wide frontier between communist and non-communist areas of mainland Asia. The fact that the Han, Mongol and Manchu cavalries did not cross this formidable range, because they could not, has contributed to encouraging some political leaders in southern and south-east Asia to believe in the myth of a *traditional friendship* with China. Nevertheless, it may well be that, when they prepared their plans for peaceful coexistence and neutralism, they took into account the protection they might expect from the Himalayan shield.

However, as recent events have shown, this unbroken chain of mountains can no longer be regarded as an impregnable barrier against communist infiltration or even against a communist military attack. Nehru is at present faced with a most arduous task in defending India's northern frontier, while at the opposite end of the same mountain-barrier, the United States is hard put to it to save Laos, Cambodia and Thailand from an impending communist annexation. This latter threat is far greater than that confronting India and Burma, chiefly because the Annamese Chain (*Truong Son* in Vietnamese) separating Laos and North Vietnam is by no means as impregnable as the Himalayan range. Moreover, Hanoi in North Vietnam is easily accessible by railway from Peking, while the journey to Lhasa in Tibet is long and difficult. Supplies and men may therefore be transported with greater speed and convenience to Vietnam. The Chinese have always regarded Vietnam as their natural gateway for eventual expansion into south-east Asia.

The map of China and Vietnam (see page xiii) suggests the image of a huge funnel whose cone is the mainland of China, with Vietnam as the long narrow spout. This analogy has historical relevance, for throughout history the Chinese have repeatedly attempted to pour through the Vietnamese corridor, the only land-route to the rice-growing plains of south-east Asia. The Vietnamese have always managed to drive them back. The successive incursions of China's expansionist dynasties—the Han, the Mongol deploying Khublai Khan's seemingly irresistible hordes, the

Ming and the Manchu—were halted by Vietnamese arms. In so doing, the Vietnamese have not only secured their own independence, but have also saved the whole of south-east Asia from a gradual but unrelenting process of *Han-hwa*, or 'Hanisation'.

According to Chinese chronicles, the whole territory south of the river Yangtze was inhabited originally by the 'Hundred Yuëh', tribes which had been entirely absorbed by the Hans after their conquest in the third century BC. Some ethnologists believe that a large proportion of these people were probably of Indonesian origin. The Vietnamese, who originally belonged to the same ethnic family, still believe that their ancestors formed one of these 'Hundred Yuëh' and miraculously escaped the fate which overtook all the rest.

In this connection, the following anecdote is revealing. During a banquet for Sun Yat-sen in Tokyo in 1911, his host, the Japanese statesman Ki Tsuyoshi Inukai, asked him unexpectedly, seeking to trap him: 'What do you think of the Vietnamese?' Caught off guard, Sun replied: 'The Vietnamese are slaves by nature. They have been ruled by us and now they are ruled by the French. They can't have a very brilliant future.' Inukai said: 'I don't agree with you on that point. Though not independent at present, they are the only one of the "Hundred Yuëh" successfully to resist the process of *Han-hwa*. Such a people must sooner or later gain their political independence.' Sun, it is said, blushed but made no reply, realising that Inukai knew that he was a Cantonese, one of a people regarded as inferior by the Vietnamese because they became so completely Sinified that they lost all their Yuëh cultural identity, considering themselves wholly Chinese. The source of this anecdote is Le Du, a Vietnamese refugee in Tokyo who was a protégé of Inukai's.

For over two thousand years, the Vietnamese have played a rôle similar to that of the Spartans at Thermopylae. The service rendered by Vietnam to her neighbours in South-east Asia for so many centuries has not received sufficient recognition from modern historians. It should be noted in this connection that the Chinese who now throng Singapore, Malaya and Indonesia came there only quite recently and by sea. Their migration to these former European colonies was encouraged by colonial powers who preferred their cheap and skilled labour to that of the more indolent local peoples.

On the other hand, Chinese culture percolated through the filter which impeded their military advance and found its way through the long tube of Vietnam. The Vietnamese people eagerly absorbed this culture and forged from it a weapon to serve their own expansion southward at the expense of the Champa kingdom, which was gradually conquered and erased from history in 1697 (see maps on page xiv). Having reached the southern extremity of the peninsula in 1780, the Vietnamese were beginning to skirt the mountain chain and enter Cambodia when they were halted by the arrival of the French in 1858. The Vietnamese, on occasion the victims of Chinese imperialism, yielded to no other country in their own imperialist aspirations, and the Cambodians have good reason to feel grateful to the French for having saved them from a process of Vietnamisation, no less inexorable than that of Sinification.

In regard to Chinese cultural influence, two further aspects of the problem must be looked at objectively. These concern the attitude of the Vietnamese élite towards China and Chinese culture.

In the first place, while the Vietnamese in general regard the Chinese as their traditional enemy (fifteen Chinese invasions in two thousand years, and a thousand years of Chinese direct rule), there have always been Vietnamese kings, rebels or revolutionaries who, when faced with internal trouble or foreign invasion, have sought military help from China. On all such occasions, the Chinese came with a huge army and simply occupied the country, refusing to leave until driven out by a subsequent revolt. Ho Chi Minh, who recently sought help from Mao, defended his action by saying: 'The Chinese and Vietnamese people have always been friendly; it was the Chinese feudalists who were the enemies of both.' We may accept this, but let us note that the majority of Vietnamese intellectuals have been somewhat reluctant to do so, regarding it as a 'sophistry'.

Secondly, the Vietnamese intelligentsia conceived an exaggerated respect for Chinese culture. For successive centuries during the period of national independence, they regarded every line and every word of Chinese texts as sacrosanct, absorbing them all indiscriminately. The veneration for Chinese culture became so excessive that the Chinese ideograms were commonly referred to as *Chu ta*, 'our characters', while the Vietnamese language itself was referred to as 'the southern dialect' *(tieng nom)*. This slavish allegiance to Chinese culture tended to keep Vietnam, even when politically independent, a cultural satellite of China. As such, Vietnam would inevitably have followed her northern neighbour into an intellectual stagnation. In this connection, it is worth noting that Confucianism and Confucianist studies were maintained longer in Vietnam (until 1917) than in China, where they were suspended officially in 1905. Significantly, the communists in North Vietnam, inspired by the current Chinese example, have acted more ruthlessly to Confucianists than to Christians and Buddhists.

It is instructive to compare Vietnam with Japan. Before either had made any contact with the West, both were followers of Chinese culture and both suffered from the same cultural subservience. There was, however, a great difference in their respective attitudes to China and its culture, and this must be made clear. While Vietnamese scholars had always regarded Chinese culture as their own, the Japanese, being insular, regarded the Chinese as aliens and their philosophical ideas as foreign imports. For this reason, the Japanese were able to be eclectic to some extent, and to accept and absorb, in a way the Vietnamese could not, new ideas originating in China but banished from the official program as heretical. Among these was the doctrine of *Leang-tche* or 'intuitive knowledge', developed by Wang Yang-ming (1472-1528), which is now interpreted as an effort to revise the teachings of Confucius, using the criterion of pragmatism.

This new doctrine, which took root in Japan about the turn of the seventeenth century, contributed notably to keep the Japanese mind open enough to accept, with less reluctance than the Chinese and the Vietnamese, the superiority of Western techniques. Japanese rulers were thus constrained to revise their policy and to open their island to Western contacts (1853-54), to achieve their Meiji Revolution (1876) and in due course to modernise their country.

It is worth mentioning that, at approximately the same time, efforts to propagate the same philosophy completely failed in

Vietnam. The attempt was made by a certain Chi Chi-yu, a disciple of Wang Yang-ming, who sought asylum in southern Vietnam in 1646 following the conquest of China by the Manchus.
Chi was almost immediately recognised as a distinguished scholar
and Lord Hien, the ruler of independent southern Vietnam at this
time, frequently invited him to his palace for literary disserta-
tions. The Chinese philosopher enjoyed splendid opportunities for
contacting the Vietnamese élite and was eager to convert its members to his doctrine. However, Lord Hien's lack of education impeded his understanding of Chi's philosophical subtleties, while
the entourage at the court sought his advice only about such
childish matters as palmistry and astrology. Much discouraged
after a ten-year stay, he decided finally to leave Vietnam, and
accepted the invitation of a Japanese merchant whom he met there
to visit Japan, where he settled and greatly contributed to the
propagation of the *Leang-tche* doctrine.

After a long subservience to Chinese culture, Vietnamese
scholars could not conceive of any civilisation other than that of
the Celestial Empire. They deliberately shut their eyes to the outside world and to the immense progress being made by Western
people in science and technology. While the Japanese were
speedily modernising their country, in Vietnam, Emperor Tu Duc
and his mandarins were still busy composing verses in Chinese and
still stubbornly rejecting the eight successive proposals for reforms
submitted to them between 1853 and 1871 by Nguyen Truong
To, the first Vietnamese scholar to travel in Europe. Meanwhile
the French occupied Tourane (1858), Cochin China (1861) and
Hanoi (1873), completing their conquest in 1884.

In reviewing Vietnam's history, one is forced to conclude that
the Han culture, although beneficial to the Vietnamese in the
beginning, eventually became, with the *Chu Hi* school of Confucianism, a formula which conditioned every brain to the same
conventional mould, deterring all independent thought and all
spirit of innovation. It must be seen as the main cause of the
national disaster at the end of the last century. The submission of
the Vietnamese to Western colonialism was in great measure the
consequence of their long enslavement to China's fossilised culture.

TWO

Vietnam in modern history

THE FRENCH CONQUEST

France's first direct intervention in Vietnamese affairs was in 1787 when a treaty was signed between the French and a dethroned Vietnamese prince whereby the latter was promised military help in return for some territorial concessions. But this promise was not fulfilled owing to the Revolution in France. From that time until 1847, no French government was willing to undertake the conquest of the country, an operation which was at that time thought to be too hazardous. It may be said that French interest in Vietnam was confined to individual groups, such as chauvinist officers who might well be classed by the French today as 'activists', or Catholic missionaries whose ambition was to extend Christendom, by force of arms if necessary.

Thus the French conquest of Vietnam was carried out with much hesitancy during various periods of political and economic stability in France and subject to interruption during periods of internal revolution and external wars. It was only after 1880 that France, spurred on by national prestige and her rivalry with other European powers, adopted a systematic colonial policy and determined on the complete occupation of Vietnam.

The ultimate objective of the French at that time was not simply the conquest of Vietnam. This merely served to strengthen the French position in the Far East so that France could be assured of an eventual share of an even greater prey, China. They began their conquest by occupying Cochin China in 1859, with the idea of reaching the Chinese mainland by way of the Mekong (see Map No. 3, page xv). However, they very soon realised that this river, which has its source in Tibet and flows through the rich province of Yunnan, was totally unsuitable for navigation over most of its course. Making a second effort, the French occupied Tongking in 1882, hoping this time to get into China by way of the Red River. Later, in 1884, they conquered Annam, linking Cochin China with Tongking, and also Cambodia and Laos which they claimed as Vietnamese possessions.

The Chinese had tried to force their way down into Vietnam; the French colonial forces attempted to reverse the process by moving upward through the narrow tube into the cone of the funnel. But the Vietnamese, though unable to stop the French advance, resorted to continual revolts and guerrilla warfare. Thus French progress was delayed by the need for repeated campaigns of pacification until it was too late to go any further. China awoke from its long slumber after the Revolution of 1911, and Japan, finding itself a world power, looked upon the whole of south-east Asia as its own 'sphere of co-prosperity'. In 1940 the Japanese army occupied Indochina. For an appreciable period of time they allowed the French administration to function. It was not until the March of 1945 that the Japanese finally brought French rule to an end.

THE FRENCH UNION OF INDOCHINA

Prior to 1884, Vietnam had enjoyed diplomatic relations with most of the big powers—China, Japan, Britain, France, Spain and the United States—but after the French conquest, the name of Vietnam was practically forgotten by the rest of the world. This was because the French deliberately partitioned the territory into three separate regions giving each an arbitrarily chosen name and a different administrative status. These new regions were called: Annam, Tongking (in French spelling Tonkin) and Cochin China. Vietnam had been divided into two halves during the Secession period (1628-1788), and subsequently into three parts during the short reign of the Tay Son brothers (1788-1802). The country had been reunited by Emperor Gia Long in 1802, *i.e.* half a century before the French conquest. Despite the fact that Annam, Tongking and Cochin China are arbitrary names, we must use them in this book because they are universally known, and because the terms North and South Vietnam are now subject to confusion due to the division of the country in 1954 whereby the communist-dominated part is known as North Vietnam and the southern part as South Vietnam.

Annam (derived from 'An-Nam', meaning 'Pacified South') was the name given to the whole country by the Chinese, but the French employed it to designate only the central part which became an *indirect* protectorate. The emperor, the royal court and the hierarchy of mandarins were allowed to continue, but complete overall authority was vested in a French *résident supérieur*.

Tongking (meaning 'the Eastern Capital') is the former name of Hanoi. The French gave this name to the northern part of Vietnam, which became a *direct* protectorate. Local mandarins were recruited by and responsible to a French *résident supérieur* who, paradoxical as it might seem, assumed the status and function of a viceroy, or representative of the Vietnamese emperor. From all the evidence, this subordination to the emperor was purely theoretical and served merely as a pretext to provide the *résident supérieur* with full authority over the country under his administration.

The name *Cochin China* is a corruption of 'Ke Chiem' (the capital in Quang Nam province of the Nguyen overlordship in the seventeenth century) which foreign traders pronounced *Cochin*, adding the word *China* to distinguish it from the Indian port of Cochin. This name was used by the colonial administration to designate the southern part of Vietnam, which became a French possession completely cut off from the so-called authority of the Vietnamese emperors.

This partitioning by the French meant that the Vietnamese acquired different 'nationalities' and lived under different administrations, depending on which part of the country they had been born in. The people in Cochin China were *French subjects* and, as such, enjoyed a relatively more liberal régime than the Tongkingese or the Annamese, who were *French protégés*. The difference was greatest in the matter of legal jurisdiction. The inhabitants of Cochin China lived under a French system of jurisdiction, while their compatriots in Tongking and Annam were permanently placed under the 'Annamite' system, one which was based on a medieval judicial code of extreme severity. Needless to say, this Imperial Code and the mandarinic hierarchy were employed in such a way as instruments of repression that direct responsibility did not fall on the Colonial administration. The royal court in Hué and the mandarins simply served as a screen behind which the French ruled with complete authority, through a French administrateur appointed in each province.

These three Vietnamese 'states' (they were not properly states, but regions of colonial administration in which certain key towns had a semi-independent municipal status), together with the two neighbouring protectorates of Laos and Cambodia, formed the so-called French Union of Indochina, under the centralised authority of a French governor-general. The French realised that, despite some ethnic and cultural differences, Vietnam, Laos and Cambodia formed a geographical strategic unit. The Annamese Chain of mountains and the Mekong extend through the whole peninsula from north to south, and can be compared to the backbone and the main artery of the human body.

United, the three countries became complementary to each other, chiefly in their economic relations, and developed a well balanced co-operation under French supervision.

It may be noted, in passing, that, due allowance made for all their bad effects, imperialist conquests often brought positive and beneficial results; they brought together small and heterogeneous states and tribes to form larger, more viable groupings, and in some cases formed whole nations. Soviet Russia, now the largest country in the world, was born out of the Tsars' empire, and Mao Tse-tung, in conquering Tibet and laying claim to Formosa, considers himself to be the rightful heir of previous imperialist dynasties in China. Certainly, a number of nations now members of UNO owe their very existence as unified states to Western colonial powers.

Unfortunately, French Indochina has not been so lucky. As soon as the French authority collapsed, the three members of the Union were quickly separated. This regrettable situation arose because the French colonial administration, while creating a union for the sake of administrative and military convenience, kept its five colonial dependencies in Indochina politically apart and fostered a feeling of hatred between the Vietnamese, the Cambodians and the Laotians, and even between the northern and southern Vietnamese.

Perhaps the French were not entirely to blame for this. It was, of course, in their own immediate interests as rulers to follow the principle of 'divide and rule', but, as 'protectors', they were also under a certain obligation to defend underpopulated Cambodia and Laos against a peaceful but relentless penetration by the Vietnamese. Accordingly, emigration from Tongking and Annam into Laos and Cambodia, and even into Cochin China, was severely restricted by the French. Indeed, before the Second World War, the idea was seriously considered of sending Vietnam's excess population to the French Cameroons. Dr Tran Van Lai led a mission to the Cameroons in 1938 to study the possibility of settling people from Tongking province in that colony. But during his visit he caught yellow fever and the project was abandoned.

History has proved, and recent events in Laos have shown, that the Vietnamese are no less imperialist than the French. For instance, that part of Laotian territory at present controlled by the Pathet Lao corresponds roughly to the area 'liberated' in 1828 by Vietnamese forces from Siamese occupation. The Siamese in 1827 invaded Laos, but were forced to abandon their conquest under diplomatic and military pressure from Vietnam. As a result, four Laotian provinces (Tranninh, Samneua, Cammon and Savannakhet) were annexed to Vietnam. It is these four provinces which now correspond roughly to the area under the control of the Pathet Lao.

This is one example of the ever-present predisposition of Indochina to fly apart into separate units. This tendency is responsible for the break-up of the large confederation which was perhaps the proudest achievement of French colonialism in the Far East. Today a further complicating factor has been added by the establishment of a communist régime in North Vietnam which is promoting communist infiltration into Laos. It is thus doubly difficult for the states comprising the peninsula to survive as free and independent countries.

history books used by Vietnamese children, the chapters dealing with the French Revolution of 1789 were glossed over. It was not until long afterwards, through reading Chinese translations of European books published in Shanghai, that a few Vietnamese intellectuals became aware of the existence of Western philosophies superior in many respects to traditional Confucianism. Awakening at last to the gravity of their errors, they sent their children to the modern schools they had boycotted for a whole generation. When the schools became too full, they asked the colonial administration to open more. It was reluctant to do so. On their own initiative, therefore, they began to build a nation-wide network of private schools which popularised all kinds of Western ideas, including those of political economy (1907). The colonial administration suppressed these schools and sent their organisers to jail. Progressive scholars retaliated by extending their battle-front and mobilising during the next year (1908) large numbers of peasants to congregate in front of the offices of the French provincial *résidents* demanding tax reduction and educational reform. The mass demonstrations in Quang Nam province ended in bloodshed, many scholars being executed. In other provinces there were arrests and deportations.

After this incident, the French decided to fulfil, in spite of themselves, their mission as civilisers. They opened more Franco-Annamite schools, admitted a selected number of Vietnamese children into the French Lycée at Hanoi, abolished the traditional triennial examination (1917), and created the University of Hanoi (1918). These educational reforms, coupled with a rapid industrial development during the same period, produced in a group of scholars the belief that peaceful co-operation with the colonial power would lead to the modernisation of the country and to a democratic administration. The leader of this group, Phan Chu Trinh, was saved from prison by the League of Human Rights and brought to Paris in 1911. He adopted the republican ideal and courageously attacked the institution of monarchy. Although his unceasing efforts aroused great enthusiasm among the Vietnamese intelligentsia, they did not, however, achieve any material progress towards democratisation. He fell ill and died in March 1926. At the news of his death, students throughout the country went on strike as a sign of mourning. This spontaneous demonstration provoked a new wave of repression.

The Dong Du or Pan-Asian Movement

There were other scholars in the early years of this century who believed that no form of collaboration with alien rulers was possible. They were convinced that only a national emancipation through force of arms could ensure the modernisation of the country. Revolutionary undercurrents in southern China at the turn of the century, and Japan's tremendous victory over Russia in 1905, created in these Confucian minds a feeling of Asian solidarity and a hope for a general Asian emancipation under the guidance of a technically advanced Japan. A secret 'exodus to the East' began, organised by a brilliant scholar named Phan Boi Chau, who refused an appointment as mandarin and fled to Canton and Tokyo. In these places, with other refugees, he formed the Viet-Nam Quang-Phuc Hoi or Association for the Restoration of Vietnam, with headquarters in Canton and a network of secret cells inside Vietnam. Phan also went to Bangkok, Hong Kong and Singapore where, with other Asian leaders he built up the Dong-A Dong-Minh or League of East-Asian Peoples.

In the course of these activities, Phan gained the friendship of Sun Yat-sen, Ki Tsuyoshi Inukai, and other Chinese and Japanese political leaders—Asian idealists like himself—and through their friendship obtained funds for his organisation. He also secured scholarships for a large number of Vietnamese youths who left Vietnam at his suggestion and fled to China and Japan with the idea of acquiring the political and military training not available to them in their own country. Phan arranged for four of these young men to be admitted into the Japanese Military Academy, at least two into the Waseda University of Tokyo, and about thirty others into the Whampoa Political and Military Academy of China. Graduates from these schools later participated in an attempted uprising in Cochin China during 1913, in an attack on a frontier post in 1915 (using a few arms received from the German consulate in Bangkok), in a military putsch in Thai-nguyen in 1917, and, finally, in the attack on Lang Son in 1940.

The movement was gaining momentum when, in June 1925, Phan was tricked by the communist leader Nguyen Ai Quoc (now known as Ho Chi Minh)[1] who had arranged to betray him to the security police for the sum of 100,000 *piasters* (a buffalo cost five *piasters* at that time). Having complete confidence in Nguyen Ai Quoc, whom he knew as a communist but refused to consider as a rival, Phan was persuaded to go to an address in Shanghai, not realising it was just inside the French Concession. He was at once arrested by the French police and sent back to Vietnam. This information has been obtained at first hand from Phan's associates and the affair was widely known among the Vietnamese revolutionaries in China at that time. It was reported by some of Nguyen Ai Quoc's followers that, after this act of treachery, the communist leader gave these reasons for his action: Phan was growing too old to be of any further use to the Revolution; his arrest and subsequent trial in Vietnam would produce a surge of patriotism which the Revolution greatly needed; and, finally, the money received from the French would serve to pay for new recruits.

Nguyen Ai Quoc was assisted in this betrayal by a representative of Phan's in Hong Kong, a certain Lam Duc Thu (his real name was Nguyen Cong Vien), the two dividing the money equally.[2] Nguyen Ai Quoc used his share to finance a crypto-communist organisation he had formed in Canton—the League of Vietnamese Revolutionary Youth. Lam Duc Thu spent his in night-clubs in Hong Kong.

The 'common cause' links between the genuinely nationalist revolutionary movement and the communists enabled such treachery to flourish for many years. All new recruits sent to China by Phan's organisation had to submit to Lam Duc Thu in Hong Kong, or to his representative in Canton, two copies of a photograph of themselves. This was necessary, Thu explained, to complete their files before admission into Whampoa Academy. The day came when these recruits, having finished their military and political training, were ready to return to Vietnam and to carry

[1] The career of Nguyen Ai Quoc (Ho Chi Minh) is related in Part II.
[2] Two other exiles were also involved in this affair: Tong Oanh, Phan's own son-in-law; and Nguyen Thuong Huyen, son of Phan's best friend, Nguyen Thuong Hien.

out their revolutionary activities; but, unknown to them, one of two very different fates awaited each of them. Those who, during their stay in China, had been attracted by Nguyen Ai Quoc's propaganda and had joined his Youth League, were allowed to go home in secrecy. The rest who remained faithful to Phan's organisation and to the nationalist cause always found a French agent waiting for them near the Sino-Vietnamese border, armed with copies of their photographs. On receipt of a prearranged signal from Nguyen Ai Quoc, Lam Duc Thu sent these photographs to the French consulate in Hong Kong, receiving a sum of money for each. The unfortunate nationalists were put in jail, and thus the nationalist organisation in Vietnam gradually lost all contact with its headquarters in Canton. Messengers sent to China from Vietnam to renew contact found their way either to a French jail or into the communist camp. This process continued with such regularity that eventually graduates from Whampoa Academy who refused to become communists dared not go home, and, instead, joined the Kuomintang army. In this way the nationalist organisation almost collapsed, while the communist movement progressed, acquiring more and more importance.

From these transactions which were humorously termed the 'raising and selling of pigs', Lam Duc Thu became immensely rich and lived luxuriously in Hong Kong. However, a few years later, having no more 'pigs' to sell, Thu was reduced to wretched poverty and forced to go home and to seek assistance and protection from the French colonial administration. After the Revolution in 1945, Thu became very frightened and sought to find a way out of his difficulties. Making his way, in secret, to see Nguyen Ai Quoc, who had become Ho Chi Minh, President of the Democratic Republic, he came to yet another arrangement with him. Thu was promised protection and safety on condition that he kept silent concerning his past activities in Hong Kong. Thereafter, Thu lived peacefully in his native village in Thai Binh province until 1950, when a French attack threatened the area. Following the prearranged instructions to be carried out in such an eventuality, local communist cadres put him into a bamboo basket and threw it into the river.

As for Phan, after a lengthy trial before a special criminal court, he was sentenced to be beheaded. This sentence provoked that violent wave of protest throughout the country which Nguyen Ai Quoc had predicted. Thanks to this and to the softer attitude of the 'cartel de gauche' government in Paris, represented in Indochina by a socialist governor-general, Alexandre Varenne, Phan was granted an amnesty but kept under house arrest in Hué. He remained there until his death on October 20, 1940, a few days after the arrival of Japanese troops in Vietnam. This was what he had hoped for from the day he began his career as a revolutionary. He firmly believed that Japan would do all in its power to help the Vietnamese to regain their independence.

The Japanese began their occupation by attacking the French garrison of Lang Son in September 1940, and at the same time they helped a group of Phan's former followers to start a general insurrection throughout Lang Son province. But a few days later, having obtained the concessions they wanted from the Vichy government, the Japanese astonished Vietnamese opinion by restoring Lang Son to the French, who promptly put to death many of those who had revealed pro-Japanese sympathies. For Phan, the news of the killing of his last followers was the final blow. Already disillusioned by the Japanese war against China, he became a very sick man. A few days before he died he signed, at the request of the French *résident supérieur* who professed to be his best friend, a letter recommending a peaceful relationship between France and Vietnam. No one knew whether Phan's complete change of attitude was the result of an agonising reappraisal of his life-long policy —which had ended in utter failure—or whether his mind had become sick as well as his body. Despite this *volte-face*, Phan is still regarded as an outstanding hero of Vietnamese nationalism in recent times.

The Viet-Nam Quoc-Dan Dang or National Party of Vietnam

The three movements already described were developed by those members of Vietnamese society who were, for the most part, born before the formal establishment of French rule in 1884. Educated in the traditional Confucianist way, they had little, if any, knowledge of Western culture. This fourth nationalist movement, however, was brought into being by a younger generation, born about the turn of the century, which had absorbed a certain amount of Western knowledge in Franco-Annamite schools. These early Westernised intellectuals formed a transitional link between the traditional and the modern intelligentsia. They were traditional enough to maintain the struggle against foreign domination and modern enough to adopt a republican outlook. On the other hand, they were as impractical as their fathers in starting a national revolution without first formulating any definite program of social reforms. Another difference was that this new generation did not base its hope of success upon foreign intervention and its watchword might have been taken from a similar movement in the West, *Sinn Fein* of Ireland.

Lacking political maturity, and having little revolutionary experience, they could not hope for success against either of their rivals. The communist group already enjoyed the allegiance of half the patriotic elements in the country, while the French, who had a vast network of informers at their disposal, carried out severe repression with the aid of the local mandarins. The fourth embodiment of nationalist agitation was, in the last analysis, a delayed consequence of Phan Boi Chau's arrest and Phan Chu Trinh's death. It might best be described as a spontaneous outburst of anger against colonialism by a large section of those half-educated intellectuals who had been awakened to nationalism a few years previously by the *Student's Movement* of 1925. This movement (not to be confused with the Scholars' or Private Schools' Movement of 1907-8) was touched off by the trial and condemnation to death of Phan Boi Chau. Repressed, it broke out again in March 1926 following the death of Phan Chu Trinh. Many of these intellectuals had participated in the general strike which followed Phan Chu Trinh's death and, as punishment for this, had been expelled from school and prevented from taking examinations. Of middle-class background, they formed the cream of the Vietnamese society at that time. After the First World War, the upper class (mandarins and urban bourgeoisie) were seduced from their ideals by the privileges which the colonial administration granted to them, and by the Western pattern of life with its modern comforts and pleasures. They were no longer capable of the sacrifices demanded by the revolution, but a few of their sons, who were idealists—as sons of rich families not infrequently are—adopted a new faith—Marxism—and started another kind of revolution.

Nguyen Thai Hoc, the promoter and political leader of the new nationalist movement, was a teacher in a Franco-Annamite primary school. Other members of this group were small tradesmen, minor officials in the public services, employees in private business enterprises and junior officers of the Indochinese troops. A minority of workers, and women too, played an important rôle.

It is interesting to note that Nguyen Thai Hoc and his followers were somewhat closer to the proletariat than their communist rivals. It is a fact that no big landlords, rich bourgeois or eminent intellectuals joined or supported the nationalist movement. On the other hand, the veteran communists were for the most part sons of mandarins and big landlords. Many of them were graduates from Hanoi University or students returned from France.[3]

In fact, most of those who participated in the nationalist revolution of 1930 were of humble origin, people who had suffered directly from colonial oppression and were impatient to be free of it. In contrast, those joining the communist movement were comfortably off, well educated, and endowed with sufficient patience and foresight to find and adopt a 'scientific ideology' which they realised would be necessary in the future.

In 1927, Nguyen Thai Hoc and his friends set up a publishing house in Hanoi with the idea of providing financial resources for their political activities. They hoped at the same time, by publishing political literature, to inform the Vietnamese reading public about world affairs and to make it familiar with modern conceptions of freedom and democracy. This enterprise was very quickly closed down by the police, but its premises continued to serve as a meeting place for the group which ultimately decided to form the Viet-Nam Quoc-Dan Dang, or National Party of Vietnam.

Being ill-informed about political theory, this group simply

[3] A story runs that Phan Tu Nghia, a veteran communist, when speaking in Paris in 1935, proudly began: 'We sons of peasants . . .' But a voice in the audience called out: 'No! Sons of mandarins!' Nghia was in fact the son of a provincial governor.

imitated contemporary Chinese political methods. They adopted the name of Kuomintang for their own party (Quoc-Dan Dang is the Vietnamese pronunciation of 'kuo', 'min' and 'tang', Chinese characters meaning 'National Party'), and proclaimed Sun Yat-sen's principles of nationalism, democracy and socialism as formulated in the Kuomintang's doctrine of the 'Three People' *(San-min-chu-y)*, i.e., 'min-chu' (People's Sovereignty, or Democracy); 'min-so' (People's Family, or Nationalism); 'min-sing' (People's Welfare, commonly rendered as Socialism).

Well aware of the difficulty of escaping the vigilance of the French police, Nguyen Thai Hoc resorted to a stratagem which for some time proved very effective. He divided his party into two separate sections, one overt (a 'front' organisation), and one clandestine. The former was in the main composed of personalities already known to the police; it was more or less a diversionary group whose task was simply to arouse general enthusiasm and interest. It operated quite openly from the Viet-Nam Hotel, a restaurant set up by the party in the centre of Hanoi.

Operating under the very eyes of the police, and doing nothing that was actually illegal, this group served as a screen behind which the other section, composed entirely of activists, operated in secrecy. By using these tactics, the Viet-Nam Quoc-Dan Dang rapidly increased in importance. The Viet-Nam Hotel became very popular. By January 1929, there were no less than 120 cells comprising 1,500 members, over a hundred of whom were military personnel. Nguyen Thai Hoc and his friends hoped to continue with this dual activity (overt agitation combined with clandestine revolutionary organisation) for several years until the party became strong enough to rid the country of colonial rule by a general insurrection. But events beyond its control forced the group to take direct action before its preparations had matured.

On the evening of February 9, 1929, a French settler named René Bazin, who recruited labour in Tongking for the rubber plantations in Cochin China, was shot dead by an unidentified Vietnamese youth.

This affair still remains something of a mystery. The youth waited outside Bazin's bungalow and, when the settler returned home, handed him a letter. As Bazin was opening the envelope, the assassin pulled out a pistol and shot him. Bazin was found dead on the path, clutching a sheet of paper on which was written: 'You vampire sucking Vietnamese blood.' The French police never discovered (or, if they did, never revealed) the murderer's identity. A Marxist historian, Le Thanh Khoi, asserts in his book *Le Vietnam* (Paris, 1955, p. 439) that the murderer was an *agent-provocateur* of the French security service. But this seems improbable. It is hard to believe that the colonial administration, at that time all-powerful, would sacrifice the life of an important member of the French community as a pretext for repression. A more widely accepted theory is that the assassin was acting on behalf of the communists who sought a double objective: to thwart the plans of the Quoc-Dan Dang, and to stimulate further unrest among the coolies in the French plantations.

The French reaction to the murder was swift. The police at once arrested the whole of the overt section of the VNQDD and sent its best-known members to the prison-camp on Poulo Condore Island. Eventually some two hundred of them were released since incriminating evidence could not be found against them. Nguyen Thai Hoc himself remained at liberty. But after this incident, the clandestine section of the VNQDD became known to the police, and Nguyen Thai Hoc was beset with the fear that, if they did not act quickly, it would be soon too late to act at all to further the planned revolution. He therefore ordered preparations for a general uprising with the greatest possible speed.

Among its other preparations, the party started to make bombs. But, through entrusting the production of the explosive to a seventeen-year-old amateur chemist,[4] a series of accidents occurred which left the police in no doubt as to what was going on. Many important party members were arrested and Nguyen Thai Hoc himself was located. In this desperate situation, with the risk of failure imminent, he gave orders for a general attack to be launched

---

[4] This was Trinh Van Yen, at that time a third-year student at the Collège du Protectorat, a middle school for Vietnamese boys in Hanoi. While in prison, he continued his studies in chemistry and later became a talented chemist. He joined the Vietminh during the Resistance War of 1946-54 and became a leading technician in the arms and ammunition service of the Vietminh army.

on February 10, 1930. But later he made a second order, postponing the attack until February 15. Because of communication difficulties, notice of this change in the plan was not received by the military garrison at Yen Bay, with the result that it staged an uprising on its own on February 10th.

Not surprisingly, the repression which followed the uprising was both rapid and severe. Co Am, the village in which the conspirators had taken refuge, was heavily bombed, and in a matter of a few weeks the whole party-apparatus was captured. A score of the leaders were sentenced to death and went to the guillotine together at Yen Bay on July 17, 1930. They went bravely to their execution, each shouting: 'Long live Vietnam!' One woman, Nguyen Thi Giang, a companion of Nguyen Thai Hoc's who had escaped arrest, mingled with the crowds gathered to watch the executions. Immediately afterwards, she went to the dead leader's native village and shot herself under a banyan tree outside the village gate.[5]

A few participants in this revolt escaped to China where they set up a new VNQDD. This was the group which returned to Vietnam in 1945 and fought with equal zeal both the communists who had seized power and the French who were trying to re-occupy the country. Their physical courage was unquestioned, but they failed to win mass support from the Vietnamese people because of their almost complete lack of experienced political leadership. The Chinese troops looked favourably on their activities, but on the withdrawal of Lu Han's army (sent to northern Vietnam to disarm Japanese troops), the neo-VNQDD was quickly crushed by the communists. The French gave the communists both passive

[5] By committing suicide in her companion's village, the nationalist heroine forced the local authorities to bury her in the neighbourhood of the burial place of Nguyen Thai Hoc's ancestors. This gesture signified her desire to be associated with him for ever in the hereafter. It is to be regretted that Le Thanh Khoi, in his book, Le Vietnam, should assert, without any vestige of proof, that the banyan tree under which she shot herself 'sheltered their first rendezvous', thereby suggesting that her heroic action was motivated by nothing more than romanticism. This suggestion is more consonant with the rantings of a communist propagandist than with the judgment of a serious historian.

and active assistance in return for certain compromises (*see Communism in South East Asia* by J. H. Brimmel, p. 181).

Again forced back into China, the defeated group set to work to reorganise itself. But a new threat materialised with the advance, in 1949, of Mao Tse-tung's army on southern China. The group's new leader, Vu Hong Khanh, formed an army of ten thousand men, most of whom were Chinese, and led them to Vietnam. The communists in the north evacuated all the villages through which his army passed on its way from the Sino-Vietnamese border. But the intervention of the French army and air force compelled him to accept the authority of the Bao Dai government. From then on, the Viet-Nam Quoc Dan Dang ceased to exist as a political party.[6]

[6] This information is taken from the mimeographed text of an unpublished work, *Forces Politiques du Vietnam* (p. 181), by Pierre Dabezies.

PART II

INDEPENDENCE FOR THE Nth TIME

'. . . We have sometimes been weak, and
sometimes powerful, but at no time have
we lacked heroes.'

Proclamation of Emperor Le Loi
in 1418, at the start of a ten-year
war of independence against the
Chinese.

THREE

Ho Chi Minh, The National Hero

The Vietnamese Revolution might be said to have begun with nationalism and ended with communism. Two successive generations of Vietnamese patriots had fought for national independence but had achieved no success other than to keep the revolutionary spirit alive. Their failures, however, prepared the way for the communists who finally emerged as the liberators of the country after a comparatively short period of clandestine activity and with smaller losses, by comparison with the nationalists, of their rank-and-file followers. Communism achieved its relatively easy success for several different reasons. Among these were the skilful leadership provided by the Comintern, the sound organisation at the core of the party, and the courage and determination of its members. Moreover, it proved itself capable, by its progressive ideology, of attracting intellectual idealists, while at the same time mobilising the underprivileged masses by promising a short cut to better living standards. All these factors contributed to the growing strength of the Communist Party and to the consequent weakening of the nationalist movement. But its final success was due in large measure to the suppleness of its tactics which enabled it to appear communist or nationalist as changing circumstances demanded, while keeping well concealed the unchanging strategic objective.

The Vietnamese communist movement began in 1925 when Ho Chi Minh formed the Association of Revolutionary Youth, recruit-

ing his first followers from a small group of Vietnamese patriots
sent to China by the nationalist organisation. He was still posing
as a nationalist leader when, twenty years later, he seized power
at Hanoi in 1945 under the banner of the Vietminh, or League for
Vietnamese Independence.

Whenever the Vietnamese communists resorted to the ortho-
dox class-struggle, they achieved a slight strengthening of their
influence over the masses, but failed to bring off any major vic-
tories. These have always come at times when they acted as
nationalists aiming solely at the liquidation of French colonial
rule. Proof of this is to be found in the period from 1946 to 1951,
when the Vietnamese Communist Party[1] was obliged by circumstances to declare itself voluntarily disbanded and to go underground, despite the fact that it never lost control of the government or the army. In a country like Vietnam, which is quite without native capitalists,[2] class-conflict clearly contributed little to
the cause of communism, and the insignificant quasi-proletariat in
fact played no rôle of any importance in the emergence of communism. The factors which in the event contributed most to the
communist cause were those which, under more normal circumstances, might have sustained a purely nationalist revolution, *i.e.*
French domination, which created a feeling of racial inequality
(and hence of solidarity within the race), and the despotic rule of
the feudalist-minded hierarchy of mandarins, which generated
widespread dissatisfaction and extinguished all hope of modernisation and democratisation. The communists succeeded because the
nationalist movement proved unable to fulfil its historic mission.
Admittedly, the latter's failure was due to its inability to resist
colonialist repression. But the communists encroached on the
nationalists' preserves and progressively eliminated them by competition, by trickery and, finally, by military force.

In the circumstances prevailing, the kind of leader the com-

---

[1] Its official name from 1931 to 1946 was 'Indochinese Communist Party' (ICP); from 1951 onward the name was the
'Lao-Dong Party'.
[2] The only wealthy man in North Vietnam who could con-
ceivably be described as a capitalist was Ngo Tu Ha, the owner
of a printing firm. But his sympathies lay with the communists whose cause he served unswervingly.

munist movement in Vietnam needed for its success was not a
scholarly theoretician, but a professional agitator who would ex-
pertly play the nationalists' game. In 1925, the Comintern chose
Ho Chi Minh for this difficult rôle, and he played it brilliantly, for
Ho possessed all the qualities essential to a communist-cum-
nationalist leader.

The name of Ho Chi Minh became known to the Vietnamese
public for the first time in August 1945, when Hanoi newspapers
on August 28 (nine days after the Vietminh revolution) published
the composition of the newly-formed provisional government of
the Democratic Republic of Vietnam. Ho was named as President.
No one had ever heard of him before and all were puzzled by his
somewhat unusual name. Educated Vietnamese concluded that it
must be a pseudonym, for it means 'Ho who-aspires-to-enlighten-
ment'; this had too literary a flavour to be a genuine name.[3]

There was lively speculation about the new President's identity
especially among the members of the new administration whose
anxiety to discover who their leader was can readily be imagined.
The answer was not long delayed, for only a few days later the
rumour began to circulate that Ho Chi Minh was the pseudonym
adopted by Nguyen Ai Quoc, the mysterious but well-known
'father of the Vietnamese Communist Party'.

At this news, the French police lost no time in searching
through their files to find a photograph of Nguyen Ai Quoc who,
according to the official records, had been reported dead in Hong
Kong in 1933. On comparing their rather faded photograph with
those on sale on almost every street-corner in Hanoi, the French
security police became convinced that Nguyen was still alive and
that after a decade of total obscurity he had reappeared on the

---

[3] All Vietnamese names are made up of Chinese characters,
although they are not necessarily of Chinese origin. In
the case of Ho Chi Minh, Ho is a common family name, *Chi*
means 'aspiration', and *Minh* means 'enlightment'. The practice of joining the second and third names to form a com-
pound word is more Chinese than Vietnamese. It is sometimes adopted in Vietnam, but usually for pen-names and
pseudonyms. Similar differences exist in the romanised orthography: the Chinese put a hyphen between the second and
third names (*e.g.* Mao Tse-tung), but the Vietnamese do not
(*e.g.* Ho Chi Minh).

political scene as Ho Chi Minh. Although physically greatly changed after twenty years of hardship, Ho was positively identified by French experts as Nguyen Ai Quoc. For example, the right ear in both photographs was seen to be pointed, while the left was regular in shape. But Ho persistently denied he was Nguyen, and even when General Salan, the French officer in charge of truce-negotiations in 1946, asked him face to face whether he was the same man, he categorically denied it.[4]

To Vietnamese questions, Ho gave no straight denial but hedged, avoiding a direct answer one way or the other. For instance on being asked by Vo Quy Huan: 'Do you know, Mr President, where Nguyen Ai Quoc is at present?' Ho merely smiled and replied: 'You'd better ask him, not me!' This question was asked on board the SS *Dumont d'Urville* when Ho was returning to Haiphong in 1946 from the Fontainebleau conference in company with four Vietnamese technicians brought back with him from Paris. Vo Quy Huan was one of the four.

It was not only his identity he kept secret, but also his origins. In an official declaration made by him in 1946, he stated that he was a native of Ha-Tinh; but it is now known that his birthplace was in Nghe-An province. This was revealed in 1958 when a group of diplomatists from the embassies of socialist countries paid an official visit to the house where Ho had spent his childhood. After this visit, official publications in Hanoi admitted that Ho was indeed Nguyen Ai Quoc. The photo-magazine *Viet-Nam Dan-Chu Cong-Hoa* (Democratic Republic of Vietnam), published by the Vietnam Press Agency, in its August issue, 1960, contained a photograph of Nguyen Ai Quoc with the caption—'Comrade Nguyen Ai Quoc (Ho Chi Minh) at the age of thirty, carrying out his activities abroad.'

However, although his identity has been established beyond doubt, the Free World still knows very little about this remarkable man, and most of his activities remain the secret of the Comintern. All that is known about Ho is based upon fragmentary police records and a few individual testimonies obtained from people who have met him.

[4] Jean Lacouture, *Cinq Hommes et La France* (Editions du Seuil, Paris 1961), p. 12.

While the French were busy examining Ho's photographs and scrutinising his ears whenever he appeared in public, the Vietnamese were already unanimous in accepting the fact that Ho was Nguyen, for they could not believe that any country could produce, in the same epoch, two men of Ho's genius. He spoke a dozen foreign languages with great fluency and had travelled all round the world under a score of different names, spending half his time in prisons—possibly in a Soviet prison too—and the rest in clandestine political activity. He outshone all his rivals in both revolutionary tactics and political experience. He studied Chinese classics in his boyhood, then continued his education by wandering through Europe and America where he worked, observing and learning all the time from friends and through books. Later he received a careful, methodical training from the Comintern. Thus he had ample opportunity to learn from three different, but equally valuable sources: Oriental, Western and Marxist. He was equally at home with a Vietnamese peasant, a Chinese warlord, an Indian philosopher or a Western journalist.

In the course of his long experience as a conspirator, he had to resort to many tricks and subterfuges in order to escape from police traps and confound his enemies' plans. This long training in intrigue rendered him a truly formidable opponent, for over the years he developed an amazing capacity for throwing everyone off the scent. He has at one time or another successfully evaded the Vietnamese nationalists, the Chinese Kuomintang, and the British and American Intelligence Services.

In addition to his remarkable intelligence, Ho is endowed with an outstanding personality. He has in fact all the qualities necessary in a leader, and his austerity, perseverance, iron determination and whole-hearted devotion to the cause of the Revolution are an inspiration to all who serve under him and to the nation as a whole. It is often said by Vietnamese that Ho has inherited his revolutionary spirit from his forefathers and provincial fellow-countrymen—perseverance, austerity and fanaticism are qualities common amongst the people of Nghe-An province, his birthplace. Ho has developed these attributes to the highest degree. The people of Nghe-An possess all the moral qualities attributed to the Japanese, but differ from them in that the Japanese are, generally speaking, a highly disciplined race while the people of Nghe-An are inclined to rebel against all forms of government. Nghe-An was a hotbed of revolution throughout the period of French domination, and more recently, in 1956, it was the centre of a peasant uprising against Ho's own régime.

During the years of the Resistance, and prior to the mass-killings occurring in the Land Reform campaign, Ho became, with the help of good propaganda and inspiring but quite false legends, a living idol amongst his people. Not only was his photograph placed on every family altar, but in a few places, such as Quang-Ngai, people even bowed before his image as they set out to work in the ricefields.

Ho lives the life of an ascetic, never indulging in any comfort that is not strictly necessary—his one weakness is for American cigarettes which he smokes incessantly. For years he dressed as a peasant, wearing a Canadian windcheater (these garments were surplus American stock and flooded North Vietnam in 1946) and a pair of sandals made from a discarded tyre. His whole appearance was an assurance that he had devoted his life to the service of the people. Having renounced his family early in life and being un-married,[5] Ho stands above all suspicion of nepotism and corrup-tion, and would thus seem beyond the reach of calumny. To quote Paul Mus, the envoy sent by the French government in 1947 to meet Ho and negotiate a truce: 'He is an intransigent and incor-ruptible revolutionary in the manner of Saint-Just.'[6]

This comparison is high praise for any statesman, since com-plete incorruptibility is exceptional among politicians of our era, particularly in underdeveloped countries. Thus, by his moral standing alone, Ho acquired the respect and confidence of the whole Vietnamese nation. His reputation for honesty and sin-cerity has contributed greatly to his success, for in Vietnam, as in many underdeveloped countries, the masses put their trust in the

---

[5] According to reliable sources, Ho took a Chinese wife while in Hong Kong and had a daughter by her. The same sources have disclosed that, in 1949, he asked the Chinese Communist Party to make enquiries as to her whereabouts, but no trace of this woman could be found.
[6] Paul Mus, *Vietnam, Sociologie d'une guerre* (Editions du Seuil, Paris, 1952) p. 88.

personal character and behaviour of a leader more than in the political party he represents.

In retrospect, it appears obvious that none of Ho's rivals ever had any serious chance of success. Nguyen Hai Than, disciple and successor of Phan Boi Chau, was beyond doubt a genuine patriot, but during his forty years' stay in China he had fallen victim to the attraction of opium smoking. The former Emperor Bao Dai, whom the French reinstated as 'Head of State' in 1949, for more than twenty years had had the reputation of being a playboy and of leading an immoral life. Last, but by no means least, is Ngo Dinh Diem, brought to power by American pressure in 1954 and now ruler of South Vietnam. Diem differs from Ho in every possible way. Whereas Ho renounces his family, Diem is surrounded by brothers, sisters, nephews and other relatives, close and distant, on whom he has bestowed all the key positions in his government and in the army. Also, while Ho will chat with workers and peasants in a friendly manner, Diem sits on a gilded chair as his feet are ceremonially washed by tribal chiefs, following a centuries-old practice symbolising the acknowledgment of a monarch's suzerainty.

An important factor usually unnoticed by outside observers was the moral indignation generated in ordinary decent Vietnamese people by the corrupt practices sanctioned by the colonial régime. This of itself was sufficient to stimulate very large numbers of them to support the Revolution. Any rebels, no matter what ideology they supported, would have been regarded by these people as the courageous protagonists of right and justice. The mandarins serving the colonial administration, whose comfortable lives were made more conspicuous by the general poverty surrounding them, personified for the people not only treachery to the national cause, but corruption and depravity as well. Revolutions may spring from many causes but the Vietnamese Revolution was motivated in the first place by the people's eagerness to get rid of mandarinic despotism and insolence. For the Vietnamese people, the Revolution was a conflict between virtue and vice. The ideological dispute which later developed was regarded as a complicating, but subsidiary, factor. This attitude partly explains why neither Bao Dai, the ex-Emperor, nor Ngo Dinh Diem, the ex-

mandarin, have ever had any chance of success against Ho Chi
Minh, the model revolutionary and symbol of virtue: the Saint-
Just of the twentieth century.

Ho Chi Minh was born in the village of Kim-Lien in the Nam-
Dan district of Nghe-An province. His birthday is officially given
as May 19, 1890. Like every Vietnamese of his time, Ho was given
two names: a first name at birth, and a second, 'literary' name
when he went to school. His first and 'sacred' name was Nguyen
Van Coong (Coong is a modification, required by superstitious
custom, of *Cung*, and means 'respectful'). His second name, intended for ordinary use, was Nguyen Tat Thanh ('Nguyen-who-
will-inevitably-succeed'). In the course of his long life, he has been
known by various other names: Nguyen Ai Quoc, Ho Chi Minh,
Ly Thuy, Vuong Son Nhi—these are some of them, all invented by
him to suit his purposes at different periods of his life.

He is descended from a long line of brilliant scholars, who were,
for the most part, junior mandarins and small landlords, as were
most Vietnamese intellectuals. His grandfather received the degree
of *Cu-nhan* (Master of Arts) and was appointed a district governor, but was later dismissed for insubordination. His father,
Nguyen Sinh Huy, later known as Nguyen Tat Sac, obtained the
Pho Bang (Doctor of lower degree), but, refusing to accept a man-
darinal post, he joined the Scholars' Movement of 1907 and was
subsequently arrested. After release from Poulo Condore prison in
1910, Ho's father was placed under house-arrest in Saigon where
he earned a meagre living as a practitioner in Chinese medicine. It
is said that he never charged for his services. At that time it was
customary for the practitioner in Chinese medicine to remain at his
patient's bedside all day, and he was always given two meals a day
by the family. This was the limit of Sac's needs. Since he was hardly
ever short of patients, he rarely went hungry.

Ho was the youngest child of the family. In contrast to his
brother and sister, he was permitted to abandon his Confucian
studies to become a pupil in a Franco-Annamite school. He
passed his *certificat d'études primaires* in 1907 and was appointed a teacher in an elementary school. But after the
nationalist unrest of 1907-8, he became fired with patriotism and,

as soon as he got news of Sac's release, went south to join his father in Saigon.

Ho's sister, called Bach Lien ('White Lotus'), enjoyed a reputation for learning and for revolutionary political ideas. While still a child, she became engaged to Mai Ngoc Ngon. Her fiancé's death on the prison-island of Poulo Condore so grieved her that she never married. She died in 1953.

Ho's brother was Nguyen Tat Dat ('Nguyen-who-will-inevitably-arrive'), a mediocre student who failed in all his examinations and who had to live a simple life as a teacher of Chinese characters. Dat was in his native village when he heard, in 1946, that Ho had become President of the Republic, or more precisely that Ho Chi Minh, the new President of the Republic, was none other than his own brother. Uninvited, Dat set off immediately for Hanoi, eager to meet his brother again after more than thirty years of separation. However, at this time Ho was still anxious to keep his identity and background secret; he did not therefore receive Dat in the presidential palace. Instead, he sent him to a relative in the suburb of Thai-Ha. One night he went out to the suburb to see Dat. The brothers conversed for an hour, after which Dat returned home in silence. Two years later, he died without seeing Ho again.

Ho journeyed to Saigon to see his father and ask for the older man's political advice before setting out on his revolutionary career. Sac consulted his friends and after discussion with them decided that young Ho ought to go to France. Arrangements were therefore made to secure a job for Ho aboard one of the liners sailing between Saigon and Marseilles. In 1912, the young man boarded the SS *La Touche-Tréville*, carrying only a small suitcase and a letter of introduction from his father addressed to Phan Chu Trinh, the veteran nationalist of the Private Schools Movement, who had been saved from jail and brought to Paris the year before by the League of Human Rights (see page 16 above). Sac had known him in the prison on Poulo Condore and hoped that he would tutor his young, inexperienced son. No doubt he impressed upon Ho how important it was for him to listen to Phan's advice.

On arrival in Paris, Ho gave Phan his father's letter and lodged

with him for a little while. But he soon discovered that he could
not accept Phan's political opinions, particularly the latter's theory
of peaceful co-operation with the French. Disillusioned, Ho resumed his job as 'boy' on international liners, travelling all over
the world—to America, Africa and Europe—before settling for a
while in London. On one of these trips Ho visited Saigon and went
to see his father. Their meeting ended by Sac's seizing a cane
and putting Ho to flight: a letter from Phan had told him of what
had taken place in Paris. The young man returned to his ship
and never visited his father again. This incident more than any
other led Ho to his decision to sever all ties with his family. Ho
is today its sole survivor, for his brother's marriage proved child-
less.

Ho lived in London from 1913 to 1917, working in the kitchens
of the Carlton Hotel under Escoffier, the famous French chef.
During these years he devoted much of his free time and his attention to the Overseas Workers' Union, a clandestine anti-colonial
organisation established in London by Chinese and Indian workers.
Towards the end of the First World War, his fellow-members
urged him to go to France and initiate similar activity amongst the
sixty thousand Vietnamese then living in France (or serving in
the French army). In Paris, he met a chemical engineer called
Nguyen The Truyen, who introduced him to a group of patriots
from other French colonies living there in exile. The group built
up the 'Union Inter-coloniale' which published a periodical named
Le Paria; at the same time Ho and Truyen edited on their own
account the Viet Nam Hon (The Soul of Vietnam) and, using
Vietnamese employed in French ships, smuggled copies into Vietnam. Availing himself of material collected by the group, Ho began
to write the Procès de la Colonisation Française—an indictment of
French colonialism. The foreword was contributed by Nguyen
The Truyen who was well known at that time in the leftish political circles in France. Also in collaboration with Truyen, Ho produced an eight-point program which he intended to lay before
President Wilson during the latter's visit to Versailles to sign the
Peace Treaty. In this program, Ho demanded autonomy, democratic freedom, amnesty for political prisoners, equality of rights
between French and Vietnamese, and the abolition of forced

labour, the salt-tax and 'the forced consumption of alcohol'.[7] In the event, Ho was unable to gain access to the President, and his attempt to gain American support for the Vietnamese revolutionary cause ended in failure. Returned from Versailles, he published his eight points in the newspaper, Viet Nam Hon. They were received with great enthusiasm in the country. The articles were signed by Nguyen Ai Quoc ('Nguyen-the-Patriot'), the name by which he was known to the ordinary Vietnamese up to the day he became Ho Chi Minh.

Nguyen The Truyen introduced Ho to many left-wing political figures in Paris: Léon Blum, Marcel Cachin, Marius Moutet, and many more. Under their influence, he joined the Socialist Party and produced some articles for the socialist organ, Le Populaire. He was a delegate to the Socialist Congress at Tours in 1920 and voted for the Third International and for communism. From that moment on, he parted company with Nguyen The Truyen and the other Vietnamese patriots in Paris. While these continued to struggle for their country's independence, Ho devoted himself to the cause of international communism.[8]

Three years ago, on the occasion of his seventieth birthday, having admitted that he was Nguyen Ai Quoc, Ho explained his case as follows:

> In the beginning, it was patriotism and not communism which induced me to believe in Lenin and the Third International. But little by little, progressing step by step in the course of the struggle, and combining theoretical studies of Marxism-Leninism with practical activities, I came to realise

[7] The production of rice-alcohol was the monopoly of a French firm, the Société des Distilleries de l'Indochine, whose products were so bad that the Vietnamese preferred to drink their own distilled alcoholic concoctions. To safeguard the French firm's interests, the government made frequent raids on Vietnamese property, imposing heavy fines and imprisonment. Despite these stringent measures, the private production of alcohol persisted. In the end, the government adopted the policy of distributing a fixed quantity of 'official' alcohol to every village, obliging the inhabitants to pay for it.

[8] Nguyen The Truyen is now living in Saigon in South Vietnam. He stood as a candidate in the presidential election of 1961.

that socialism and communism alone are capable of emancipating workers and downtrodden people all over the world.

There was in Vietnam, as well as in China, the legend of the magic bag; anyone faced with a great problem would simply open the bag to find a ready solution. For the Vietnamese Revolution and people, Marxism-Leninism is not a magic bag, or a compass, but a real sun which lights the road to final victory, to socialism and communism.[9]

It becomes clear from the above quotation that Ho at first regarded communism as a convenient instrument for his patriotic purposes, and then, under the charms of its 'open Sesame', his mind was made receptive to it as an end in itself. The process is quite common amongst convinced communists, but his use of terms like 'magic bag' and 'real sun' denotes a certain mysticism and a quasi-religious fervour of his own.

Ho went to Moscow for the first time in 1922 as a first colonial delegate to the Fourth Congress of the Communist International. It can hardly have been a coincidence that this Congress decided to create a south Asian section. He returned in 1923, this time to attend the Peasants' International Congress, and again in 1924 to become a student at the Eastern Workers' University. On this last occasion, Ho remained in Moscow for more than a year, taking courses in Marxism-Leninism and bolshevik tactics. To get to Moscow, Vietnamese communists used to buy, at low cost, a Kuomintang passport from the Chinese embassy in Paris; they pretended to be Chinese citizens wanting to go back to China by way of Moscow and Vladivostok.

In 1925 he was sent to Canton, entrusted with the task of introducing communism into Vietnam. The day he set out for China marked the beginning of another period of his revolutionary career which ended with his disappearance from the Asian scene in 1933. Since all his activities during this period were closely and directly connected with local events, these will be considered in the next chapter which deals with the development of communism in Vietnam.

[9] Ho Chi Minh, 'The path that led me to Leninism', article in the July issue, 1960, of *Echo du Vietnam*, a semi-official organ of the Vietnamese communist group in Paris.

FOUR

Emergence of Communism

The complete evolution of communism in Vietnam, from the creation of the first communist cell in 1925 to the imposition of agricultural collectivisation on the whole of North Vietnam in 1956, divides conveniently into six successive movements. Each one marked a particular phase in the general development, and each differs from the others in its short-term program, political orientation and revolutionary tactics as well as in the external leadership acknowledged by Vietnamese communists. They paid allegiance sometimes to Peking, sometimes directly to Moscow, or indirectly by way of intermediary staging posts in Canton, Shanghai, Bangkok and Paris.

The phases of revolutionary activity were interspersed by periods of relative stagnation, due either to severe repression or to internal difficulties. The six principal movements were: the *Thanh-Nien* (1925-28), the *Nghe-An Soviets* (1930-31), the *Popular Front* (1936-37), the *Viet-Minh* (1941-46), the *Resistance War* (1946-54) and the *Land Reform* (1953-56). From 1951 the communists began to clear the way for Land Reform, which is, in effect, the establishment of a 'dictatorship of the proletariat' by the imposition of the Agricultural Tax and by a wave of terror. The first five movements will be reviewed here by way of historical background, while the sixth, the Land Reform, which is the implementation of Mao's technique of gradual communisation, will be described more fully in the remaining part of the book.

THE THANH-NIEN MOVEMENT

Thanh-Nien or 'Youth' is the current abbreviation of the term *Viet-Nam Thanh-Nien Cach-Menh Dong-Chi Hoi* (the Association of Vietnamese Revolutionary Young Comrades).[1] This was the name that Ho Chi Minh gave to a crypto-communist organisation which he founded in Canton in 1925, a few months after he had been sent there by the Comintern. The ostensible reason for his presence in Canton was to act as a Chinese translator for the Soviet consulate, but his real task was the introduction of communism into Vietnam. He was known as Lee Suei (Ly Thuy in Vietnamese spelling) to the Chinese authorities, to whom he passed himself off as a Chinese national. But to the Vietnamese whom he met in Canton he admitted to being a compatriot and asked them to call him Vuong Son Nhi, or plain Mr Vuong.

It is significant that, at this early stage of his revolutionary career, Ho had yet to acquire discretion. In inventing two names for himself, he had been unable to resist playing a Chinese word-game prevalent at the time amongst Chinese and Vietnamese scholars. The game consisted of splitting the ideogram representing one's own name into its component parts, each part being an ideogram by itself, and then using these parts as a pseudonym. In this case the character *Suei* (pronounced Thuy in Vietnamese) is made up of the three characters *Vuong, Son* and *Nhi*. This slight indiscretion enabled the better educated Vietnamese—and many Vietnamese *émigrés* were highly educated—to discern at once that Ly Thuy and Vuong Son Nhi were one and the same person. Other indiscretions revealed before long that he was none other than Nguyen Ai Quoc, already well known in Vietnam and France as an ardent communist. The next time he visited the same area (in 1941) he was far more careful to keep his identity a secret, which is indicative of his greater maturity.

Canton, which had been the centre of Sun Yat-sen's revolution, was still at that time the administrative and political capital of the Kuomintang government. The establishment of the Whampoa Military Academy nearby had made Canton a kind of anti-

---

[1] The word *Dong Chi* (in Chinese *T'ung Chi*) meaning 'comrade' reflects the communist tendency of the movement. This is the first occasion of its use in the Vietnamese language.

imperialist Mecca, and large numbers of south-east Asian intellectuals were attracted to this revolutionary city for political guidance and military training. Of these revolutionaries, by far the most numerous were Vietnamese.

On his arrival at Canton in the spring of 1925, Ho set to work to build up a political organisation designed to achieve his own ends. However, most of the Vietnamese refugees there already belonged to one of the existing nationalist groups and Ho found it necessary to represent himself as sharing the same aims as the leaders of these groups in order to contact the individual members of their organisations. He hoped in this way to attract the younger and more capable elements to his side. He was well aware that the more mature Vietnamese had, for the most part, a solid Confucian background, and were therefore practically immune to Marxist indoctrination; consequently he devoted his time almost entirely to the younger elements who had received some measure of Western education in the new Franco-Annamite schools. A golden opportunity for applying his indoctrination on a scale far greater than he had hoped occurred during the next year when he encountered large numbers of young men who had escaped from the repression following the Hanoi Students' movement in 1925. Of these new *émigrés*, Pham Van Dong, now Prime Minister of the Democratic Republic of Vietnam, had received the highest education. He was preparing for the baccalauréat in Hanoi when the Students' movement took place, leading to his expulsion from school. The others were of a lower educational standard, but the whole group had one thing in common: none of them had received any training in the traditional culture, that is to say, Confucianism, although all were sons of Confucian scholars.

Ho instructed his young disciples in the history of the Russian Revolution and the Marxist conception of the class-struggle, and he taught them some of the new revolutionary techniques. He showed them how to produce leaflets using the 'jelly' duplication method, how to conduct mass meetings, how to provoke workers' strikes, and so on. It took him only six months to complete the training program. By the end of 1925, he was ready to select the most brilliant among his followers to join him in forming the central committee of his Youth Association. The remainder he sent back to Vietnam to organise secret cells, to propagate the new doctrine and to help new recruits to journey secretly to Canton. The central committee, which remained in Canton, was responsible for printing the party newspaper, *Thanh-Nien*, and for translating communist breviaries from Chinese into Vietnamese. These hasty translations were often far from clear and correct. The main fault lay with the Chinese translators who had previously translated the documents from the Russian, for they were still unversed in Marxism. The word 'communism', for instance, was rendered as 'community of wealth', while 'proletariat' appeared in Chinese as 'wealthless'. These mistranslations persist even today in the Chinese and Vietnamese vocabulary, but people now understand what is meant by them. Such mistakes created some confusion at the time and rendered Marxism unintelligible to most people. Accurate translations became available only some years later, when communist documents published in France reached Vietnam.

Ho had received his political education in Moscow during the early years of Stalin's power, and he firmly believed in the two fundamental principles which formed the basis of the Stalinist orthodoxy. These were:

1. Dictatorship of the proletariat should be achieved in two stages as it had been in Russia—a bourgeois-democratic revolution preceding and paving the way for a communist revolution.

2. Workers alone are capable of good revolutionary leadership; peasants can only be regarded as 'long-term allies'.

The first of these principles determined Ho's attitude towards the various nationalist groups; he regarded them as temporary allies for the achievement of the first stage who could be expendable when occasion required. He competed with them relentlessly for political supremacy, and even betrayed certain individual nationalists to secure funds for his party. His belief in the second principle led him to devote more of his time to organising workers than to controlling peasants. His main concern at that time seems to have been to secure the spread of Marxist ideology in Vietnam by indoctrinating the intellectuals so that they, in turn, might organise workers into a network of communist cells in all the important industrial centres.

Though aiming all the time at unchallenged supremacy over his

nationalist rivals, Ho determined to wait until the latter had successfully accomplished their bourgeois-democratic revolution before attempting to snatch political power from them. His rivalry
with the nationalists secured for his followers a measure of tolerance from the colonial administration, which probably saw in the
communist movement a force which could rid them of the
nationalists and their uncompromisingly anti-French attitude. The
communist slogans, though anti-colonialist, were far less violent in
character than those of the nationalists. However, several unforeseen events changed the public image of the communist movement and led to unexpected consequences.

In the first place, the communist cells in Vietnam ran short of
money and, in order to secure the necessary funds, their members
resorted to numerous robberies with violence throughout the
country. Owing to some oversight in their training, these people
looked upon all rich Vietnamese as their enemies and robbed them
of their money and jewellery, using violence if necessary, whenever they thought fit. Such acts of open robbery soon caused public
opinion to identify communism with gangsterism and antagonised
the Vietnamese bourgeoisie. They also provided the colonial administration with an excuse to condemn all communist agents as
bandits and send them to jail.

Secondly, the arrest of Phan Boi Chau, for which Ho was held
mainly responsible, caused the nationalists to regard the communists with grave suspicion. All co-operation between them
ceased; although there was no open conflict at this stage, from
then on an undercurrent of hostility between the two groups
developed.

Thirdly, the sudden rift in 1927 between Chiang Kai-shek and
his communist colaborators brought to an abrupt end the first
Russian impact on China and eastern Asia. Michael Borodin, the
head of the Soviet consulate in China, who had acted for years as
political adviser to the Kuomintang, was obliged to leave China in
a hurry taking with him to Moscow all his collaborators, including
Ho Chi Minh.

When Chiang attacked the Chinese communists and massacred
many of their number, Ho was still busy teaching in Whampoa.
The course had to be stopped at once and the students were obliged

to return home as best they could. A few days later, Ho met a
group of them at Canton, and sought to hearten them by saying :
'Don't be discouraged by the recent setback. Remember that a
storm is a good opportunity for the *Tung* (pine) and the *Ba*
(cypress) to show their strength and their stability.' (Ho was
making use of an old Chinese proverb.) He then accompanied
Borodin to Hankow, where, in an effort to oppose Chiang's military dictatorship, Wang Ching-wei, a political adherent of Sun
Yat-sen, had set up the so-called Wu-han government. Borodin
offered Wang Soviet aid to fight against Chiang on the condition
that he adopted a more leftist policy and implemented land reform,
confiscating land from the rich for redistribution among the poor.
But eventually Wang chose to surrender to Chiang, and the Soviet
delegation, including Ho, left for Moscow. The communist movement in Asia was thus driven off the course determined for it by
the Comintern; the consequences of this deviation were not slow
to follow.

Before leaving China, Ho appointed Ho Tung Mau, the oldest
of his followers, to succeed him as secretary-general of the Youth
Association. It was a good choice since Mau was as wise and
cautious as Ho himself. Ho advised Mau to stick firmly to the
political line that he had laid down for the Association, *i.e.* to continue to spread Marxist ideology under the cover of the anti-
colonialist struggle. He also insisted that there should be no
parading of communist slogans, since these might frighten away
the Vietnamese bourgeoisie whose sympathy the party still needed.
Mau faithfully carried out Ho's instructions until his arrest by
the Kuomintang authorities the following year. The leadership of
the movement then fell to Lam Duc Thu whose doings have already been described in Chapter Two.

In May 1927, Thu convoked delegates from Vietnam to a
national congress in Hong Kong. Three of the four who arrived
were shocked by Thu's bourgeois way of life : he resided in a
luxurious hotel, drank whisky and smoked expensive Manila
cigars. They accused the central committee of bourgeois tendencies
and rightist deviations. When their demand for an overt communist agitation was outvoted, they walked out in disgust. On
their return to Vietnam they organised on their own initiative a

communist group which they called the 'Indochinese Communist Party'. Greatly perturbed by the rapid progress being made by these three activists, the central committee decided to transform the Youth Association into an overt communist organisation. To distinguish it from its rival they called it the 'Annamese Communist Party'. At the same time some members of the *Tan-Viet*, a party composed exclusively of intellectuals of the social-democrat type, founded a communist party which they called the 'Indochinese Communist Union'. Thus there were now three communist parties in Vietnam, each one hostile to the other two. The ensuing conflict between them provided the French authorities with a pretext for making mass arrests which led to the rapid collapse of the whole communist movement in Vietnam.

THE NGHE-AN SOVIETS MOVEMENT

Following his return to Moscow, Ho's first assignment was to the Anti-Imperialist League in Berlin, but it was short-lived, and he was then sent to Bangkok where a Comintern South-Sea Bureau had been set up. There he worked under the supervision of a French communist agent, Hilaire Noulens, at the task of organising Vietnamese immigrants and converting them to communism: there were many such immigrants in the north-eastern provinces of Siam, close to the Laotian border. This Vietnamese colony was made up of two distinct groups known as the 'old' and the 'new' Vietnamese. The 'old' were the descendants of former waves of *émigrés* who had followed their exiled prince to Siam at the end of the eighteenth century, during the period of civil war. The 'new' were traders who preferred to settle in Siam where they could acquire wealth more easily than was possible in Vietnam. Among them were a few revolutionaries who had come through Laos to escape French repression. Although many of them had forgotten the Vietnamese language and had adopted Thai customs, their attachment to their own country was still very strong.[2] Ho employed the same strategy here as he had used in south China.

[2] Firmly controlled by agents of the Democratic Republic of Vietnam, this colony of immigrants has become in recent years a permanent threat to the security of Thailand.

C

While working in this area during 1929, Ho met quite by chance a man from his native village who immediately recognised him in spite of his disguise. On returning home, this man, a trader, reported to some local communists that he had seen Ho, and they, in turn, informed their leaders. The latter at once sent a delegation to Siam imploring Ho to use his influence in settling the quarrel at home. He agreed to do so, but it took him a whole year to obtain the necessary authorisation from the Comintern. It is significant that Ho was removed from the Chinese arena, which culturally included Vietnam, and sent to an area of unrelated culture, and that he was given a modest task under the supervision of a European communist.

This, along with other measures taken by the Comintern at that time, suggests that Stalin had had more than enough of the Chinese communists after the spectacular Russian failure in China, and especially after Mao's impertinent deviation from Leninist orthodoxy. He wanted to leave them to their own fate. The communist movement in Vietnam, an offshoot of Chinese communism, was similarly neglected by him. Concluding that European communists were more obedient and reliable, Stalin planned to attack Western imperialism by intensifying communist subversion in south-east Asia. He hoped to accomplish this through the good offices of the French, Dutch and British Communist parties. This was the real reason for the increasing importance attached by the Comintern to its South-Sea Bureau at the expense of the Far-Eastern Bureau in Shanghai, whose activities were greatly curtailed. Not until the 1930s did Stalin realise that, even in these non-Chinese countries, nothing could be achieved without the direct participation of the Chinese inhabitants who were more politically minded than the local people. The centre of co-ordination was thus moved first to Shanghai and later to Hong Kong. Meanwhile, since Mao had moved his headquarters westward, leaving the coastal area of China free from his influence, Stalin resumed his interest in this relatively industrialised zone. He sent a team from Moscow to salvage what they could in the area and to restore some order and organisation. This new policy was the reason why Ho Chi Minh was sent back to Hong Kong at the end of 1929 to rejoin his former disciples with whom he had been prevented from making contact for three years.

Ho summoned representatives of the three rival Vietnamese communist factions to Hong Kong, where he resolved their differences and reunited them into a single 'Vietnamese Communist Party'. Later, in 1931, the name was changed to the 'Indochinese Communist Party' so that Laos and Cambodia might be included in its field of activity, and the headquarters were transferred to Vietnamese territory. As a result of his success, Ho was appointed head of the Far-Eastern Bureau of the Comintern, and became responsible for liaison between Moscow and the various communist organisations all over south-east Asia.

The onerous duties of his new office made it impossible for him to exercise close control over the movement in Vietnam, and he was forced to rely on the ability of local leaders. For the most part, unlike Ho, these men were hot-headed and impetuous, and difficult to control. Most of them had served their communist apprenticeship in China and had been impressed by Chinese examples— the commune of Canton, the peasant movement in Hunan and the like. They were eager to inaugurate radical changes. The quelling of the nationalist revolt of February 1930 had produced in them a bitter eagerness to take over from their unfortunate rivals. Moreover the world economic depression had had a most serious effect upon the Vietnamese peasantry. Crops were as abundant as ever but it was impossible to export rice. The result was that big landlords as well as wage-earning peasants were reduced to utter poverty. The ruin of the peasantry very soon affected the urban bourgeoisie which, in its turn, also became bankrupt. Thus general dissatisfaction was prevalent in all classes of Vietnamese society, with the exception of the public servants who continued to receive the same salary as before despite the deflation which reduced prices to a quarter or a fifth of their former level, and with the exception also, to some extent, of workers in large enterprises, whose salaries, though somewhat reduced, still gave them a regular income. These two groups were in marked contrast to the rest of the population who were without the means to obtain money to buy food and to pay taxes.

Under these circumstances it was practically impossible for the communists to recruit and to organise workers in industrial centres, as the Comintern wished. Those lucky enough to command a regular salary thought only of keeping their jobs. On the other hand, the situation in the villages was highly explosive. Peasants starved whilst food was ridiculously cheap. The communist leaders saw in this situation an opportunity to imitate their Chinese comrades, and to lead the angry peasants into open revolt. So, on May Day 1930, huge meetings were organised in the villages, followed by hunger marches which, advancing on the administrative centres, developed into bloody riots. At this point the colonial administration called out the Foreign Legion whose machine guns were turned on the long marching columns.

Driven to despair by the failure of the revolt and in a final bid to save the movement, the Indochinese Communist Party decided on the creation of peasant soviets in several districts of Nghe-An province still under their control. This was a repetition of Mao's campaign four years previously. Backed by the peasant militia he had organised, Mao was able to resist the attacks launched against him by the inefficient Kuomintang army. But the Vietnamese communists, without militia, were unable to withstand the counter-measures taken by French forces. The Nghe-An soviets collapsed within a matter of a few months. By the end of 1931, complete order had been restored throughout the country. All communists of any importance were captured and imprisoned. Ho, who had returned to Hong Kong at the end of 1929, was arrested there on June 6, 1931. On being released, probably in 1932 (the exact date is in question), he immediately went to Singapore where he was arrested a second time and sent back to Hong Kong where he was admitted to hospital because of tuberculosis. He then disappears without trace in 1933. The British authorities have not disclosed the circumstances of his disappearance, escape from custody, whatever we may call it, but it is believed by some that Ho was released in return for a promise to do secret work for the British Intelligence Service.[3] This is not improbable, for it is known that he concluded a similar agreement with the French security police (see Chapter Two). A news-item published in the Daily Worker (the organ of the British Communist Party) and

[3] Bernard Fall: Le Viet Minh (Librairie Armand Colin, Paris, 1960), p. 31.

accepted by French as well as Vietnamese communists, stated that Ho died of tuberculosis in a Hong Kong prison. As early as 1933, the French security police noted in Nguyen Ai Quoc's dossier that he had 'died in Hong Kong' in that year.[4] At all events, Ho leaves the scene, and his influence is not apparent in any policy formed by the Indochinese Communist Party during the rest of the 1930s.

Nobody, apart from Ho himself and a few senior officials of the Comintern, knows for certain what he did and where he lived between this disappearance from Hong Kong in 1933 and his reappearance in Moscow in 1941. Even Nguyen Khanh Toan, who lived in Moscow from 1927 onwards, teaching Vietnamese at Moscow University, honestly believed that Ho had died. Toan has since told his friends of his utter surprise when Ho appeared unannounced at his house one morning in 1941. Ho suggested that Toan should go with him to a place near the Vietnamese border to foment a revolution in their own country. When Toan agreed, arrangements were hastily made, and a few days later the two Vietnamese boarded the Trans-Siberian railway for Yenan (officially Fu-shih).

Another of Toan's disclosures throws some light on Ho's marital affairs. A few hours after their hurried departure from Moscow, a Russian woman arrived at Ho's house saying she had been appointed Ho's wife by the party for the duration of his stay in the Soviet capital. There are reasons for thinking that Toan's story is not wholly reliable, but there may be elements of truth in it. There is such a dearth of information about Ho's life at this period that we must 'make do' with what we can find. It certainly was the custom of the Comintern to provide 'temporary wives' for important government officials and party-servants whose continual clandestine travels made it impossible for them to live a normal married life. Toan himself had been given a wife during his prolonged stay in Moscow who bore him several children. He abandoned her when he departed and was supplied with a Chinese wife for his four years' residence at Yenan. The 'wives' of departing cadres were normally given to the newly-arrived activists, so that they became 'professional party-wives' to a succession of itinerant communist officials. It would seem that arrangements of

[4] Jean Lacouture: *Cinq Hommes et la France*, p. 35.

this kind were the responsibility of the local communist women's organisations.

Toan's amazement when Ho suddenly reappeared lends weight to the theory that the Vietnamese communist leader had been secretly hidden in the Soviet Union—somewhere far from Moscow —between 1933 and 1941. One thing is quite certain: Ho had never been in Yenan prior to his going there with Toan in 1941. There is a second reason for accepting this interpretation of events. During the period when the Nghe-An soviets were being organised, Ho's attitude was somewhat ambiguous. While he most certainly did not approve of the action taken (a repetition of Mao's Hunan campaign which Stalin held to be anathema), he took no steps to stop it. During a Thought Reform course in 1953, it was disclosed that Ho had voted against the resolution calling for a peasant uprising, but he was in a minority of one and submitted to the will of the majority. (This story was published to illustrate Ho's strict observance of democratic rules.) Whatever the truth, there is no doubt that this was the first occasion on which Ho lost control of the movement under his charge. This failure in Ho's leadership may have determined Stalin to entrust the political guidance of the Indochinese Communist Party, and the responsibility for correcting its deviations, to Maurice Thorez, leader of the French Communist Party. Stalin consequently would be anxious to remove Ho so as to avoid any division of authority. If Ho remained in eastern Asia, most Vietnamese communists might be tempted to look to him, not to Thorez, for leadership. His absence left his former field of activity open to the French Communist Party which acted as intermediary between Vietnamese communism and Moscow. This situation persisted for ten years, until the Second World War severed contact between France and Vietnam.

THE POPULAR FRONT

The use of communist parties in 'metropolitan' countries to control party-members in colonial territories on behalf of Moscow implied a radical change in political tactics. Since the official line of the party now required leadership and initiative in the work of communists in the colonies to come from the relevant European communist party, nationalist fervour was discouraged and anti-colonialist slogans retracted. Anti-capitalist slogans took their place, for under the new dispensation the main target was not the colonial administration as such, but the capitalists, metropolitan and local.

Arrangements were made for Vietnamese communists who had been active in France, and a few who had been trained in Moscow, to slip into Vietnam. Most of these had to stay in Cochin China where they enjoyed relative freedom to pursue their activities. Here they organised the workers to protect proletarian interests against the 'yellow and white sharks of finance and industry', and presented themselves as opposition candidates in local elections. The movement quickly gathered momentum, but the communists did not have the field entirely to themselves. Trotskyites returning to Vietnam from France competed vigorously with them for political supremacy; being better educated on the whole than the communists, they soon won the sympathies of the intellectuals and petty-bourgeois in Cochin China. But the bulk of the workers and the peasants remained under the control of the communists of the Third International.

In the meantime, those in jail were brushing up their Marxism-Leninism, and organising secret political courses for their fellow prisoners as well as for themselves. It was in this period that many nationalist prisoners were persuaded to accept communism. So numerous were the conversions to Marxism that a despairing nationalist on Poulo Condore Island gathered his former comrades about him, and, before their eyes, cut his throat. Later nationalism came to be regarded as a spent force, and the average Vietnamese felt that the emancipation of his country depended entirely on the future success of the left-wing parties in France. The rise of the Popular Front in France encouraged them in this view. Faced with such a change in the French political scene, the colonial authorities in Vietnam hesitated over the course they should adopt and temporarily relaxed their control. Widespread agitation immediately followed.

In the south, Stalinists and Trotskyites intensified their activities, but since the latter had no confidence in the French communists or in the Popular Front, they became more vehement in

their attacks than the Moscow-aligned communists and so won
for themselves greater prestige. Through being obliged by the current line in Moscow to advocate the acceptance of colonialism, the
'official' communists were placed at a disadvantage. In the northern
parts of Indochina, intellectuals of all political leanings combined
to found a French-language newspaper, *Le Travail*, since only
newspapers in French could be published without a special licence.
This group comprised a large number of politically conscious Vietnamese who were members of no party, a few Moscow-orientated
communists newly released from prison, one Trotskyite from
Saigon (though strong in the south, Trotskyism was virtually non-
existent in Hanoi), and two former members of the *Tan-Viet*:
Dang Thai Mai and Vo Nguyen Giap, who had been communist
party members since 1930.[5]

For some months, they all co-operated successfully, and
aroused the interest and enthusiasm of intellectuals in northern
Vietnam. It was not long, however, before the French socialists
belonging to the SFIO in Vietnam began building up a branch of
the party in Hanoi and another in Saigon, admitting Vietnamese
intellectuals freely to membership. Since the branches were off-
shoots of the party in government in France, they were free from
repression and played an active rôle in fighting social injustice in
Indochina. The communists collaborated secretly with these two
branches and used their influence among the workers to foment
strikes and demonstrations in support of the socialists' actions.

[5] Mai and Giap at this time had both become protégés of
Louis Marty, the director of the Political Affairs and General
Security Service in Indochina. Under his protection, they lived
quietly and comfortably in Hanoi until the emergence of the
Vietminh, in which they both became influential members.
Giap later became commander-in-chief of the DRV's army and
was responsible for making possible its success at Dien Bien
Phu in 1954. He gained his *licence en droit* in 1937 but failed
to obtain the Certificate of Administrative Law in the following year, nor did he gain his Doctorate of Law, as many writers
assert. He spent a few months at the military training course
in Tsin-tsi run by American officers, but it is not true, as is
often claimed, that he ever went to Yenan. For long, Giap
and Mai regarded themselves as 'brothers by mutual adoption',
a relationship which was transformed into that of father-in-
law and son-in-law by Giap's marriage (his second) to Mai's
daughter in 1946.

The measure of success attained by the socialists and the communists working together may be judged by the events of May Day 1937, when twenty thousand people assembled and paraded through the streets of Hanoi.

Meanwhile, a general amnesty was proclaimed for all political prisoners. Communists released from jail very soon resumed their political activities. They were now more cautious, however, than they had been in the past. They reorganised themselves into two sections, an overt group designed to engage in legal activities, and a clandestine group whose task it was secretly to reconstruct the network of communist cells. This wise precaution later enabled the communists to survive the repression which followed the fall of the Popular Front government in France. The overt group, led by Truong Chinh, infiltrated the organisation publishing *Le Travail* and undermined, and eventually destroyed, the Trotskyite element on the paper. But while this was going on, the paper was suppressed by the authorities. The communists thereupon organised another body entirely under their control which published two newspapers: one in French, the *Rassemblement*, and another, *Tin Tuc* (News), in Vietnamese; but neither achieved any marked success.

Gradually, the early enthusiasm melted away. The Popular Front government proved itself to be no less colonialist than its predecessors, often resorting to repressive measures and always restricting its revolutionary activity to empty promises for the future. The fall of the Popular Front in France in 1938, and the advent of the Second World War, ended the Popular Front movement in Vietnam. The Socialist Party disbanded and the communists went underground. Since normal traffic between France and Vietnam was interrupted, the French Communist Party ceased to have any control over its sister organisation in Vietnam. Although non-violent in its methods, the Vietnamese Popular Front left a deeper imprint upon the general trend of the Vietnamese revolution than any previous movement. During the relatively short period of its existence, communist publications from Paris and Moscow flooded the Vietnamese market and contributed to the spreading and consolidation of the Marxist ideology among the intelligentsia and in petty-bourgeois circles. Consequently, the new foreign doctrine began to replace the more rudimentary creed of simple Vietnamese nationalism. The desire for national independence was outweighed by a longing for democracy, and communism came to be regarded as the most perfect form of democracy.

The workers, who had acquired a few social privileges during the Popular Front period, looked upon the communists as the only effective defenders of their class. The large peasant masses, still largely illiterate, were not yet capable of absorbing any kind of ideology although a number evinced interest in the promise of the equal distribution of land. They were attracted into various co-operatives and mutual aid associations, discreetly controlled by communists who, for the most part, belonged to the village bourgeoisie. The majority were well-off peasants or small landlords who had failed to secure for themselves positions in their village communities secure enough to protect them against the oppression of higher authorities.

When the communists went underground, they organised a vast network of secret cells, formed by more than ten thousand party members and many more sympathisers. Between 1939 and 1941, however, these were paralysed into inactivity by the measures of the colonial administration and by the sudden upsurge of nationalism when Japanese troops entered Vietnam. Moreover, since Soviet Russia had signed a non-aggression pact with Nazi Germany and was maintaining a neutral attitude towards Japan, the Vietnamese communists, along with communists in other countries, found themselves in difficulties over the best course of action to adopt. Despite these setbacks, however, their faith was unshaken and their organisation stood firm, so that they contrived to prevent nationalist enthusiasm from gaining control over the masses. They were eventually rescued from their political embarrassment when Japan declared that she respected French sovereignty in Indochina and Russia became an ally of the Western democracies. The Vietnamese communists then produced their slogan: 'Remove the double yoke imposed by the French and Japanese; fight against both the colonialists and the fascists!' Their latent reserve force was ready to emerge into the open when communist leaders, who had fled to China, returned as 'liberators'. This is known as the 'Vietminh Revolution'.

FIVE

The Final Triumph

The movement which brought the Vietnamese communists to
power (the fourth movement in the struggle for freedom from
French rule), followed as a direct result of the Second World War.
Many writers have described it in great detail. In this book, its
general historical background, rather than a detailed study of its
history, will be given; only such facts as are essential for understanding developments will be presented, so as to leave more space
for a description of the less widely known Chinese technique of
imposing the dictatorship of the proletariat. Our interpretation of
a given event may possibly differ slightly from that of an observer
studying events from the outside. This is because the present
writer is drawing on his own first-hand experiences of the whole
evolution of the Resistance movement of which he was a member.
It has not been necessary for him to rely either on Vietminh or
French accounts and documents. Both are often contradictory and
not always relevant.

THE VIETMINH MOVEMENT

Only three months after the defeat of France by Germany in
1940, Vietnam came under Japanese occupation. At that time,
having signed a non-aggression pact with Germany, Russia
adopted an uncommitted attitude towards the war between the
'fascists' and the 'imperialists'. After a careful study of the situa-

tion, the Comintern was probably able to foresee what would happen to French imperialism following the entry of Japanese troops into her colony. Anticipating the inevitable collapse of French power in Vietnam, and possibly that of Japan at a later date, Moscow very probably realised that the resulting situation in Indochina would be most favourable to the emergence of communism. Ho Chi Minh was recalled to Moscow and from there sent to southern China to resume the task he had been forced to abandon ten years earlier.

As we have already related, Ho set off for China in the spring of 1941, accompanied by Nguyen Khanh Toan. But in the course of the long journey on the Trans-Siberian railway, Ho discovered to his regret that Toan would never be the kind of revolutionary for whom he had hoped. For the past fifteen years, Toan had lived in Moscow as a 'foreign teacher', a status which assured for him a large salary and a quiet, comfortable life. Observing that Toan ate and drank too much, Ho concluded that his companion had become too addicted to good living to be able to withstand the privation and hardship which were an integral part of the life of a clandestine revolutionary. And so, on arrival at Yenan, Ho immediately arranged with Mao to have Toan retained there for the time being. Telling Toan what he had done and why, Ho promised to send him news if and when his revolution was successful. Senior members of the Indochinese Communist Party have remarked on the fact that, of all the Vietnamese communists, Ho and Toan have led the most widely differing lives. Ho's experiences have been hard and often perilous, whereas Toan has always enjoyed a quiet, almost bourgeois, way of life.

So Toan remained idle in Yenan, enjoying once more the privileges of a foreigner, possessing the ration card normally reserved for Europeans, and provided with a Chinese wife. He remained there long enough to beget two children. After the success of the Vietminh revolution on August 19, 1945, Ho was so busy that he forgot to communicate with Toan. On learning of these events from a Canadian correspondent, Toan decided to return to Vietnam. When Mao accorded him the necessary permission, he set out in company with Nguyen Son, a Vietnamese who had joined the Chinese Communist Party in 1927. In December 1945, they reached Hanoi, where Toan was appointed vice-minister of Education, controlling the minister, Nguyen Van Huyen, who was not a party-member.

Having left Toan in Yenan, Ho secretly slipped into the zone controlled by the Kuomintang and went alone to southern China to a spot close to the Vietnamese border, where he made contact with a group of Vietnamese nationalists already active there. He kept his identity a secret, and for the first time began to call himself Ho Chi Minh, pretending to be an anti-fascist Vietnamese whose aim was to deliver his country from Japanese occupation. He lost no time, however, in summoning to him such of his former colleagues as were still in China (amongst them was Ho Tung Mau). With their help, he founded the Vietminh Front. 'Vietminh' is an abbreviation of *Viet-Nam Doc-Lap Dong-Minh*, or 'League for the Independence of Vietnam'.[1] Some of his associates were sent over to Vietnam to renew contacts and revive the dormant network of communist cells. Before long, many of the communist leaders who had been arrested by the colonial administration and kept in concentration camps escaped in groups and fled to China. The French had arrested these leaders and placed them in prison camps before Russia entered the war against Germany. But after the Japanese occupation of Vietnam, the communists and the French ceased to be enemies, having a common foe in the Japanese. Thus it was not difficult for the communists to escape from their French captors.

Ho offered to place his clandestine organisation inside Vietnam at the disposal of the British and American intelligence services. He was given the task of reporting on Japanese troop movements

[1] Foreign correspondents and writers customarily refer to the Vietnamese communists as the 'Vietminh', sometimes rather crudely shortened to 'Viet'. It should be noted that 'Viet' is a generic name for the whole people in south-east China and in Vietnam, and that 'Vietminh' initially was a national movement for independence in which a large number of non-communists participated. To distinguish between Vietminh as a national movement and the Vietnamese communists, the press in Saigon since 1956 has referred to the latter as 'Vietcong', *Cong* (an abbreviation of *Cong-san*) standing for 'communists'. The new term is precise and accurate and, contrary to what many foreign correspondents believe, does not have any disparaging meaning.

and of helping Allied pilots shot down by the Japanese to escape
into China. The British freed all communists who had been exiled
to Madagascar and parachuted them into the Vietminh guerrilla
zone,[2] while the Americans provided them with portable radio-
equipment and hundreds of light machine-guns. Ho used these to
seize a few military posts from the French, but was careful not to
risk an encounter with the stronger, better armed Japanese. His
plan was to preserve his American supplies intact if possible in
anticipation of the defeat of Japan and the emergence of new
rivals.   Everything happened in the way Ho had foreseen. Following the liberation of France, the French authorities, now compromised by the oath of allegiance they had sworn to the Vichy
government and wishing to redeem themselves, planned a revolt
against the Japanese occupying forces. The Japanese learned of the
preparations and anticipated the uprisings. On March 9, 1945,
three days before the date fixed by the French for their revolt, the
colonial administration was overthrown by the Japanese and all
French soldiers and civilians imprisoned. Bao Dai was retained as
emperor and a pro-Japanese government was set up; it was a
government in name only, for it possessed no military power, no
arms and no ammunition. Its members were men of strong
nationalist leanings who showed their patriotism by ordering the
release of all political prisoners, including communists. These
latter immediately joined the ranks of the Vietminh.

On August 19, 1945, five days after the Japanese surrendered to
the Allies, the Vietminh, by means of popular demonstrations
and a few revolver shots, captured undefended Hanoi. Bao Dai
was made to abdicate in favour of Ho Chi Minh who proclaimed
himself President of the Provisional Government of the Democratic Republic of Vietnam. A few days later, in accordance with
the Potsdam Agreement, British troops landed at Saigon and
Chinese troops entered Hanoi to disarm the defeated Japanese.
Both these occupying forces used their influence to prevent the
Vietminh from extending its control. The British in the south did
what they could to assist French efforts to regain control of the

[2] Among these was Hoang Huu Nam (the real name of Phan
Boi), who became vice-minister of the Interior in 1946. He was
assassinated by a nationalist while crossing a river ferry in
1947.

country, and the Kuomintang officers supported the attempts of
the Vietnamese nationalists to weaken the Vietminh position.
The opposition to the Vietminh came mostly from the *neo-Viet-
Nam Quoc-Dan Dang* (led by Vu Hong Khanh), the *Viet-Nam
Cach-Menh Dong-Minh* (led by Nguyen Hai Than), the *Dai-
Viet Quoc-Dan Dang* (led by Truong Tu Anh), and the *Ngu-Xa*
movement (led by Phan Quang Dan).[3] They employed normal
constitutional tactics in opposing the Vietminh, but also resorted
to the murder of Vietminh cadres and to military action in order
to assert their control in certain provinces.

Faced by a growing opposition to his policy, Ho was forced to
compromise with the nationalists. By guaranteeing them a number
of seats in a National Assembly constituted by 'democratic elections',[4] he contrived to form a coalition government, and appealed
for national unity to face the expected French attack. The Communist Party declared itself voluntarily disbanded in a spectacular
gesture designed to show communist devotion to the nationalist
cause. But it continued to operate secretly and never relaxed its
grip on the population. The nationalists, on the other hand, con-
solidated their position and intensified their anti-communist propaganda. Assailed from both sides, Ho Chi Minh found himself in
a desperate situation when, quite unexpectedly, an agreement between Paris and Nanking gave him the chance he had been waiting for. Marshal Chiang agreed to withdraw his troops from northern Vietnam and leave the way clear for the French army to
move in.

[3] Truong Tu Anh was assassinated by the communists in
1946, whereupon the leadership of the Dai-Viet devolved on
Nguyen Ton Hoan, now in exile in Paris. Phan Quang Dan
led a legal opposition to the Ngo Dinh Diem government in
South Vietnam, with the result that he is now in prison. Dan's
successor, Pham Huy Co, is in Paris.
[4] The names of official candidates (the majority of whom were
communists and party sympathisers, including the ex-Emperor
Bao Dai) were versified and also inscribed in three lists called
A, B and C. When illiterate voters, who then formed 80 per
cent of the population, arrived at the ballot box, the official
responsible for marking the ballot paper on their behalf would
ask them: 'For whom do you want to vote?' All they had to do
was simply to recite the verse they had memorised, or to say
'A, B and C', and that did the trick.

Following the departure of the Chinese, the communists in the Vietminh soon crushed all nationalist resistance and then endeavoured to come to terms with the French. On March 6, 1946, an accord was signed whereby France 'recognised the Republic of Vietnam as a Free State having its own government, parliament, army and treasury, and belonging to the Indochinese Federation and the French Union'. Ho made further efforts to rewrite the terms of the accord on lines more favourable to the Vietminh policy of complete independence, for the agreement involved the continuation of the presence of French occupying forces in Vietnam. Conferences were held in Dalat (April and May 1946) and in Fontainebleau (July and August), but neither of them produced what Ho wanted despite his going to Paris himself to negotiate. All he had to show at the end was an agreement (confirming the provisions of the earlier accord) signed in September 1946 by Ho and Marius Moutet, the Minister for Overseas Territories and an old French socialist whom Ho had known for more than twenty years.

The French paid little heed to this document and, on various pretexts, occupied one stronghold after another until finally, on December 19, 1946, Ho retaliated with a surprise attack. He made his decision at 11 a.m. and the attack was timed to start at 8 p.m. Vo Nguyen Giap, who was in charge of military affairs, immediately transmitted the order to all the Vietminh troops scattered throughout the country. At 2 p.m., however, Giap received news that Marius Moutet was on his way to Vietnam; accordingly he returned to the presidential palace to ask whether, under the circumstances, Ho wished to postpone the attack. But Ho did not revoke his decision. That night saw the beginning of a war which lasted for more than eight years.

Ho had pursued a policy of compromise with the French in order to gain time for the Vietminh to consolidate its political and military strength. He probably bided his time also to see what progress was being made by his Chinese counterpart, Mao Tse-tung. But there is no doubt that all along it was his conviction that, if it came to a war with the French, he would triumph in the end. Vietnam, he was well aware, is a long way from France, and the French people had not fully recovered from the German occupa-

tion. Moreover, as a result of the Second World War, the international situation had altered so radically that colonial reconquest
was no longer possible. The war, provoked by the French, would
itself strengthen the hitherto uncertain authority of the Vietminh
for it would make Ho and his supporters the genuine defenders of
their country and give validity to their hitherto baseless claim of
being its 'liberators'. Ho became a symbol of national unity and
many Vietnamese joined him in the fight for their country's
independence.

THE WAR OF RESISTANCE

The Vietminh leaders planned to repeat the Japanese coup of
March 9, 1945, by attacking the French garrisons at 8 p.m. while
their officers were still at dinner. On this occasion, however, the
French had been warned of the impending attack in good time by
a Eurasian serving in the Vietminh ranks. Although forced to
surrender in a few places held by only a handful of men, the
French successfully defended the towns where they outnumbered
the Vietminh. The outcome of this first attack established the
pattern which was to last for three years: the French afraid to
venture outside the towns; the Vietminh in control of the countryside, destroying bridges, removing railway lines and cutting roads.
Any enlargement made of the area controlled by the French was
offset by greater improvements in the Vietminh's military
organisation. The stalemate was still continuing when the Kuomintang collapsed in China and Mao proclaimed his People's
Republic in Peking on October 1, 1949. Ho's appeals for help were
answered when, in the February of 1950, Mao dispatched one of
his most able lieutenants, General Lo Kwei-po, to act as military
adviser to the Vietminh army. He was soon followed by a flood of
Chinese experts arriving to serve in every branch of Vietminh administration. In addition, President Mao ordered the two Chinese
provinces adjoining Vietnam—Kwang-si and Kwang-tung—to
supply the Vietminh with foodstuffs, arms and ammunition. Large
numbers of Vietminh officers began to travel to China to receive
military training.

With Chinese military support, the Vietminh launched a

general offensive against the French positions along the Sino-Vietnamese border, forcing the French to retreat southwards into the delta of the Red River. Emboldened by his initial success, General Lo, who had little experience of air attack, advised the Vietminh to pursue the retreating French and attack their positions in the low-lying delta. Fierce French aerial bombardment with napalm inflicted heavy casualties upon the Vietminh, forcing them to withdraw in disorder. Realising the gravity of his mistake, General Lo changed his strategy and attempted to lure the French back into the jungle. The first part of his new plan was to attack the French posts in neighbouring Laos. Lying behind the protection of the Annamese Chain, these positions had long been considered safe from attack and had consequently been allowed to lapse into a state of complete unpreparedness.

The Vietminh began to prepare stocks of food—chiefly steamed rice and salted fish—since Laos was so sparsely populated that no help could be expected from the local inhabitants. They also requisitioned all available bicycles, previously smuggled out of the French-occupied zone, to transport provisions and ammunition. In this way Vietminh troops crossed the Annamese Chain and moved through the Laotian jungle so quickly that the French were taken completely by surprise.

The Vietnamese launched three major campaigns against Laos. The first campaign was in the direction of Luang Prabang, the royal city. During this campaign, they reached a point thirty miles north of the city on April 30, 1953. To prevent the Vietminh from repeating this menacing thrust, the French occupied Dien Bien Phu on November 20, 1953, by parachuting there six battalions. The Vietminh then launched a second campaign, this time in central Laos, and occupied Thakhek on December 28. Thereafter, they moved southwards in the direction of southern Laos. Their aim in doing this seems to have been to force the French to scatter their forces throughout Laos and so exhaust their air force in the task of supplying a great number of isolated posts. Finally, the Vietminh launched a third campaign directed once again towards Luang Prabang. On February 8, 1954, they arrived at a point within twenty miles of the capital. The Laotian king crossed for safety to the other side of the Mekong. The French parachuted more and more troops into Dien Bien Phu.

Although little more than a village, Luang Prabang, as the royal capital, had to be defended at all costs, hence the French plan to halt the Vietminh advance by cutting off their supply route at Dien Bien Phu, a post deep in the jungle and just behind the Vietminh's lines. The latter laid siege to this outpost. The operation of parachuting more and more troops to hold it cost the French several aircraft, for the Vietminh were using accurate Czech-manufactured anti-aircraft guns.

It is almost certain that the Vietminh launched their campaigns against Laos, not with the aim of occupying it (there was, in fact, little possibility then of their being able to hold territory in Laos for any appreciable length of time), but simply to trap French troops in the jungle where they would be at a disadvantage. De Lattre de Tassigny was a good strategist, but his successors were not equal to him and they wholly failed to cope with the challenge presented by Vietminh tactics. The move to attack the Vietminh army in the rear turned into a trap for the French. Relying on conventional Western tactics, they were forced on to the defensive by guerrilla tactics. Dien Bien Phu became impossible to hold.

At this juncture, the Russians suggested to the government in Paris a means whereby the war might be ended without involving the French in too great a loss of face. As a result, in 1954, a conference was held in Geneva. At first, the French were reluctant to accept the conditions imposed by the Vietminh. While they were wavering, General Lo launched a massive assault on Dien Bien Phu, overwhelming the garrison and forcing it to surrender on May 7, 1954. This major defeat caused general alarm in France, with the result that the Mendès-France government signed rather too hastily an agreement giving the Vietminh more than their leaders had hoped for.

The truce came at the very moment when the province of Thanh-Hoa was on the verge of famine. This province, formed by the rich delta of Song Ma, called the second granary of northern Vietnam, was never occupied by French troops. In historical times, it had repeatedly served as a Vietnamese bastion against Chinese

invaders. During the Indochinese war, it was the major source of
food for the Vietminh army. The French army was perhaps in-
capable of conquering that vast plain, separated from Tongking
by a straight chain of mountains; but the more probable explanation is that French strategists, paying no heed to the lessons to be
learned from Vietnamese history or to the precepts of Sun Tzu,[5]
simply neglected to conquer the province.

A measure of the province's importance during the war is the
fact that it supplied the communist troops at Dien Bien Phu with
76 per cent of their provisions. This figure was cited in an official
message of thanks to the population of Thanh-Hoa. The size of
this contribution can be appreciated only when it is realised that
the prevailing method of transporting the rice—known as the
'walking grain process'—permitted no more than 10 per cent of
the rice levied in Thanh-Hoa province to reach Dien Bien Phu.
The other 90 per cent was eaten *en route* by hundreds of thousands
of porters, men and women, each of whom carried 15 kilos (about
33 pounds) of rice on his or her shoulders, travelling at about 15
kilometres (about 10 miles) every night. To avoid French air
attacks, all travelling took place between sunset and midnight.
Endless lines of porters wound along the roads every night, each
fifth man carrying a hurricane lamp, dousing it immediately at
the sound of an approaching aircraft. Seen from above, this long
procession of lamps looked like an illustration from a book of fairy
tales.

[5] Sun Tzu was a famous strategist of the third century BC
whose military precepts are still respected and carefully
studied by Mao Tse-tung. In an offensive action, Sun Tzu
recommended three operations: 'First conquer the heart (of
the people), second conquer (the source of) supplies, and
thirdly conquer the fortresses.' Looking back on the War of
Resistance, it is apparent that the Vietminh observed the first
principle and the French the third. Similar neglect of the first
principle by the Vietminh's opponents is apparent today in
South Vietnam in the struggle between the American-
supported government of Ngo Dinh Diem and the Vietcong
(Vietnamese communists). For further details of Sun Tzu's
and Mao's strategy, see *Mao Tse-tung on Guerrilla Warfare*,
translated and edited by Brigadier-General Samuel B. Griffith,
Praeger, New York, 1962, and Cassells, London; and *Sun Tzu:
The Art of War*, by the same translator, Oxford University
Press, 1963.

It is clear that, if the French were exhausted by the war in Indochina, the DRV was close to complete bankruptcy, at least so far as material resources were concerned. Victory came to the side which maintained greater equanimity and whose internal difficulties were successfully hidden from the opposite camp. In retrospect, one may conclude also that the French attempt at the reconquest of Vietnam had the effect of putting the Vietminh troops through an arduous course of training in modern warfare which, after nine years of compulsory practice, led to the final defeat of the colonialist enemy. When the Vietminh forces began their fight in 1945, their only weapons were sticks, a few pistols and some light machine-guns provided by the Americans or bought from corrupt Kuomintang officers. But today they can boast a highly-trained, well-equipped army, the fighting spirit of which is recognised by the whole world.

Contrary to what some maintain, the Japanese never gave any of their arms to the Vietminh. During the first days immediately after their surrender, the Japanese inclined to the idea of offering part of their arms and equipment to the Vietminh, but they changed their minds when Vo Nguyen Giap, *en route* from Viet-Bac to Hanoi, attacked their garrison at Thai Nguyen on August 17, 1945. The Japanese thereafter burned all their commissariat stores and later on handed over to the Chinese at Haiphong 400,000 tons of arms and ammunition.

In the area controlled by the Resistance, it was unanimously accepted that, apart from the arms and ammunition taken from the French in battle, the five material factors, indirectly provided by the French, which contributed most to the communist victory were:

1. Anti-malarial medicines, making possible operations in malaria-ridden areas;

2. Nylon sheets which served as lightweight waterproofs and were sometimes bundled up by troops to serve as floats to carry their clothes and personal effects when crossing rivers;

3. Discarded tyres which were used to make strong sandals for the rocky terrain in the hill country;

4. Bicycles for transporting supplies;

5. Kerosene oil for lamps.

All these items were imported into Vietnam from France and subsequently smuggled into the communist zone by local merchants, sometimes with the connivance of French local commanders.

The war was brought to an end on July 21, 1954, when France and the DRV, together with Cambodia, Laos, South Vietnam, Soviet Russia, Communist China, the United States and the United Kingdom, signed the Final Declaration of the Geneva conference, an agreement whereby *de facto* recognition was given to the DRV's sovereignty over North Vietnam. There followed five years of comparative calm which the communists used to complete the process of collectivisation in the North and to train their sympathisers from the South as activists. A direct result of this second activity has been widespread communist subversion in South Vietnam. This has been greatly helped by general dissatisfaction with Ngo Dinh Diem's régime. Already, at the present time, more than half of the villages in 'free Vietnam' are under communist control.

POLITICAL IMPLEMENTATION

Similar progress has been accomplished in the cultural and political spheres. In 1945, 80 per cent of the population was illiterate, but this was completely overcome as early as 1950. Thanks largely to the simplicity and regularity of the romanised orthography of the Vietnamese language, it usually takes no more than an average of one month's study for an adult Vietnamese to learn how to read and write. To compel the whole population to study the written language, measures were taken to prevent people for entering a market, crossing a river or moving along a road if they failed to spell a word correctly.

Although the cultural level is still low (because, generally speaking, indoctrination prevails over education), there is at present a primary school in every village and a middle school in every district, while there are many evening classes provided for adults from every walk of life.

Progress in the administrative sphere has been impressive. From a handful of officials and technicians, distinguished only by their

lack of qualifications, the Lao-Dong Party has created thousands
of experts in a wide range of techniques, as well as a huge army of
activists who control the whole population in every aspect of
their daily life. The process of establishing control over the whole
population—the régime's most considerable achievement—can be
divided roughly into two phases: the 'anti-imperialist' phase
from 1946 to 1949, and the 'anti-feudalist' phase from 1950 to
1956.

The anti-imperialist phase, 1946-49

The slogan at this period was 'Fatherland Above All'. Ho Chi
Minh asked the whole population to support his government to
create the national unity necessary to resist French aggression. To
promote political unity and lull the suspicions of the upper class,
the Indochinese Communist Party declared itself voluntarily disbanded and made a show of handing over political leadership to
the Lien-Viet (Vietnamese Alliance) Front. Private ownership was
carefully respected and landlords continued to collect rent for their
rice fields. In many cases, farmers were prosecuted for not paying
their rent. Intellectuals enjoyed high esteem and were retained in
responsible, or at least decorous, positions, while men of distinc-
tion received the same measure of public acclaim as before. To
satisfy the desire of those wishing to play a part in national affairs
(and also to have some control over them), several bogus political
organisations were established, notably the Democratic Party, reserved exclusively to landlords and rich tradesmen, the Socialist
Party, reserved for intellectuals, and the Lien-Viet, which catered
for revered figures in national cultural and political life who still
had some influence on the young, but were too old to engage in
any other activity. These organisations, in fact, were no more than
a screen behind which the Communist Party continued to function. Being puppet organisations, each one specifically reserved for
one particular group of sympathisers, they quickly lost their
ability to attract people.

First set up during the Japanese occupation by a group of university students, the Democratic Party very soon fell under communist control as a result of its accepting co-operation with the

Vietminh in a common fight against the French and the
Japanese. It eventually became a bogus organisation, the function of which was the control of 'bourgeois elements' as distinct
from the intellectuals who were channelled into the Socialist
Party.

The Democratic and Socialist Parties exist today in name only,
while the National Front has changed its name no less than three
times: from *Vietminh* (League for National Independence) to
Lien-Viet (Vietnamese Alliance), from Lien-Viet to *To-quoc*
(Fatherland Front), and finally from To-quoc to *Thong-nhat Quoc-
gia* (National Reunification). These changes were accompanied by
slight modifications in the official policy to suit the needs of the
moment. Many writers, after studying the official statements,
believed they could detect some genuine changes in the policy.
But in fact the frequent changes of names were symptomatic of a
gradual decline in the popularity of the 'front' rather than of any
major change in policy. For instance, the first National Front, as
we have seen, was called the *Viet Minh*, but these two Vietnamese
words were colloquially shortened into VM, pronounced *Vé-Em*
or (quickly) *Vem*. In Vietnamese, *Vem* also means parrot, so the
old expression 'to talk like a parrot' took on another meaning,
i.e. 'to talk like a Vietminh cadre' which amounted pretty much
to the same thing. This led to other expressions, such as 'to lie like
a Vem', 'as hypocritical as a Vem', and the like. Vem or Vietminh
as terms became so embarrassing to the communists that they
changed the name from Vietminh to Lien-Viet. But this proved
no better for the communists, since Lien-Viet became abbreviated
to LV. These two letters are commonly pronounced *El* and *Vé*
according to the alphabet, but in classes for illiterates they were
usually taught as *Lö* and *Vö*—to make the spelling easier to adult
beginners. But *Lö vö* is also a Vietnamese expression meaning
'giving an outward appearance of doing a particular thing', which
was exactly how Lien-Viet members were behaving. So once again
the name changed! During this first phase, in which there was
an appearance of democracy, there was a progressive consolidation
of the state machinery together with, contradictory as it might
seem, a gradual decline in the popularity of the régime as its hypocrisy became more and more apparent.

The anti-feudal phase 1950-56

The democratic façade was maintained for four years and came to an end only with the Vietminh defeat of the French at Langson in the September of 1950, a victory which gave them a common frontier with China. It was rumoured that Ho Chi Minh had paid a secret visit to Mao earlier that year, and that he had been criticised by Chinese theoreticians for being 'rightist'. They had argued that Ho was devoting too much attention to the patriotic war with the French and not enough to the establishment of communism.

On Ho's return from Peking, the Communist Party dropped its mask of secrecy and emerged once more under the name of *Dang Lao-Dong* or Vietnamese Labour Party (March 3, 1951).[6] Its new slogan was: 'The anti-imperialist and the anti-feudal fights are of equal importance.' Until that moment, slogans had been concerned with the war against imperialism, but the change of policy made it necessary for the slogans also to be changed. But an abrupt substitution of new slogans for old ones would have made the sudden swing in party policy clear for all to see, and this the communists wished to avoid at all costs. They set to work, therefore, to alter the old phrases imperceptibly, word by word, until these became so watered down that their original meaning was lost. For example, one popular slogan of 1950 which ran, 'Let us be ready for a general counter-offensive' was altered in 1951 to read 'Let us prepare a general counter-offensive', and further weakened in 1952 to 'Let us get ready for the preparation of a general counter-offensive', after which it was forgotten altogether. When the counter-offensive was eventually launched in 1954, the party was strong enough to resort to terrorism in order to command obedience. No longer tied to the necessity of getting control by 'democratic persuasion', the communists had no further need for this slogan.

When the slogan, 'The anti-imperialist and the anti-feudal fights are of equal importance', was adopted, people began to ask themselves what was its precise meaning. It had been generally under-

[6] *Lao-Dong* (from the Chinese *Lao-tung*) means 'Labour'. A close translation of the new name would be 'Labour Party' as we give it in the text; but the communists themselves choose to translate it as 'Workers' Party'.

stood that the anti-feudal fight was simply the eradication of the
last vestige of feudalism in the thinking of mandarin elements
in the state machinery. But high-ranking cadres who had studied
in China realised that this policy in fact envisaged the total liquidation of 'reactionary elements', a term which included everybody
having even the most tenuous links with the landowning class.
The true definition was only made public during the Thought
Reform of 1953 (see Part IV).

The principal campaign in the anti-feudal phase was the Land
Reform (1953-56) in which half a million Vietnamese (4 per cent
of the population of North Vietnam) were sacrificed. This 'sky-
splitting and earth-shaking' campaign had been preceded by two
others designed to pave the way for it. There were: first, the implementation of the Chinese system of taxes, the aim of which was
to impoverish the whole population and to reduce all Vietnamese
society to the level of its lowest members; and, secondly, a preliminary wave of terror aimed at liquidating all 'dangerous reactionaries'. The Land Reform program was itself divided into two
separate campaigns: the so-called 'Land Rent Reduction' campaign
and the Land Reform campaign proper. This second campaign was
followed by a 'Rectification of Errors' aimed at normalising the
situation after a long process of well organised terror. All were
accompanied by repeated 'Thought Reform' campaigns, the function of which was to prepare cadres psychologically for the rigours
of these bloody campaigns. The whole process, which had been carried out on the Chinese mainland a few years earlier, was defined
as 'Mao Tse-tung's tactics'. Because of their crucial importance and
of the light they shed upon the intentions of communist theoreticians, these campaigns will be described separately in the following
chapters. It is hoped that they will provide the reader with an
appreciation of the techniques devised by Mao for China but
thought by him to be applicable in all underdeveloped countries
just as it was in Vietnam.

PART III

FIRST STEPS TOWARDS A
TOTALITARIAN REGIME

'Better betray others than be betrayed
yourselves.'

(Attributed to T'sao T'sao, a
Chinese statesman of the third
century AD and a forerunner of
Mao in establishing agro-military
communes.)

SIX

Economic Levelling

One of the immediate results of Ho's visit to Peking was the pro-
mulgation of Mao's system of taxes which had been applied in
China two years previously. Both Chinese and Vietnamese communists have boasted that this is the simplest and most rational
system of taxes known to history. Compared with the complicated
French system employed in Indochina and that of the Kuomintang
in China, it appeared very straightforward, for the communists
reduced the whole system to five taxes only: agricultural, trade,
slaughtering, forestry and import-export taxes.

By far the most important of these was the Agricultural Tax.
This was logical since Vietnam is basically an agricultural country.
Next in importance was the Trade Tax levied on a small number
of craftsmen and traders whose turnover was exceedingly low.
The Slaughtering Tax was not very important because, owing to
the shortage of draft-animals, the sacrifice of cows and buffaloes
was strictly forbidden. However, despite the serious lack of draft-
animals, which in many cases obliged men and women to draw
their own ploughs, the communists managed to export a notable
amount of oxen to the French zone in exchange for goods which
they badly needed. Thus, the main part of the Slaughtering Tax, if
any was levied, accrued to the budget of French-controlled cities,
not that of the Vietminh. The Forestry Tax was equally insignificant. As for the Import-Export Tax, it existed only on paper, since
foreign trade, in the proper sense of the word, was virtually non-

existent under the Vietminh régime at that period.

The Agricultural and Trade Taxes were levied according to individual income or turnover, and these were not investigated; they were simply 'estimated' by the cadres and 'voted' by the 'people'. The 'estimated incomes' naturally tended to exceed the reality. The percentage of income to be paid in tax was set so high that it proved far too heavy for everybody. This was a deliberate and premeditated policy envisaged, not simply as a means for collecting revenue for the state, but also and primarily as a legal means of bringing about the economic ruin of both village and urban bourgeoisie in double-quick time. It was a preliminary step towards the gradual establishment of a proletarian dictatorship.

THE AGRICULTURAL TAX

The Agricultural Tax was progressive in the mathematical sense of the word; the tax/income ratio increased from 5 to 45 per cent of the income as the income increased.

OFFICIAL SCALE OF AGRICULTURAL TAX
(source: *Cuu Quoc*, No. 2080 of July 6, 1952)

Scale No.	Average individual income (kg. of paddy)			Per cent rate
1	From	71	to 95	5
2	„	96	„ 115	6
3	„	116	„ 135	7
4	„	136	„ 155	8
5	„	156	„ 175	9
6	„	176	„ 205	10
7	„	206	„ 235	11
8	„	236	„ 265	12
9	„	266	„ 295	13
10	„	296	„ 325	14
11	„	326	„ 355	15
12	„	366	„ 385	16
13	„	386	„ 425	17
14	„	426	„ 465	18
15	„	466	„ 505	19
16	„	506	„ 545	20
17	„	546	„ 585	21
18	„	586	„ 625	22
19	„	626	„ 665	23
20	„	666	„ 705	24

21	From 706 to 755	25
22	,, 756 ,, 805	26
23	,, 806 ,, 855	27
24	,, 856 ,, 905	28
25	,, 906 ,, 955	29
26	,, 956 ,, 1005	30
27	,, 1006 ,, 1055	31
28	,, 1056 ,, 1105	32
29	,, 1106 ,, 1155	33
30	,, 1156 ,, 1215	34
31	,, 1216 ,, 1275	35
32	,, 1276 ,, 1335	36
33	,, 1336 ,, 1395	37
34	,, 1396 ,, 1455	38
35	,, 1456 ,, 1515	39
36	,, 1516 ,, 1575	40
37	,, 1576 ,, 1635	41
38	,, 1636 ,, 1695	42
39	,, 1696 ,, 1755	43
40	,, 1756 ,, 1815	44
41	,, 1816 and above	45

This table was quoted by Bernard Fall on p. 249 of his book, *Le Viet Minh*, but Fall, like all other foreign observers, was unaware of the addition of a further amount to the official tax which the DRV authorities were careful not to publish. This further amount went to the so-called 'village budget'. The fixed tax was stated to be due to the national treasury only: this additional amount was purported to be devoted to village expenditure. In fact, it all went to the party. The extra levy was fixed at 15 per cent of the original amount of tax and the two levies were collected together. The party branch in each village kept two-thirds of the extra levy collected, handing the remainder to the provincial committee and so on up to the party's national organisation which in its turn —so many believe—sent one-third of its revenues to the Cominform in the shape of annual fees. Thus, the table of the Agricultural Tax served only as a basis for calculating the final amount exacted, which represented the amount indicated in the table plus a further 15 per cent of the official tax. To show the process more clearly, here are two examples.

Tax Scale No. 1: According to the table, each peasant in this category was required to pay 5 per cent of his income to the government. He had also to pay a further 15 per cent of this

5 per cent, i.e. ·75 per cent of his income, to the party. Thus 5·75 per cent of his income was paid in Agricultural Tax.

Tax Scale No. 41: Individuals in this category were required to pay 45 per cent of their income in tax, plus 15 per cent of this percentage (representing an additional 6·75 per cent) to the party. The total amount represented 51·75 per cent of their income. Such was the assessment for 'rich peasants' who tilled their own land. In the case of landlords whose income was obtained from land rents, this assessment of 51·75 per cent was further multiplied by $(1 + {}^{25}/_{100})$, giving 64·68 per cent. This latter figure represented the ceiling for the whole Tax Scale.

This was the general principle, but to gain a clearer understanding of the system, which had many complicated details, the following examples are given of the case of a poor peasant (Tax Scale No. 2) and of a landlord (Tax Scale No. 41). Although these two examples are imaginary ones, care has been taken to use figures (concerning the size and yield of the land held) which are as near to reality as possible. It is hoped thus to reflect correctly the current situation in the Vietnamese villages, as well as the effect of the new tax on the Vietnamese peasantry.

Example A

Giap was a poor peasant owning half an acre of land which he tilled himself. He was married and had two children and was classed as having 'four mouths to feed'. His small ricefield yielded 400 kilos of paddy (unhusked rice) each year. Now (assuming that the people of his village agreed that his income was 400 kilos, and not higher as was usually the case), in order to arrive at his 'average income' 400 kilos must be divided by four, giving 100 kilos. With an average income of 100 kilos of paddy, Giap was classed in tax category 2, the basic rate of which was 6 per cent. He paid accordingly:

To the government 6 per cent of 400 kg	=	24	kilos
To the party 15 per cent of 24 kg	=	3·6	kilos
	Total	27·6	kilos

The remaining 372·4 kilos of paddy were all that he was allowed to keep to feed his family for a whole year. Allowing that 100 kilos of paddy produce 65 kilos of rice, Giap had at his disposal 242 kilos of rice a year, which is ·665 kg of rice a day to feed 'four mouths', or ·166 kg for each mouth. The average Vietnamese requires a minimum of ·500 kg of rice per day to sustain him, for all save the very rich eat practically nothing but rice. When working hard, a peasant will consume as much as half a kilo of rice at a meal and he requires three meals a day. This is to demonstrate that even peasants who produced much less than the amount needed for their own consumption were not exempt from taxation.

Example B

Binh was a landlord who owned fifteen acres of ricefields. His wife was as old as he was, and his two sons were away from home, one serving in the People's Army and the other working as an official in the Trade Office. Unable to work his land alone, he was forced to let it to farmers who paid him 400 kilos of paddy per acre (50 per cent of the crop) or 6,000 kilos in all. Although there were four members in Binh's family, it was classed as 'three mouths to feed' as the son in the Trade Office had a salary and was not counted. Thus, by dividing the 6,000 by 3, the 'average individual income' of his family was 2,000 kilos, and Binh was classed in tax category 41, the highest group. His tax was accordingly assessed:

To the government 45 per cent of 6,000 kg = 2,700 kilos
To the party 15 per cent of 2,700 kg   =   405 kilos

Total   3,105 kilos

Since Binh did not till his ricefields himself, his total income was said to be acquired through exploitation, and for this the amount of tax was raised by 25 per cent, making the full tax imposed on Binh 3,105 kg × $(1 + {}^{25}/_{100})$ which equals 3,881·250 kg or 64·68 per cent of his income. There remained 2,118·750 kg of paddy, or 1,376 kg of rice. Assuming that the old couple ate 1 kg of rice a day, or 365 kg a year, there only remained 1,011 kg of

D

rice (an equivalent of 100 US dollars) to cover such expenses as salt, vegetables, and the like. There was nothing left for clothes or such things as a bicycle, watch or fountain pen which his sons, like most soldiers and public servants, asked for, or to provide for the change of buffaloes (exchanging an old buffalo against a younger and stronger one) eventually required by his farmers.

These theoretical examples are based upon the assumption that the 'people's estimate' was accurate, which was not often the case. As previously shown, the tax was calculated by multiplying the area of land by the average output per unit, and the latter was always greatly exaggerated by the 'people'. As far as the land surface was concerned, the 'people's estimate' was quite unnecessary, since the French colonial administration had carried out a careful and accurate survey in most areas, the results of which were readily available. But the communists had little interest in accurate figures. They refused to admit the validity of these surveys, for their aim was to compel the 'people' to make higher estimates. Strange as it may seem, it was in precisely this manner that the communists dealt with every problem. 'The people are always clear-sighted,' they said. If, for instance, a farmer owned one acre of land, the cadres and the hard-core elements[1] would unanimously declare it to be one-and-a-half acres, and the farmer could do nothing but accept the decision. Even if he had the courage to protest and perhaps produce authentic documents to prove his case, the authorities, with comic-opera logic, merely retorted: 'The French and their lackeys were bribed when they carried out their survey. The people are impartial and objective.' Such systematic distortion of the truth could only serve to impoverish the whole population, not solely the landowning class. That this was the case is obvious from the fact that the communists were forced to modify the system slightly during the Rectification of Errors campaign in 1956. The following extract quoted from the official organ of the party indicates the way in which land surface estimation was carried out:

. . . During the land surface estimation campaign, cadres in

[1] A 'hard-core' is a peasant who, though not a party member, supports party policy and carries out the orders of the cadres.

the village of To-Hieu forced the peasants to raise their *voluntary declaration* by 10 to 15 per cent. Teo, a middle-level peasant woman, owned only 1·9 *mau*² of land, but was forced to make four successive 'voluntary declarations'. Only when she said that she owned 2·5 *mau* of land, was her declaration accepted. Quan, a rich peasant, owning 5 *mau*, was warned that his entire property would be confiscated if he failed to make an 'honest' declaration. Out of fear he admitted to 6 *mau*.

Many hard-core elements dared not protest even though they knew that they were only being used as tools by the cadres to force others to accept these false estimates. Recently Tit, a female hard-core element, confessed : 'I now feel ashamed before the villagers, but the cadres "persuaded" me so that I was forced to lie.'

(*Nhan Dan*, Hanoi, No. 903, August 24, 1956)

The communists used the hard-core elements to force peasants to make false statements regarding their land surface, and again to force the same peasants to accept higher figures for their output per unit. For instance, a certain farmer owning an acre of land harvested 800 kilos of paddy. In his 'voluntary declaration' he stated that he had obtained 800 kilos or perhaps a little less. But the communist cadres chose to disbelieve him and bribed a certain hard-core to declare publicly that he himself owned a quarter of an acre of land in the same area, and that he harvested 300 kilos from it, thereby suggesting that from an acre one should get 1,200 kilos. The farmer was not allowed to appeal and had to accept this figure.

The following extract from a long report on the Rectification of Errors campaign, published in the newspaper *Thoi Moi*, confirms this method of forcing peasants to make false declarations :

. . . The discussion became particularly animated when people talked about the output of the ricefields. For the same size of holding in the same area, someone said : 'I harvested three baskets' while another said 'I only harvested two.' Mr Bieu, a middle-class peasant, became angry and said : 'A first-

² There are two kinds of *mau* : the Tongkingese *mau* which is equal to 0·9 of an acre, and the Annamese *mau* which is equal to 1·2 acres. The one mentioned here is the Tongkingese.

class ricefield in this village can never produce more than a *sao* [100 kg or one-tenth of a *mau*] and you estimate the output to be 130 kilos? Do you want to include husks and straws in your figure? You have just admitted that you had committed mistakes during Land Reform; if now you don't want to change your policy, then what kind of errors do you really want to rectify?' He was noisily applauded by the whole assembly while comrades in the tax team remained quiet and did not utter a single word.

(*Thoi Moi*, Hanoi, April 19, 1957)

With the area of the land and the output per acre raised, the land income usually reached enormous figures. As a result, a poor peasant, harvesting 100 kilos, found himself admitting to 200 kilos, so that his tax might be calculated on the latter amount. This could well have been more than double the true figure, since in a progressive tax the ratio for 200 kg would be higher than that for 100 kg; thus the government, though claiming that it only took 20 per cent of the entire land income of the peasantry, took in fact more than 40 per cent.

With the tax reaching these proportions, the middle-level peasants who owned small plots now paid the government what amounted to land rent, and this was usually as high as that previously imposed by the landlords. The Agricultural Tax was levied twice a year immediately following the summer and winter harvests, and it had to be paid in rice. Other agricultural products or money were not accepted, not even in respect to tax paid on holdings planted with other cereals or with fruit trees. Inhabited land exceeding 495 square metres (approximately one-tenth of an acre), even if paved, was subject to tax. A few who pulled up their flagstones, turning their courtyards into cultivated plots, were later prosecuted for 'sabotage of the people's wealth'.

With one stroke, the communists, who for years had relied on inflation in order to survive, became the virtual owners of all the agricultural land in the country. This was the unhappy lot of the middle-level and the poor peasants. The landlords' fate was infinitely worse. Up to 1954, the landlords' right to collect rent was still theoretically maintained but in practice, after 1951, they were unable to do so. As most of their tenants were members of, or held office in, the newly appointed village committees, the landlords considered it advisable not to exert any pressure on them to obtain full payment of their rents. But the landlords were still expected to pay the Agricultural Tax. Having insufficient rice to meet the levy, they were obliged to buy the balance from the market with their savings. Many of them had previously made large and repeated donations to the Resistance Movement and, as a result, were financially crippled. Soon they were selling their cows and buffaloes to raise money, and when these sources were exhausted, they disposed of family jewels and other personal valuables. Between 1952 and 1954, all manner of rare antiques appeared on the market; priceless Sung vases were sold for less than an aluminium basin imported from the French-occupied zone.

In order to carry out the rice-collecting program, drastic measures were applied. The party launched an intensive propaganda campaign urging competition in quick and honest payment. At first, the peasants took to soaking their rice in water, thus greatly increasing its weight, but the communists campaigned against this, demanding honest payment in dry rice. At the same time, local authorities began to humiliate the landlords and rich peasants by compelling them to carry their tax rice on their shoulders to the public granaries which were often situated as much as fifteen kilometres from their village. Orders were given to the tax collector to weigh first the rice brought by the poor peasants, making the landlords and rich peasants wait all day and sometimes until the following day. (Poor peasants enjoyed priority in everything, and most particularly in medical care, being the first to be examined and treated when they went to hospital.)

Finding that they were being ruined by this excessive taxation, landlords sought to sell some of their land or give it away to the state. But in 1953 this was forbidden; moreover those who had sold their land to poor peasants were compelled to return the money to the buyers, although the peasants were authorised to keep the land. Those who had offered their land to the state had to continue to pay taxes on the land as before. Only refugees from the towns who had bought small plots of land to cultivate in an effort to adapt themselves to their new environment, as preached by the party, were allowed to hand over their plots to the local Peasants' Association. They were required, however, to leave behind one buffalo, their ploughing implements and a sum of money as gifts to the incoming cultivator.

TRADE AND THE TRADE TAX

During the first years of the régime (from 1947 to 1950), the Vietminh carried out a policy of total blockade against the French-occupied zone. By doing so they hoped to deprive the occupying forces of necessary supplies and to crush French efforts at reconstruction in the areas they controlled. Consequently, trade or barter across the border was strictly prohibited. Goods which were occasionally smuggled into the Vietminh zone were confiscated and burned publicly.

As a result of the blockade, the French army and those living under its protection lacked the most elementary supplies. Rice had to be brought from South Vietnam by sea, whilst meat was sent from Cambodia by air. Consequently, the cost of living in French-occupied towns was far higher than in the neighbouring Vietminh villages.

The economic blockade did, however, have one good effect. By creating a severe shortage of manufactured goods in the Vietminh zone, the development of local crafts was greatly encouraged. Relatively complicated articles such as rudimentary printing machines, bicycles, bicycle tyres, and similar manufactures were produced locally. Some ingenious chemists succeeded in producing a few chemical products such as sulphuric acid, sodium carbonate, 90 per cent alcohol, etc., which made possible the manufacture of many more goods. Though completely isolated from the outside world, the Vietnamese people were able to live quite well by their own efforts. Soap, toothpaste, matches, carbon paper, hypodermic syringes (not needles), ether and liquid penicillin were produced in reasonably sufficient quantities.

Despite all this, there still remained two major obstacles, namely: the shortage of metals, and the lack of power. But by common effort and individual initiative, these obstacles were partially overcome. Engines from discarded cars and trucks served as driving power in small factories. Some waterfalls along the irrigation system were made to produce electricity, and a group of technicians produced a blast furnace which could turn out three tons of cast iron a day. This miniature blast furnace was remarkably efficient for its small size and drew real amazement from an East German delegation which visited North Vietnam in 1954. Rails and sleepers taken from the railways supplied steel, while napalm bomb-cases and the remnants of aircraft which had been shot down were quickly turned into aluminium articles such as spoons, basins, and the like.

Although the economy during the first years of the Vietminh régime could not be described as satisfactory by modern standards, ordinary people, other than public servants who were very poorly paid, lived quite easily and there was work for everyone. But the government's policy of encouraging local production was short-lived, for the Chinese, on their arrival in North Vietnam in 1950, explained to the Vietminh leaders the dangers of this capitalist pattern of economy. They said it would lead to the formation of a new class of capitalists. Following their advice, the whole economic program was abruptly reversed. Local production was discouraged and commerce between the two zones was allowed once again. French manufactured goods began to flood the Vietminh market, whereupon local producers, unable to compete, closed down their workshops. In many cases, both employers and employees fled to the French-occupied towns in the hope of finding work there, since the sudden raising of the blockade had created an unexpected revival of business on the French side.

To ensure rapid progress towards socialism, two other measures were taken simultaneously: the implementation of the Trade Tax, aimed at crushing all private enterprise; and the creation of a Trade Office. The reason for the latter was, of course, to give the party a complete monopoly of all trade.

The Trade Tax was similar to the Agricultural Tax with a few differences in regulation and method of application. It was levied monthly instead of twice a year, and was calculated on the basis of net profit with a ceiling fixed at 28 per cent of the total income, which was much lower than that of the Agricultural Tax fixed at 64·68 per cent. It was, in theory at least, more rational and less heavy than that imposed on the peasants. The amount of tax to be paid by each tradesman was determined in the following way:

1. Preliminary evaluation of the taxpayer's monthly turnover.

2. Determination of his net profit, arrived at by multiplying his turnover by the *rate of profit* assigned to his particular activity by a decree issued by the Ministry of Finance (30 per cent for grocers' shops, 50 per cent for restaurants, for example).

3. The amount of tax to be imposed was determined by multiplying the calculated net profit by a certain *rate of taxation* corresponding to the amount of net profit and duly established by the Ministry of Finance in a *scale of taxation* similar to that of the Agricultural Tax. The tax was progressive, for the rate of taxation varied in accordance with the amount of profit from a minimum of 15 per cent to a maximum of 28 per cent; this was the maximum fixed for all trading activities.

All the operations, apart from the first, were automatic calculations, since both the *rate of profit* and the *rate of taxation* were previously fixed by the government. All that was required therefore was to find the turnover of each tradesman. This was the starting point of the process and the decisive factor in determining the fate of the taxpayer.

The evaluation was carried out in the following way: every tradesman, large or small, was required to keep an account of all his trading operations and to issue a receipt, in triplicate, for any payment received from customers. These accounts, however, served only for eventual controls by governmental agencies, not for the evaluation of turnover, which was stated to be the responsibility of the people. In a people's democracy, the government merely receives the tax whereas the tax collecting and assessing are entrusted to the people, who according to the party, are clearsighted enough to make all the necessary evaluations without having to scrutinise any documents. The favourite expression is: 'One must have complete confidence in the people.'

In the party's view, tax-collecting is the people's business since tax-paying is considered to be a voluntary contribution and not, as in capitalist countries, a compulsory imposition. It is given joyfully by the citizen who is aware that, by paying his share, he is contributing to the socialist development of his country. Tax-paying is a patriotic deed and so one says: 'You have the *honour* of paying your tax', and not, 'You must pay your tax'. From this concept of taxation arise two logical corollaries: first, this great honour cannot be bestowed upon everyone indiscriminately; and secondly, the people are ready to help individuals who feel that they are not eligible to receive this honour, or those who cannot fully accomplish it. It is worth while examining these two points in more detail.

The significance of the great honour. In a people's democracy, one is not free to carry on any trade one likes, and this seems to mark a clear-cut difference from the so-called 'bourgeois demo-cracy'. Should a person wish to start a business, he is first required to put in an application to do so at the nearest branch of the Trade Office—which regulates trade in the locality—and a further appli-cation to the administrative committee for approval, since there are trading restrictions relating to certain social classes. Landlords, for instance, are forbidden by law to be hairdressers, restaurant-keepers, and so forth. In any case, approval cannot be granted with-out the consent of the secretary of the local party-cell, whose duty it is to judge the political attitude of the applicant. If a tradesman obtains a licence and later becomes suspect, then police agents in plain clothes will stand outside his shop demanding to see the identity cards of all his customers.

Thus, it is argued, while a person has the 'honour' of paying his taxes, he knows that he still enjoys a certain amount of economic freedom: a freedom which means that his family can avoid starvation and is far more precious than the political free-dom so often talked about in the capitalist press. It is the fear of losing this 'honour' that guarantees the complete submission of people living under a communist régime.

The help of the people. Despite the fact that the idea of 'honour' has been carefully explained to the population during political discussion meetings, there are always some who are not fully aware of its patriotic significance, and who are reluctant to make correct statements concerning their incomes. Therefore people living in the same neighbourhood will help the 'absent-minded' by reminding them of the amount of income that they have 'forgotten to declare'.

For North Vietnamese traders, during the period from 1951 to 1955, this collective help was provided in two stages, at two separate meetings.

The first meeting was attended by all those dealing in the same trade and living in the same area. They discussed one another's business affairs and finally classified themselves in accordance with the relative importance of each one's business. A list was drawn up but there was no mention of turnover: it was simply a list of incomes in descending order of size. The process was called 'vertical estimation' since its aim was to produce a classification, from top to bottom, of all those dealing in the same trade. It was said that people belonging to the same profession should be in a better position to give a correct judgment on the position of other members of their group. But the true motive behind this method was the realisation that a natural jealousy existed between those buying and selling the same goods which would lead them to denounce each other, thereby making sure that each one told the truth concerning his rival's income.

The second meeting was attended by all the tradesmen, whatever their trade, who lived in one street or village. They discussed and argued amongst themselves until the amount of turnover of each one was arrived at by vote. This process was called 'lateral estimation'. Every tradesman was aware of the fact that a certain amount of tax was fixed for each locality, and so he did his utmost to raise the amount paid by others in order to reduce his own share. The results of all this were twofold.

In the first place, since there is often some dissension amongst people living in the same village, the 'lateral estimation' provided an opportunity of getting even with one's neighbours. For example: A's wife committed adultery with B, another tradesman in the village. To revenge himself on B, A declared that he had reason to believe that B had an enormous income. To add weight to the accusation he said that he had frequently seen B's wife returning from the market with a chicken in her basket. Then, when the assembly began discussing A's case, B's brother, seeking to avenge B, stated that he had seen A taking coffee and milk (a luxury in North Vietnam) every evening at a café near his house. Consequently, nearly everyone found that his turnover was enormously overestimated, and the tax-collector often received more money than he had expected.

Secondly, those who know little of their neighbours' financial affairs and can only guess at their income by observing their standards of living, will undoubtedly believe that a man who eats chicken once a week, or who drinks coffee with milk every day, has a very large income.

The outcome was that nobody ate chicken or drank coffee and milk openly any more. If Mrs B wanted to buy a chicken, she hid it in the bottom of her basket, and A either drank his coffee in another locality or brewed it secretly in his bedroom. The whole population took on a woebegone appearance because of a pitiless income-estimation. They wore their oldest and shabbiest clothes, and let their hair grow long or had their wives cut it for them. Café-owners, tailors and hairdressers all closed down; hypocrisy was widespread, and trade throughout the country quickly collapsed. A veritable army of ruined tradesmen and shop assistants fled to the French zone leaving the field clear for the Trade Office to carry out its reconstruction according to the socialist pattern of commerce and industry. At that time everybody was equally poor.

SEVEN

The First Wave of Terror

Peasants and tradesmen were still struggling for economic survival after the effects of the Agricultural and Trade Taxes when, one evening in February 1953, the communist authorities launched a well organised, but quite unexpected, wave of terror throughout the whole of communist-controlled North Vietnam. Because it was entirely political in character, this campaign was later referred to as the 'Political Struggle' by those who had suffered under it.

At that time, to avoid bombing attacks by French aircraft, all meetings in the Resistance zone were held during the hours of darkness, and on this particular evening meetings were held in every village to discuss the Agricultural and Trade Taxes. There was only one question on the agenda: why were so many people failing to pay their taxes, or to pay them in full? The only answer was that, after three years of taxation of this type, rich and poor alike were unable to find any way of raising the required amount of rice. Such an obvious answer, however, did not satisfy the communists who in reality were using the question of tax-payment to conceal a calculated and sinister plan.

The cadres came to these meetings armed with sticks and ropes. Tax-debtors were arrested, tortured and asked why they had not paid their taxes, and *who had advised them not to pay*. From the method of questioning it was quite apparent that tax-evasion was not the main issue. The interrogator, when asking who had advised non-payment, mentioned specific names. 'Was it Giap or Binh?' he would ask. The beating continued until the victim, reached the limit of his endurance, nodded his head in assent. If he persisted in his refusal to implicate the said Giap or Binh, the beating might continue all night, and might even end in death.

Once the unfortunate victim had given the answer required of him, the Giap or Binh concerned would be immediately arrested. Before embarking on this terror, the communists had compiled lists of the names of those they wished arrested. The tax-debtor's part in this gruesome farce was merely to provide them with an excuse to carry out the arrests. The interrogators, having selected a name from their lists, sought to compel the unfortunate debtors, by torture if necessary, to make the required accusation. Once this was made, they were of no further use to the communists.

After being subjected to terrible tortures, the denounced person was required to sign a confession. In this he had to state: first, that he was a member of some entirely fictitious organisation— giving it any name that came into his head; and secondly, that others belonged to the same organisation. The names of these others, however, were not fictitious, but were taken from those on the lists already mentioned.

One after another, those listed as reactionaries or suspicious characters were arrested in this way and tortured. They were not necessarily landlords, rich peasants, or even reactionaries. Many of them could be fairly described as following a middle-of-the-road course. The following verses written by Xuan Dieu, the poet laureate of the Vietminh, clearly shows that such people might expect to receive the same treatment as true reactionaries.

> Hello, Comrades. Let us unite our forces,
> Destroy our mortal foes without remorse.
> Landlords, notabilities and opposition groups
> We must reduce to ash;
> Middle-of-the-roaders and reactionaries,
> Their bones we must smash.

When he wrote these lines the bard was not indulging in flights of poetic fancy, for owing to the severity of the tortures, large numbers of people did have their bones crushed. Some typical tortures were:

The victim was compelled to kneel down, supporting on his head a basket filled with heavy stones.

He was forced to hang by his thumbs or feet from a rope thrown over a rafter. In this position he could be either beaten or, by pulling on the rope, jerked violently up and down.

His thumbs were wrapped in a cloth soaked in oil which was then ignited.

Since these tortures were widely used throughout the whole country, it is reasonable to assume that they had been carefully devised and sanctioned by the leadership of the party. It was the opinion of some people that such measures had already been employed in China two years earlier and imported into Vietnam by Chinese advisers.

These 'regular' tortures were common to every village, but there were others which were the product of local ingenuity. In one village, for instance, the victims were placed in a bamboo bucket and immersed in water for a couple of minutes at a time, until confessions were obtained. In another village the victim's thumb was held in a vice belonging to the local bicycle-repairer, and with every turn of the screw the torturer repeated his question.

It is worth noting that party members and cadres were never present at these nightmarish scenes. They deliberately left such work to hard-core peasants who could not easily be identified with the party. Thus the government and the party could disclaim any responsibility for such atrocious actions, and could place the blame on the people themselves. This is illustrated in the following anecdote which was circulating in the Nghe-An province about this time.

A teacher in a village school asked her pupils to write an essay with the title 'A Scene of Struggle in Our Village'. The children wrote detailed and colourful accounts of the arrests, beatings and tortures, with the usual praise of the party and its part in these affairs. The party, however, had officially disclaimed all responsibility for terrorism and described the recent events as an 'outburst of public anger', so the teacher, on reading the compositions, was forced to reprimand the children for their 'inaccuracy'. The entire class, resentful of such unjust criticism, asserted that they had been eye-witnesses to the scenes they had described. Many went so far as to say that they had even seen the party cadres cutting bamboo sticks and bringing ropes and various other implements to the scene of the torture before the arrival of the crowd.

This wave of terror lasted for a fortnight, during which every village reported scenes of horror and death. The campaign began a week before *Tet* (New Year in the lunar calendar), a time when the whole population is busy with the preparation of food, cakes and delicacies to welcome in the New Year. At this feast the people worship the spirits of their departed ancestors who, they believe, are present at the family altar on that day. But on this occasion all traditional ceremonies were abandoned. Silence reigned in every village, and at night no house dared to show a light.

During the first days of the campaign, everything went according to the party's plan. Victims whose names appeared on its black lists were denounced and tortured. However, as the movement gathered momentum, the party cadres became intoxicated by the great power they were wielding over their helpless compatriots. Lists were forgotten, and the denunciations snowballed until nobody was safe. This phenomenon was widespread; the campaign got completely out of control. The limits set for the campaign at the outset by its organisers were everywhere exceeded. Terror, violence and death spread unchecked through the whole country. There were two main reasons for this.

1. In accordance with the party's policy, the cadres entrusted the task of torturing and extracting confessions to the hard-core peasants. But in most villages such people were not numerous, and these few soon tired of their distasteful duties. In many instances they enlisted the services of people outside their group to relieve them.

Now to find people willing to engage in such an undertaking was far from easy, so that their choice fell upon hooligans and thugs. These craven opportunists of necessity carried out their new duties with an exaggerated enthusiasm, eager to demonstrate to the crowd their pro-party feelings. Many had in fact evaded the compulsory 'citizen-labour service'[1] and others had stolen rice from the village granaries or committed some similar crime. Consequently they gladly accepted the opportunity of showing everyone what powerful members of the community they had become, and that they enjoyed the full confidence of the party. How could they be considered reactionary when they were torturing true reactionaries for everyone to see?

The situation rapidly degenerated into anarchy. Being the people they were, the hooligans' principal concern was to protect themselves from denunciation by others, and to take advantage of a wonderful opportunity to enhance their prestige in the eyes of the party. They resorted to extreme brutality and tortured indiscriminately all those unfortunate enough to come under their authority. Everyone who was denounced was tortured; to these political illiterates, for whom 'capitalism' and 'imperialism' meant very little, all honest citizens appeared equally reactionary.

2. The second reason was to some extent a natural consequence of the first. During the initial stage, when hard-core peasants were still in control, there was no doubt in the prisoner's mind about whom he should denounce, for this was always made quite clear to him. But with the advent of the thugs and hooligans, the official black list was little respected, and anyone who was denounced suffered the same fate. People very soon realised that with these new masters they were free to denounce whomsoever they wished, and the sooner they did so, the sooner they would be released.

Not unnaturally, the thought uppermost in everyone's mind was: 'If I am denounced tonight, whom I shall denounce when, or if possible before, I am tortured?' Some reasoned that, if they denounced relatives of party cadres, or the influential party members themselves, they would force the party to call a halt to the

---

[1] 'Citizen-labour' (*Min-kung* in Chinese) is a compulsory service which all citizens have to perform for a specified number of days in a year—thirty days according to the present law in North Vietnam. It consists of physical labour, such as road building and repairing, carrying rice, arms and ammunition, etc. In other words, it simply means forced labour and corresponds exactly to the former system of *corvée* under the French rule. As in many such cases, a euphemism has been invented to avoid the disparaging meaning which was inevitably associated with previous terms for the same thing.

terror. The denounced party members were arrested and brutally beaten in exactly the same way as any 'reactionary'. Local communist cells were helpless to intervene, for the campaign slogan was: 'Give the masses a free hand to fight reactionaries', and the orders they had earlier received from a higher authority stated categorically that no individual and no organisation of the party would be permitted to interfere. They were victims of a demagogy which had careered wildly out of control. Hell was let loose, and 'the devil was stronger than the sorcerer', as a Vietnamese saying has it.

On one occasion, when a victim became so frightened that his senses deserted him, he denounced the chairman of the meeting. The luckless chairman was straightaway dragged from his seat and tortured. After that the meeting had to be suspended, for nobody would volunteer to serve as chairman.

Well aware of the danger inherent in this alarming situation, the central government decided, on the fifteenth day of the campaign, that the time had come for it to act. Telegrams were sent to all the provinces in North Vietnam ordering an immediate cessation of the barbarous operations. It was nevertheless decreed that all those 'reactionaries' who had been denounced by the masses should remain in jail because 'the judgment of the masses is always correct'.

This decree made it obvious now to everyone that the detention of suspects had all along been the party's real aim; those who did not accept the party line unquestioningly had to be put out of the way temporarily so as not to cause any trouble during the next and decisive campaign—the Land Reform. It was this action which marked the abrupt transition from a pseudo-democratic to a communist pattern of society. Those arrested were confined in concentration camps and not released until the Rectification of Errors campaign in 1956.

The death-roll during the days of terror averaged between three to five in every village, and among the victims were many party members, including even one government minister, Dang Van Huong. He was spending a holiday in his native village, where not unnaturally his fellow villagers regarded him more as the man whom they all knew than as a minister of government. No man is a hero in his own country, but even so it must have been a severe shock to him to find himself denounced and beaten as a reactionary, while his colleagues in the central government did nothing to intervene. Both he and his wife committed suicide after the incident. This fate befell them in spite of the fact that their son, Colonel Dang Van Viet, known as the 'Hero of Road No. 4', had been victor of the Cao Bang—Lang Son battle a few years previously.

While all this was happening in the villages, a similar campaign was taking place in the towns, but on a much smaller scale. Feelings of hatred were not to be found to the same degree among town-dwellers for, having come from different parts of the country, they did not know each other well. It must be understood that real towns no longer existed in the communist zone. They had been completely destroyed by Vietminh forces in their scorched-earth retreat before the French troops. The real intention behind this wanton destruction was to ruin the urban bourgeoisie. 'Town' must be taken as meaning rows of thatched shanties built at important crossroads by merchants who had lost most of their wealth and were trying to survive by opening up their business again.

Generally speaking, it took the villagers about seven days to discover that a prompt confession to their supposed crimes was the only way to escape torture and beatings. But to the better educated and more resourceful town-dwellers, this means of escape became apparent more quickly. Thus it was a common sight to see the accused meekly kneel down and 'confess' in a loud voice before anyone laid a hand on him. Moreover, since the people accused each other of only very minor crimes, only very few reactionaries were discovered. The shortage of traitors and reactionaries in the towns made it difficult for the authorities to sustain the terror for the full fifteen days. Consequently the urban campaign speedily degenerated into one directed against the consumers of imported goods. A well groomed appearance, even the use of brilliantine, became a crime. Indeed, hard-core elements were posted at every street corner for the sole purpose of apprehending the users of brilliantine and compelling them to wash off the offending cosmetic in greasy dishwater stored close by for that purpose. Many people were astute enough to volunteer to wash their own hair as soon as they realised what was happening. Well dressed people and those who indulged their taste for refined cooking were also singled out for ill-treatment and humiliation.

The difference between the rural and the urban campaigns is very marked. In the villages, the terror increased in intensity until it outran all efforts at control, whilst in the towns it very quickly subsided into a relatively innocuous agitation directed against the 'petty-bourgeois' way of life. Many villagers, in fact, fled to the towns to escape the horrors at home. This explains why the communist authorities, both in North Vietnam and in China, were frequently obliged to round up these refugees in the towns and send them back to their native villages.

At the end of the wave of terror, President Ho Chi Minh addressed a message to all the villagers. In it he apologised for failing in his leadership, thus forcing the masses to take the law into their hands even to the point of ignoring the humanitarian principles of the party and the government. It was reported by the cadres that, when issuing the statement, the President was so overcome that he burst into tears. The report was probably accurate, for Ho is known to be a consummate actor, weeping and kissing being two of his favourite effects. He uses them readily at the appropriate moment. (Ho was nicknamed by an Indonesian paper 'The Kissing President' on the occasion of his official visit to Djakarta in 1959.)

He next ordered that all village committees should submit a full report of these excesses to the higher authorities. At the same time, they were to draw up lists of all those who had been clear-sighted enough to recognise the wrongs which were being committed and who had made some attempt to stop them.

Many citizens, most of them party members, had refused to participate in the campaign, and some had even tried to intervene on behalf of relatives. Their names were now carefully listed and forwarded to provincial committees, which at once invited them to come forward and be congratulated. After receiving their commendations, they were promptly dispatched to 're-education camps' for three years, to employ their time in manual labour and in studying in more detail the unfailing principles of Marxism-

Leninism. They were released in 1956, thanks to the Rectification of Errors campaign which concluded the Land Reform program. This is a typical example of the cunning way in which the party eliminated those of its own members who, although faithful to communist doctrine, did not approve of the terrorist policy.

Only a month after President Ho had wept and apologised, he sent the same cadres, accompanied by the same advisers from Hunan in China, to the Fifth Zone to repeat the same gruesome pattern of terror. The Fifth Zone was in South Vietnam and was controlled at the time by the communists.

The immediate effect of this first wave of terror was to spread fear of the party amongst all classes of the population. Before these terrible events the prestige of the party had been at a very low ebb. Peasants whose homes had been destroyed by French bombing openly reproached 'Uncle Ho' for having indirectly caused their misfortunes; while thousands more, carrying rice to the front, suddenly went on strike and returned home, leaving their baskets still full of rice by the roadsides. In one village, at a time when the Communist Party was still in 'voluntary dissolution', the guards surprised a communist cell in animated discussion and arrested all its members on the ground that they were holding an illegal meeting.

After the wave of terror, however, there was a complete reversal of the situation. Far from refusing to participate in 'citizen-labour', thousands volunteered for it, and taxes were collected in a matter of a few hours.

Although many people believed this to be the primary aim of the campaign, such was not, in fact, the case. The long-term intention, as we shall see later, was to pave the way for the impending Land Reform (this will be dealt with in detail in Part V). But the immediate short-term aim was to strengthen the authority of the party, and this was achieved by frightening the people—rich and poor alike—and by eliminating those among them who, although participating in the war against the French, were suspected of being potential opponents to the communist régime.

The unexpected wave of terror lasted for a fortnight. Beginning at the command of the party's central committee, and ending with President Ho's tears and apologies, it left behind it a state of relative tranquillity in the villages. People who had fled to the towns or elsewhere were able to return to their villages and live undisturbed for a few months.

One further task remained for the party to accomplish, and that was to re-establish the validity of the most sacred principle of Maoism: 'the judgment of the masses is always correct' and 'the peasantry is, of itself, capable of good revolutionary leadership'.

But some of the effects of this campaign were adverse. Many people who had wholeheartedly supported the communists now began to lose confidence in the régime. They discovered that Ho Chi Minh, falling under the influence of Mao Tse-tung, had imported from China a type of primitive barbarism which had been unknown in Vietnam for centuries and which was intolerable in a civilised country. They were also convinced that the party, now all-powerful and possessing an elaborate technique for provoking 'mass anger' at will, would unhesitatingly employ this rather than a just and humane policy to attain its end. Those who were still capable of reasoning—and indeed many had lost that precious intellectual faculty through intensive indoctrination—began to compare the new communist régime with the former colonialist system. They remembered that, although under colonial rule there had been little justice or freedom, there had at least been a form of legality. The French killed, but by the guillotine, not by mob violence.

Even faithful party members began to have doubts about the peasants, and feared what might result if these simple-minded people, driven on by the spirit of hatred, were given a free hand. While they knew that a society in which the rich kick the poor is a hell, they also realised that people who squeeze one another's thumbs in a vice could not be capable of building a paradise on earth.

In order to fight such dangerous trends of thinking, the party resorted to two methods of persuasion, one for the uneducated masses and the other for intellectuals.

1. In every province public trials directed against 'traitors' were held. These were to demonstrate to the masses that the recent 'spontaneous outburst of popular anger' was not completely un-

justifiable. On the contrary, there were dangerous spies and saboteurs working for the French amongst those whom the angry villagers had denounced and arrested.

2. There was a campaign of brain-washing for all the nation's intellectuals—party members and public servants at all levels—to persuade them of the rightness of the party's policy in insisting on giving a free hand to the masses.

These two methods, which embody certain characteristics of Mao Tse-tung's tactics, will be described in full in the next chapters.

EIGHT

The List of Traitors

Such victims of the 'Political Struggle' as had escaped execution and had by some miracle survived the most barbarous tortures, were sent to jail pending further investigations. An interval of a few weeks elapsed, and then the results of these 'investigations' were made public. It was officially proclaimed that many of those arrested were members of a dangerous clandestine organisation working for the French imperialists.

Two years earlier, in 1951, heavy bombing by the French had annihilated the entire irrigation network in the communist-controlled zone. The party now saw in this military disaster a possible solution to its present problem. Its leaders revealed that the idea of destroying the irrigation system had been suggested to the French by these very traitors whom the angry masses had denounced. It was even said that they had provided the French with accurate maps giving the location of dams and lock-gates. The absurdity of this accusation was immediately apparent to all but the blindest followers of the party, since every Vietnamese knew perfectly well that it was the French who had built the dams, and that all the ordnance maps of Vietnam and of Indochina had been compiled by the French. To suppose that they had forgotten the whereabouts of these gigantic constructions, and needed map references from local spies to locate them again, was patently ridiculous. But communists, in their propaganda, have never considered absurdity to be a serious obstacle to mass persuasion. It was their habit when dealing with peasants constantly to repeat simple statements, and their propagandists knew from past experience that the villagers would believe without question any story, however fanciful, about the French and the Americans; many of them had probably never met a Frenchman or an American in the whole course of their lives. One communist officer, who had valiantly fought at Dien Bien Phu, was heard to enquire whether or not Americans had red skins. Obviously he had confused Americans with American Indians, the Redskins—a name introduced into the Vietnamese language by its French equivalent, *Peaux Rouges*. Clearly, an ignorant man; all the same, he typifies the abysmal ignorance which was so widespread. Thus, the simpler the argument, the more suited it was to the peasants' understanding.

Public trials were accordingly arranged in every province, long lists of traitors being drawn up and sent to the central committee of the party for approval. These lists included the names of the following types of people living in each province: the richest landlord; the most senior Buddhist monk; the Catholic bishop; the most influential Confucianist (*i.e.* the scholar having the highest degree under the former system of education, based on the study of canonical texts, and who thus enjoyed greater prestige as a moralist); and the highest mandarin who had served under the previous monarchist régime in the days of the French Protectorate.

While awaiting trial, the 'traitors' were transferred from jail to jail, and were led under military escort from one place to another to be exhibited to the people, after the fashion of the parade of animals prior to a circus's opening performance. Their feet were chained together and their arms were tied by a single rope joining the whole suffering line. They staggered along the dusty roads under the glaring sun holding in their manacled hands pieces of string by means of which they lifted the foot chains and prevented these from dragging along the road. The continuous clanking of their iron fetters produced a cheerless noise which could be heard at surprisingly long distances.

The preparations for the trials were nearly complete and the juries were on the point of being sworn in, when a sudden postponement was announced. It was rumoured that the central committee had not closed the list of 'traitors' compiled in the provinces as their Chinese advisers had found them to be incomplete. The latter had pointed out that these lists did not contain the names of any reactionaries belonging to a class known, in Mao's classification, as 'compradorist bourgeois'.

According to the Chinese leader, and this is regarded by his disciples as probably his most valuable pronouncement, the capitalist class in underdeveloped countries can be divided into two groups: the *national bourgeoisie* or the industrialists, and the *compradorist bourgeoisie* or those engaging in foreign trade. These two kinds of capitalist acquire different political attitudes because of the different ways in which they invest their money.

The national bourgeoisie or native industrialists, being producers of local goods, carry out a bitter fight against foreign capitalists. They possess, therefore, a certain degree of patriotism, and because of this are prepared to collaborate with the communist government until the socialist stage is set. They are allowed to live undisturbed, their affairs being closely controlled by their own workers, during the short period between land collectivisation and the socialisation of private enterprise. In China and Vietnam this period lasted about two years.

Those classified as the compradorist bourgeoisie, on the other hand, are completely lacking in any nationalist feeling, their interests being closely integrated with those of foreign capitalists. They are but the slaves of foreign imperialism and must be classified as 'Enemy Number Two' of the people ('Enemy Number One' being the landlord). But in order to be defined as compradorist bourgeois, as the term was defined by Mao Tse-tung, one had to fulfil two conditions. One had to be a bourgeois (or capitalist) and also a comprador (a dealer in foreign trade). Therefore, when the provincial committees were asked to provide the higher authorities with a list of compradorist bourgeois, they had to pick out from among local 'capitalists' those supposed to be engaged in foreign trade. But this was no easy task since there were no capitalists left in the Resistance zone and in any case foreign trade was non-existent at that time in the zone. Vietnam boasted few native capitalists, and almost all that she had remained in the comparative safety of the big towns which were controlled by the

French, thereby confirming Mao's dictum that these slaves of foreign capital always side with imperialism. Others, of less importance, who had fled to the country when war was still raging in the towns, had returned after a few years of life under the communists. A number of rich merchants—all these terms are relative, and these rich merchants would be regarded as small shopkeepers in Europe—had stayed on in the guerrilla zone for reasons of family rather than out of patriotism, but they had suffered financial ruin for their pains. Their misfortunes were caused by an insufficient turnover (the result of a severe shortage of goods, the absence of regular traffic, the abysmally low purchasing power of the population), and, of course, the heavy exactions of the Trade Tax. Runaway inflation obliged them to operate with a permanent deficit (between 1946 and 1955 the Vietnamese *piaster* was reduced to a thousandth part of its former value), and they were constrained by the military authorities, on the pretext of avoiding French parachutists, to move from one place to another at frequent intervals.

The problem of finding capitalists was not insoluble, since the term 'capitalist', like that of 'landlord', is capable of elastic extension in the communist dictionary. The authorities could always find some one who might be termed 'capitalist' on the grounds that he enjoyed a higher-than-average standard of living. Such a man could be held up to the masses as apparently possessing a certain amount of capital. But to find someone who was involved in foreign trade was far more difficult, and the Chinese advisers, by insisting on this, were making a great mistake. They probably imagined that this type of capitalist was as readily discoverable in Vietnam as in Kuomintang China; but while there were many businessmen who traded in the Shanghai region under the Chiang Kai-shek régime, there were none in Vietnam, where foreign trade had, for almost a century, remained the monopoly of a few French firms.

To suppose that, under the French colonial occupation, there were Vietnamese who engaged in foreign trade was ridiculous enough, but to pretend that such persons actually existed in the communist-controlled zone was utterly nonsensical. But Big Brother's principles must be respected, come what may, and orders from higher authority must be carried out. Accordingly, in order to provide this supplement of 'traitors' so insistently demanded by the authorities, the provincial committees ordered the arrest of a few party functionaries whose job was to organise the smuggling of bicycles, medicines, lamp-oil and other necessities from the French-occupied zone. Their reason for doing so was simple. In the complete absence of any foreign trade, the smuggling of a few foreign goods across a no-man's land could, by a stretch of the imagination, be considered as such. Those who enjoyed the confidence of the party sufficiently to be entrusted with this dangerous but necessary task now found themselves charged with 'spying activities' and sent to jail along with the other 'traitors'.

After the list had been approved, a special war tribunal was formed. Moving from one province to another, it brought to trial the various groups of traitors in each region. The presiding judge was a well known lawyer, who had previously been a professor of Hanoi University, while the assessors and public prosecutors were faithful party members. There were no barristers, only 'defenders'. These were people from every walk of life—in one instance, a teacher from a private school and a midwife—who were appointed by the tribunal to defend the 'interests of the people' rather than the rights of the prisoner at the bar. They pleaded indulgence for a few 'confederates' who had been arrested only in order that they might denounce the leaders of the 'gangs', but demanded severe punishment for these alleged ringleaders.

The trials were public, which meant that they were attended by two delegations of party members, one from the villagers and the other from workers' organisations. The delegates were granted at least two weeks to study the case and to memorise all the slogans they would be required to shout at appropriate moments.

However, sentences were not unduly numerous, for in all matters of national importance and of a symbolic character, the régime took the opportunity of proving itself to be both just and magnanimous. In Thanh-hoa province, for example, only the wealthiest landlord and the senior Buddhist monk were sentenced to death, while the Catholic bishop and the two compradorist bourgeois received sentences of twenty and fifteen years' hard labour. The mandarin and the Confucianist did not appear before the tribunal because both had died in jail prior to the trial. The death sentences were not carried out for some time, so that people began to speculate about the possibility of a pardon or a reduction of sentence. But on the eve of the exchange of prisoners between the French and the DRV prescribed by the Geneva Agreements, the two prisoners under sentence of death were taken out during the night and shot. The executions were carried out without the customary cheering crowds. On the following day, the other 'traitors' were released.

PART IV

THOUGHT REFORM

'A true but complicated idea has always less chance of succeeding than one which is false but simple.'

Alexis de Tocqueville

NINE

Ideological Operations

Most of the Vietnamese intellectuals who had joined the Vietminh and were still serving the Resistance government found it difficult to believe in the fanciful stories of the so-called conspiracies. The alleged existence of French spies in the villages, and the improbable story of the Buddhist monks who were supposed to have drawn maps to aid French pilots, all this deceived nobody save the abjectly ignorant. The hand of the party was easily detected by those with any degree of discernment, and it became obvious to them that the party was using both legal and illegal means to rid the Resistance of its non-communist participants. Feeling that the military aid provided by China would ensure an immediate victory over the French, the Vietnamese communists concluded that the propitious moment had arrived to launch their program for the communisation of the country. A cardinal item in preparing for this was the elimination of all potential sources of opposition.

Some well-informed people went so far as to assert that Ho Chi Minh's *volte-face* towards his nationalist supporters was occasioned by his experience of Chiang Kai-shek's change of attitude towards his communist allies twenty-four years earlier. At that time there existed in China a military coalition between the Kuomintang and the Chinese Communist Party, and the troops of both had gone out to fight against the warlord Chang Tso-lin. This expedition ended with the massacre of all the communist participants, on the orders of General Chiang himself, after the capture, in the May of 1927, of Shanghai, whose city gates had been opened from inside by Chou En-lai and his followers.[1]

Ho Chi Minh, who was in Canton at the time, was fortunate in possessing a Russian passport, enabling him to escape with the whole Russian advisory group to Moscow. Mao Tse-tung and other surviving communists had to fight their way out, and subsequently began the longest retreat in military history: the Long March, which lasted for more than two years (1934-36) and which led them to Yenan where they remained until 1949.

Both Ho and Mao had been placed in personal danger by this incident, and both have used it ever since to strengthen the advice they give to new recruits, viz. that when co-operating with nationalist elements, communists should keep the upper hand or at least remain at a safe distance. Mao Tse-tung is reported to have declared in the course of a lecture on Chinese literature which he delivered at Yenan that he has unbounded admiration for T'sao T'sao, the Chinese Machiavelli of the third century BC, whose oft-repeated principle was: 'Better betray others than be betrayed yourselves'. T'sao was a principal, if not most edifying, character in the novel San Kuo Chi (Romance of the Three Kingdoms).

To return to the Vietnamese intellectuals serving with the Viet-minh: these were completely unprepared for the party's sudden change of attitude, because they had never been told of the Shang-hai incident and the cynical philosophy of reciprocal betrayal. They had joined the Resistance and had fought under communist leadership with no aim other than the achievement of Vietnamese independence. They believed that their actions would bring free-dom and justice to their beloved country. But this hope quickly vanished after they had witnessed the Political Struggle during which the party massacred so many of its former friends and col-laborators in an 'outburst of popular anger'. They wondered how such pa-tao[2] could ever lead to the noble objective of universal

---

[1] Asian Who's Who: Pan-Asian Newspaper Alliance, Hong Kong, 1937; pp. 617-18.

[2] The Chinese have divided the different means used by poli-cians into three categories: Ti-tao or 'emperor's way', mean-ing noble means; Wang-tao or 'prince's way', meaning dignified means; and Pa-tao or 'duke's way', meaning machiavellian means.

brotherhood. In their muddled and disturbed minds, the scepticism they had once learned from the pages of Montaigne gained ascendancy: 'Truth on this side, error on the other.' Viewed from different angles, justice, independence, freedom and the rest of the currently popular words took on different meanings. In the face of these rapidly changing political strategies, unfailingly accompanied by a veritable flood of Chinese terminology, Vietnamese intellectuals who had been nurtured on algebra, physics and chemistry in the French schools, were completely lost. Oriental and Western philosophies, even Marxism, offered no help, since Mao and his theoreticians had given to every word a new meaning. In their utter confusion they were even in doubt as to who was their chief enemy—the French colonialists, the American imperialists, Vietnamese landlords, monks, compradorist bourgeois or the petty-bourgeois intellectuals themselves.

Many party members, too, experienced great disappointment. They had studied Marxism and accepted the principle of a proletarian dictatorship. They had even believed that the peasants and workers would rule the country with justice and equity, for these people, after all, were honest. But 'proletarian dictatorship', they discovered, accorded the honest peasants and workers no more voice in affairs than they had ever had. It was the hooligans and thugs who were endowed with a new authority and encouraged to direct events. 'Only one's standpoint is important, not one's social class,' it was later explained. In 1952, Professor Tran Duc Thao, who had received the highest French degree in philosophy, left Paris to return to Vietnam and serve the communist régime. Only four years later, in 1956, on the occasion of the Hundred Flowers movement (a description of which is given in Chapter Seventeen), the same professor wrote: 'Our organisation at the district and provincial levels has been reshaped in accordance with a policy which I can only describe as the hooliganisation of the peasantry.'[3]

It would be reasonable to assume from the articles which they wrote during this short period of greater freedom that the Vietnamese intellectuals who had faithfully served the Resistance had

[3] Tran Duc Thao, *Freedom and Society* (Giai Pham Mua Dong, Hanoi, 1956).

I

become greatly disillusioned, although fear of the party prevented them from voicing their dissatisfaction openly. The over-all numbers of the intellectuals were small, but as a class they had proved invaluable to the party. Their contribution during the period of the Resistance War was out of all proportion to their numbers. Their services were still essential, but their importance diminished with each succeeding year.

About a thousand youths had been sent to China, Russia and East European countries every year for education and training, but these had not yet returned home. All the technicians and activists during the Resistance period were therefore still of colonialist and feudal background. President Mao expressed the view that intellectuals who failed to accept Marxism were of less use to the community than excrement, for, he said, excrement could at least be used as manure. But since there was no alternative, they had to be retained in service for a few years, and it was precisely with a view to making them at least as useful as excrement that they had to be encouraged and re-educated. The particular kind of education they received is known in communist terminology as 'ideological revolution' and was, from the communist viewpoint, more important than anything else. It was a kind of psychological warfare directed, not against the enemy himself, but against the bad influence exercised upon the intellectuals' mind by enemy thought-processes.

Keeping pace with military operations, political implementation, social reformation, and even with socialist reconstruction, the ideological revolution was similarly divided into separate stages, each based upon the shrewd principle of 'one enemy at a time'. Just as Horace, in Corneille's drama, killed his three opponents by separating them and then fighting them one at a time, so ideological operations were launched against a variety of non-communist ideologies one by one.

The first stage, 1946-54 (during the Resistance War) was directed against 'French cultural influence'—idealism, scepticism, romanticism, individualism, 'Art for Art's sake', and so forth.

The second stage, 1953-56 (during the Land Reform campaign) was aimed at 'feudalist conceptions' of private ownership and social order, at the Confucian system of morality, confidence in the omnipotent ability of the intellectuals, contempt for 'ignorant peasants', and so on.

The third stage, 1957-59 (after the Hundred Flowers movement) was against 'bourgeois ideology'—free enterprise, admiration for Western techniques and Western parliamentary systems, regret for 'petty freedom' (individual freedom, freedom of the press, of movement) and the like.

In its final stage, from 1959 onwards (after the collectivisation of private enterprises), the campaign was turned against the 'petty-bourgeois ideology'. The main characteristics of this non-proletarian ideology have recently been enumerated by Truong Chinh, the theoretician of the party, as follows:

> ... no firm standpoint, a rigid and subjective viewpoint, pre-disposition to unfounded optimism and pessimism, narrow-mindedness, short-sightedness, hesitancy, conservatism ... lack of discipline, absence of respect for labour discipline, in-subordination to the new pattern of life, reluctance to follow the path of collectivism, regret for individual production, lack of courage to improve techniques and organisation, failure to seek out the new, fear of thinking and acting, re-luctance to buy requisitioned foodstuffs taken from families who have them in excess, reluctance to carry out the tax and debt collecting policy and reluctance to repress active gangs of counter revolutionaries.[4]

As the fight against reactionary ideologies proceeded, a progres-sive Marxist indoctrination was simultaneously and systematically carried out. This constructive part of the work was also divided into stages to enable party members, cadres and the masses to climb the multi-storey Marxist-Leninist edifice without becoming too dizzy. The reasons for such a program may be set out as follows:

1. Teaching Marxism-Leninism to any layman is extremely difficult and cannot be explained in one lesson, or even in one year. Like Euclidean geometry, Marxism starts from one precon-ceived postulate—that of internal conflict—from which derive a

[4] Truong Chinh, 'Speech at the Third Congress of the Party, 1960', in the literary magazine Van Hoc, No. 113 (September 1960, Hanoi).

sequence of theorems and corollaries which progressively lead to acceptance of the communist pattern of life as the most rational one. Students of Marxism must be graded into different 'classes' and must pass successively from one 'standard' to the next.

2. Marxism is comparable with chemistry in so far as it is an applied science, developed by experimental research but explained by hypothetical presumptions. Just as no one can expect to become a chemist purely by reading books on chemistry, so no one can expect to become a good communist, or even to understand communism, simply by reading books on Marxism or by attending political courses. Practical application is of prime importance, for only through daily practice can one get the 'Marxist substance' to flow through one's veins. The students of Marxism require, therefore, a certain period of probation after each successive 'ideological operation'.

3. To communists, reactionary thoughts in the mind closely resemble pathological germs in the body, because both exist in many varieties, and each variety produces its own outward symptoms. There are feudal, bourgeois, petty-bourgeois and a score of other 'non-proletarian' thoughts—usually termed as *diseases*—all of which are harmful, and require specific treatment. A complete cure requires a series of prescriptions, well spaced over a long period of time. Patriotism, for instance, has been used successfully in the treatment of the disease of 'decadent French culture', the manifestations of which are scepticism, romanticism, individualism, etc., while the 'enlightenment to socialism' is today used to combat the 'petty-bourgeois sickness'.

4. Marxism-Leninism is a medicine designed to cure ideological disorders, but, in common with a number of medicines, it demands a gradually acquired tolerance. If the initial doses are too large or too frequent, they are liable to produce an unpleasant reaction. Thus, to be effective, Marxism-Leninism should be administered in graduated doses at carefully calculated intervals.

5. There is a more important reason, however, for conducting the ideological struggle by progressive stages, and this is stated with some clarity in the following extract from Truong Chinh's speech at the Third Congress of the party in September 1960:

The ideological task is always determined by the political

task and must be subordinated to it. It is impossible to separate the two, and even more impossible that the two should
conflict. (*Van Hoc*, No. 113, September 1960.)

It follows from this that, whenever the party plans to change
its policy, a new ideological campaign must be carried out beforehand or simultaneously.

The organisation is not unlike that of an enormous school, with
the entire nation as pupils. While the indoctrination program is
arranged in successive stages, the pupils themselves are divided
into two categories. All are allocated to classes, party members and
government-cadres—both groups are predominantly formed by
intellectuals—filling the upper classrooms and the remainder
making up the 'junior school'. All is based upon the assumption,
which must never be questioned, that it is necessary for the whole
nation to progress along the path of Marxism-Leninism. As party
members are supposed to have a higher ideological standard than
non-party members, there is a slight difference between the teaching programs respectively reserved for each group. Of two programs arranged in recent years, one is for party members and one
for non-party members. Truong Chinh in his speech describes
their aims as follows:

> For *non-party members*: The targets for the educational and
> ideological struggle are a steadily increasing understanding
> of the desire for national reunification and of the fact that
> our people are their own masters. Students must also be
> taught to *fight* against every manifestation of bourgeois
> ideology as well as to *criticise* the petty-bourgeois ideology
> itself. A sustained effort must be made to erase every vestige
> of feudal ideology and all other non-proletarian ideologies.
> For *party members*: In the case of party members, the ideo-
> logical program is aimed at strengthening their proletarian
> ideology by means of a well-planned education in Marxism-
> Leninism. Members must also be encouraged to *fight* the
> influence of bourgeois and petty-bourgeois ideologies, and to
> continue their efforts to eradicate feudal ideology as well as
> other non-proletarian ideologies. (*Ibid.*)

Comparisons of these two programs reveals significant differences. Nationalism (the desire for national reunification) is still

put to effective use in the education of people who are not party members, but it is altogether banned from the teaching program devised for party members who have to accept the leadership of Moscow or Peking. Moreover there are subtle but highly important distinctions between the two groups in regard to 'incorrect' ideologies. By communist logic, petty-bourgeois ideology, though incorrect, is less 'criminal' than bourgeois (or capitalist) ideology; and 'criticise' is a milder form of action than 'to fight'. But it all depends on who you are.

What Truong Chinh is really saying is, first, that party members as well as those who are not members of the party must fight against bourgeois ideology; and secondly, that, while non-members are simply to *criticise* petty-bourgeois ideology, party members must actively *fight* against it. When a non-party cadre shows a petty-bourgeois tendency, he will be criticised for it; but when a party member shows the same tendency, he will be severely punished. In short, petty-bourgeois tendencies are to be tolerated to some extent among non-members, but among party members they are to be rooted out.

The pattern of the ideological program takes shape in three stages. In the *first stage* (up to 1960), petty-bourgeois ideology is tolerated in non-party cadres and criticised in party members; bourgeois ideology is criticised in non-party cadres and fought in party members. In the *second stage* (as adumbrated in the text of Truong Chinh's speech), petty-bourgeois ideology is criticised in non-party cadres and fought in party members; bourgeois ideology is fought both in non-party cadres and in party members. In the *third stage* (that of the full future perfection of the system) petty-bourgeois and bourgeois ideology alike are to be fought with equal vigour in non-party cadres and in party members.

This process implies a gradual movement from 'tolerance' to 'criticism' and finally to 'fighting'. All sections of the population are to go through these three stages (party members, non-party cadres and the masses), but at different rates.

The dose administered to party members is obviously stronger than that given to non-members. During the next campaign, non-members will receive the dose now given to party members, while the latter will receive something stronger still. Thus step by step, party members, non-party intellectuals, workers and peasants will be led forward towards a state of ultimate perfection. As Truong Chinh puts it :

> The aim of the present revolution is that the entire people, and particularly the working people, should thoroughly absorb the socialist ideology, that they should abandon their previous outlook on life and on the world and replace it with the Marxist viewpoint. Thus Marxism-Leninism will assume a leading rôle in guiding the moral life of our country and will become the framework within which the thoughts of the whole nation are formed. It will serve as the foundation upon which the ethics of our people will be built.
>
> *(Ibid.)*

The above passage demonstrates clearly that Marxism is becoming a religion in the full sense of the word—a new faith which is relentlessly striving to take the place of all existing faiths and which does not tolerate any trace of 'pantheism' or 'atheism' among the people it controls.

To achieve this state of ultimate perfection (somewhat comparable to the *Tao* of Lao-tse or the Eightfold Path of Buddha), the Eastern communion of the Communist Church employs two inquisitorial methods known as 'control-discussion' and 'correctional training', a detailed description of which will be given in the following chapters.

TEN

Control-Discussion

During the early years of the régime, from 1946 to 1950, the Leninist method of 'criticism and self-criticism' was fairly widespread, but practised only by party members who operated in great secrecy. The party itself was a secret thing during this period of apparent democracy. Restricted to a limited circle and carried out only after careful investigation, the Leninist process yielded satisfactory results. In most cases, the criticised party member was required to confess, and this he usually did without much collective pressure.

But after the establishment of direct relations with China's new régime in 1950, a new practice, known as *kiem-thao*, or control-discussion, was imported and implemented in a far wider circle. The term derives from the Chinese *kien-t'sao*, based on *kien* meaning 'control' and *t'sao* meaning discussion. The method was said to have been developed in southern China—not in Peking. It far surpassed in severity the old method of 'criticism and self-criticism'. The person to be criticised was called to attend a special meeting at which other persons in turn reported his alleged shortcomings. These were supposed to have been jotted down in a notebook at the time when they were observed. By a process of psychological analysis and deduction, the meeting decided that the criticised person had reactionary thoughts. The whole group then resorted to 'collective pressure' to induce him to confess to the shortcomings reported of him.

Several special techniques were applied, to each of which the Vietnamese attached a descriptive term.

1. *Hat-cramming.* This means the use of pressure or threat in order to force an accused person to confess to a crime he has never committed, without permitting him to defend himself. The term conveys the idea of cramming of a hat forcibly over someone's head in spite of his ineffective attempts to resist.

2. *Hunt-the-criminal.* This involves the ceaseless bombardment of the victim with searching questions, regardless of the fact that many of the questions relate purely to his private life or activities. In this way the unfortunate man is mercilessly hounded down and afforded no opportunity for evasion. People compared this eager pursuit of 'reactionary thoughts' to a stag hunt, or to the tracking down by the police of an escaped prisoner. Control-discussion sessions often lasted several days when a victim was thought to be too long in confessing.

3. *Chain deductions.* This term is used to describe a series of seemingly obvious deductions which, starting from an insignificant revelation, lead inexorably to the conclusion that the accused person is a dangerous reactionary. The following anecdote reported by the head of a middle school demonstrates this technique in action.

In the course of a control-discussion session held by students, a teacher was reported to have given a certain pupil's work a mark higher than it was thought the work merited. The indictment against the offending teacher ran as follows:

> *Basic deposition:* You gave X a higher mark than he deserved. *Deduction:* (i) by favouring one individual amongst us you hoped to create dissension; (ii) when there is dissension in a class, the students spend most of their time quarrelling among themselves instead of studying; (iii) so they make little progress; (iv) this makes their parents dissatisfied; (v) and leads them to say that our system of education is inferior to that of the French; (vi) they will say that a colonial régime is better than a people's democracy; (vii) therefore, in giving an undeserved mark, you are deliberately serving colonialism; *Conclusion:* you are a servile lackey of the French and the Americans.

Such admonitions to teachers were widespread, and in very few schools was a teacher to be found who, at some time or another, had not received similar insulting treatment. This was the main reason for the large exodus of teachers from the Resistance zone to the French-occupied areas in 1950 and 1951.

4. *The use of big knives and heavy axes.* This term refers to the use of excessively strong and often vulgar language to reprimand the defaulter in the hope of curing him of the reactionary thought-processes still believed to be active in the mind of all intellectuals. The following incident reveals the violence of the technique.

At a control-discussion session held in a peasant's house by the staff of a government office (such offices were itinerant at the time and civil servants lodged in peasants' houses), there was a great deal of noise and shouting. The peasant's wife, hearing the uproar, thought there was something seriously amiss, and hurried to see what was happening. She saw a young man standing in front of a furious group of men who were hurling abuse at him. So angry did they appear she thought they might kill the young man. So she said as calmly as she could: 'Please, gentlemen, don't be so abusive toward the poor fellow! You should be more tolerant, whatever he has done. Just remember he is a colleague of yours and a compatriot into the bargain!' The uneducated woman did not realise that this uproar was simply a weekly control-discussion session in which everyone criticised and was criticised in turn.

These repeated scenes of collective violence, interspersed with long intervals in which people behaved normally towards their fellow workers, induced in the participants an uneasy feeling that they were leading a double life.

5. *Mourning weeping.* From the very outset it was an accepted convention of *kiem-thao* that the criticised person should produce a few tears to prove to the audience that, thanks to the lesson he had received from his generous fellows, he was deeply ashamed and filled with remorse. But in a number of cases, chiefly in schools, some of those who had already made their confessions stayed on to jog the memories of their colleagues, and themselves joined with the victim in crying. These were, for the most part, young party members filled with an overpowering urge to impart

the newly acquired truth to their compatriots. They would have considered they had failed their sacred mission on earth if they could not claim at least one convert to the Marxist truth, and so constantly set themselves the task of preparing the minds of these defaulters to receive the glorious teachings of Uncle Mao and Uncle Ho. Sobbing bitterly, the young men lamented their failure to accomplish the task the party had entrusted to them. They were deeply grieved, they said, to see that the party's sustained efforts to re-educate the people were achieving no results. Weeping came easily to these young people for they were in a permanent state of nervous tension. Intensive political education combined with complete sexual continence was a main cause of their exaggerated emotionalism and, hence, their excessive fanaticism. There were, in fact, quite a number of cases of actual madness. In a class of the Politico-Military School of Viet-Bac in 1952, eight of the students became mental cases.

At first, fits of weeping were resorted to only occasionally, but later they became general practice. This provoked the common observation that the party had discovered the secret of rejuvenation, since under this system grown-up people became children again.

Group-weeping was, of course, used in the *kiem-thao* process as a means of persuasion—a form of collective pressure—to hasten the confession. On one occasion, a whole class was called upon to help a student who had refused to write down his 'suggested' self-criticism. On arriving at the house where the student was staying, the class began to weep in chorus, thoroughly alarming the peasant owners of the house[1] who not unnaturally concluded that some occupant of their house must have died suddenly. But weeping, when employed mechanically in this way, soon loses its effectiveness, and the sight of a number of people crying together without shedding a single tear came to be regarded as comic. No one, however, dared to laugh at the weepers, for their ridiculous solemnity indicated that they were performing what they conceived to be

---

[1] Vietnamese peasants always have two houses, one to live in and the other reserved for ancestor-worship—the reunion of relatives to celebrate the anniversaries of the death of parents or grandparents. These second houses were used during the war as government offices or as schools, or for such purposes as sheltering refugees.

their duty. In consequence, the practice continued for a considerable time—from 1951 to 1953.

Two different theories have been advanced about the origin of this Chinese method. Some people believe that it was a popular derivation from the method developed in Peking which had not by then reached southern China in its correct form. In Mao's China, all political innovation must be carried out in an orderly manner, following the oil-stain principle, which, though it lacks speed, allows some measure of control and assures a uniform application throughout the country. It was thought, therefore, that some over-zealous cadres in the south of China, fired with enthusiasm for the Peking technique, had on their own initiative anticipated the movement and implemented the process before they had been trained in its techniques. Others asserted that *kiem-thao* had originated in southern China, and had been applied in Hunan many years earlier when Mao Tse-tung made his first start in that province. From there it spread all over the south of the country, arriving in North Vietnam in its crude and somewhat childish form, while the Peking method, identical in basic essentials, had embodied the refinements which the technique had undergone during thirty years of application in Yenan.

It is difficult to say which of these theories is correct, and it is even possible that some people in the south of China, being impatient for the elaborate process, temporarily resuscitated the archaic version they had experienced thirty years before. The difference between the earlier method (control-discussion) and the later method (correctional training), is only one of technique, reflecting the tremendous progress that the Chinese communists have made in human psychology over the last decades. Their rapid advance is almost certainly due to the mature and brilliant culture inherited from their resourceful ancestors.

Whatever the whys and wherefores, one is forced to the conclusion that, despite all its imperfections, the southern Chinese method of control-discussion has produced a marked change in the general behaviour of the Vietnamese people. Instead of being the open-hearted and communicative people they once were, they have become very reserved and quiet. In restaurants or canteens people eat in silence, and exchange only an innocuous smile when they meet in the street. Current opinion describes them as 'more phlegmatic than the British' and 'more discreet than the Japanese'. Like these two peoples, the Vietnamese have, in fact, become 'islanders', but in the sense that each of them has become a separate 'island' with almost no communication with other surrounding 'islands', his fellow-citizens. Everyone withdraws into himself and communicates with others only in cases of strict necessity. A common practice, even among high-ranking party members, is the secret classification of one's relatives, friends, colleagues and acquaintances into one of two categories: those who might report any nonconformist views to someone else; and those who, after some precautionary tests, can be trusted completely. If a person is obliged to express his views to people who cannot be entirely trusted, his wisest course is to repeat the views of the party as stated in its most recent publication. This explains why, in contrast with a general state of complete destitution, party newspapers have an exceedingly large circulation and why people, although extremely busy from dawn to dusk, attend evening meetings with great assiduity.

This dreary mental exercise of cautiously classifying friends and relatives into separate categories, of laboriously studying the party's press which is full of boring phraseology, and of regularly attending political meetings—all this imposes a terrible mental strain.

ELEVEN

Correctional Training

The first attempt to implement the Chinese process of 'correctional training' in Vietnam was made in 1948 by General Nguyen Son, who was commander-in-chief of the Fourth War Zone (northern Annam) at the time. During the previous twenty years, he had served as a high-ranking officer in the Chinese Red Army. It is perhaps worth pausing to take a brief glimpse at the career of this man who, by the strength of his character and a singular chain of circumstances, became a national hero in China and might well have become a Vietnamese Tito.

Nguyen Son, known in Red China as Hung Suei (Deluge), was a native of Bac-Ninh province in the French colony of Tongking. Son of a scholarly Vietnamese patriot, he was sent to train as a teacher in Hanoi, where, at the age of seventeen, he took an active part in the Students' Movement of 1925. Hunted by the police, he fled to China and was immediately admitted to the Whampoa Military Academy. After graduating from the school he joined the Chinese communists at the time of the insurrection of the Commune of Canton (1928), and thereafter remained a member of the Chinese Communist Party. His outstanding qualities as a military officer became apparent in the course of the Long March (1934-36), and until 1945 he continued to serve with the Chinese Red Army under the command of Marshal Peng Teh-huai, commander of the Eighth Route Army. As one of the few survivors of the Commune of Canton and the Long March, he was made a National Hero in 1949.

Son was in Yenan at the end of the Second World War when he learned from a Canadian correspondent that Vietnam had won independence, but was at war with the French who were seeking to recover their former possession. Son's repeated requests eventually prevailed upon Mao to allow him to return to Vietnam in order to serve in the ranks of the Resistance Movement. It was arranged that Son should join Mao's delegation going to negotiate a truce with Chiang at Chungking, whence he secretly crossed the Kuomintang-controlled zone, and entered Vietnam. Accompanying him was Nguyen Khanh Toan, Ho Chi Minh's travelling companion from Moscow in 1941 who had remained in Yenan.

Son's apparent patriotism in choosing to return to Vietnam incurred criticism on the grounds that he was more nationalist than internationalist, and he was very coolly received by Ho Chi Minh when he reached Hanoi in 1946. Nevertheless, so great was Ho's need for his undoubted military talent, that Son rapidly rose from rather modest beginnings to become commander of the Fourth War Zone with the rank of brigadier general. This placed him two ranks below Vo Nguyen Giap, commander-in-chief of the Vietminh army, whom he despised as a military illiterate since Giap's high rank derived solely from his political importance. Giap had, in fact, been a law student and had had no military education other than a short training in guerrilla warfare at an American camp in Tsin-tsi during the Second World War.

But the real cause of the dispute between Ho Chi Minh, Truong Chinh and Vo Nguyen Giap on the one hand, and Nguyen Son on the other, lay in the fact that Son persistently objected to the policy of seeking help from China. Son wanted to continue the fight against the French with arms taken from the enemy, arguing that during the Sino-Japanese War, Mao had never begged aid from Stalin, who had indeed preferred to help Chiang. Angrily, Son left Vietnam to return to China. Mass meetings were held to greet him along the route from the Sino-Vietnamese border to Peking. Ho, however, sent a secret report to Mao, accusing him of many misdeeds, including the rape of a peasant girl. One sequel to this episode was that the whole Vietminh army was required to study a special document in which Son was described as 'typical of bad military cadres'.

In consequence of Ho's report, Son was brainwashed in China. Much disheartened, he volunteered to enter the Military Academy at Nanking in order to study modern military techniques under Soviet experts. In August 1956, suffering from a stomach cancer and feeling himself to be on the verge of death, he took his wife and children back to Hanoi, where he died two days after his arrival. Vietnamese opinion was unanimous in its verdict on Nguyen Son: 'He was a communist by career, but a nationalist by faith.' He was perhaps the only Vietnamese communist leader who might have become a Tito.

Whilst Son was commander of the Fourth War Zone, he wrote a few pamphlets advocating the system of 'correctional training' as he had seen it performed in Yenan. But his disagreements with Ho and the other communist leaders led to the rejection of his suggestions. Son spoke about *Chinh Dang* (Rectification of the Party), and *Chinh Phong* (Rectification of the Movement, or of the Cadres' Behaviour). These were two distinct types of thought reform, the former being reserved for party members, the second for officials and others in responsible positions who were not members of the party. A third type, *Chinh Quan* (in Chinese, *Cheng Kun*), was especially designed for military personnel of all ranks. But when thought-reform was at last implemented throughout the communist-controlled zone in 1953 (by Chinese advisers, for Nguyen Son had already returned to China), both party members and other civilian cadres were sent to the same camp for re-education. The whole process for civilians was then referred to by one name: *Chinh Huan* (in Chinese, *Cheng Hiun*), or Correctional Training.

There existed in fact at least three different kinds of correctional training, each devised for a particular kind of 'trainee'. The one described here was the mildest and most 'constructive' of the three, since it had been specifically devised for 'friends'. A second type, which was excessively harsh and completely devoid of any educative character, was reserved for 'home enemies' (local landlords and reactionaries).[1] The third type, standing midway between

[1] A description of the second type of correctional training (that reserved for 'home enemies') can be found in the author's *The Fate of the Last Viets* (Hoa-Mai Publishing Co., Saigon, 1956).

these two, was reserved for 'foreign enemies' (*i.e.* captured French soldiers and European missionaries). Reports from liberated prisoners of war and intelligence operators have made this third type better known to foreign observers who refer to it as 'brain-washing'.

Chinh Huan, or correctional training, was described as the new and officially approved form adopted by Mao after the establishment of the People's Republic in 1949. From that time onwards, it became a rule that, whenever the party planned any major change of policy, the entire personnel of both government and party—from members of the central committee and ministers down to the humblest office clerk—had to be re-educated along the new line. It is widely thought that even the leaders of communist movements in countries of the Free World who periodically visit Moscow or Peking for a few weeks at a time, ostensibly for health reasons, in fact go there for a session of thought-reform.

Truong Chinh has pointed out that all ideological operations are devised to serve some predetermined political end. Thus, each correctional training campaign is designed to prepare a suitable psychological atmosphere before the introduction of any new policy radically different from the existing one. The party's aim is to make party members and cadres accept the new policy beforehand, so that the critical period of implementation goes smoothly. The whole process might be compared with an orchestral concert, the conductor representing the party and the orchestra representing the whole apparatus of party and government. Thus, like an orchestra which obeys the slightest movement of its conductor, those cadres directly in charge of the new policy will play to perfection the parts ascribed to them. Others must suffer in silence, offering no protest, like a well mannered audience at a concert.

The task of implementing a new political idea is always a hard and complicated one. This is particularly true in backward countries where, because of a difference in cultural standards, the reactions to the innovation may be varied, depending on particular consideration and local conditions. *Linh Dong* (in Chinese *Ling Tung*) is a catchword repeated daily, and no cadre is allowed to forget it. It means that cadres in charge of implementing a new

policy are expected to behave, not like automatons, but like intelligent beings capable of the quick decisions which are sometimes
called for when dealing with unforeseen difficulties. For these
reasons, the kind of discipline imposed upon cadres must not
derive from compulsion or the threat of punishment by some
higher authority, as is usually the case with military discipline.
On the contrary, it must be voluntarily accepted as though it were
a necessary prerequisite for the fulfilment of a sacred mission. If
such a discipline is to be accepted, then the cadres must be convinced of the importance and necessity of the task assigned to
them. They must have a firm belief in the rightness of the new
policy and in the infallibility of the leadership. In order to achieve
this result, which is the aim of every correctional training course,
the party uses every argument to demonstrate and prove that only
the party is right, and that it is entirely and always right. In the
case of an acknowledgment of some previous 'mistake', it is
asserted that Marxism-Leninism is right and always will be. The
party's next task at the correctional training course is to persuade
the students of the absolute necessity of the new change. Without
it, the instructors argue, the Revolution would fail, and if that
happened the imperialists would return.

It was often the case, however, that a number of cadres, though
willing enough to learn, found it hard to accept the new teaching
simply because they had been told the same things before but with
completely different interpretations or conclusions. For instance,
when the Revolution first began, the party promised that the
country would be ruled by four classes: workers, peasants, petty-
bourgeois and national bourgeois. Later, the party explained that
only workers, peasants and petty-bourgeois would hold the power,
and finally it explained that the real partners in the people's dictatorship were the workers and the peasants, since the other classes
were either treacherous or worthless.

The habit of telescoping or changing all the major declarations
at frequent intervals, and of twisting the meaning of all the usual
terms, not unnaturally produced doubts in the cadres' minds concerning the sincerity and good faith of the party. Consequently,
they often refused to listen to the latest explanations, for they
could not believe them to be final. Whenever one of the students

attending the correctional training course refused to co-operate further, his mind was said to be 'blocked up'. Clearing these obstructed minds became the second task of every correctional training course.

So, like a plumber, the party set about the task of finding the exact location and cause of the blockage. It encouraged, and sometimes commanded, free and open criticism of the party and its methods. The students were allowed to unburden themselves fully of their grievances and individual resentments against the party, without any fear of retaliation. This promise was solemnly made beforehand and was always kept. Once their grievances were out in the open, the instructors then answered all the questions raised, just as a good-humoured Prime Minister might answer questions put to him by the Opposition. This unaccustomed liberty was in sharp contrast to the usual atmosphere of daily life, where no such criticism was permitted. Freedom to criticise, not allowed in normal circumstances, was tolerated simply in order to remove the obstruction from the 'blocked up' minds and to 'redeem redeemable souls'. All souls were not considered to be capable of redemption, and these were never admitted to correctional training courses. They were classed as enemies despite the fact that they had, until then, been 'friends'. Thus, those people who received invitations to a correctional training course were overjoyed, realising that they were still classed as 'friends'. It was clear to them that, provided they successfully accomplished their training, they would remain 'friends' for a few more years at least. So every cadre went enthusiastically to correctional training.

To convey some idea of a correctional training course, an outline is given here of the one devised for 1953, the object of which was to pave the way for the Land Reform 1954-56.

EXAMPLE OF CORRECTIONAL TRAINING COURSE

I. DIVISION OF THE STUDENTS

All the students attending the course designed for 'friends' were party and government personnel together with a certain number of 'progressivist personalities'. The teaching program was exactly the same for them all, but they were divided into four categories on the basis of their relative importance and levels of political education.

1. High-ranking members of the party and senior civil servants, plus some influential personalities, went to Viet-Bac, a kind of Vietnamese Yenan. The school was at some place geographically close to the central government so that the group might be taught directly by Truong Chinh and Ho Chi Minh.

2. Middle-ranking members of the party and cadres, plus some not very influential personalities, were sent to their respective war zones where the zonal committees looked after their education. (Each war zone comprised three to six provinces.)

3. Low-ranking party members and cadres went to their own provinces to attend courses run by the provincial committees.

4. Workers in offices and factories received their education on the spot. A teaching team was sent to instruct them during the afternoons and evenings.

Since everyone was compelled to attend correctional training courses, the sessions had to be staggered. One-third of the office personnel would go for instruction while the remainder worked harder and shared all the work between them. When the first trainees had completed their course, another group would go, and finally the third group. A month was required for preparation and for completing administrative arrangements (for security reasons the school moved from one place to another after each course), and each course lasted three months. Thus it required a full year to complete three successive courses. The whole campaign, however, took eighteen months as the Viet-Bac course had to finish before the others could begin. The reason for this was that the teaching teams had to receive their training first.

II. PRACTICAL ORGANISATION

Schools were organised, as a general rule, in remote villages in the jungle. Students lived in the villagers' houses, but the school itself was built by the students themselves of bamboo and logs. Firewood was gathered by the students at weekends from the surrounding forests. This manual labour was a deliberate part of the educational program, devised to make the intellectuals feel closer to the workers. Students had to bring with them all the personal belongings which they might need, such as clothes, blankets, mosquito-nets, a bowl and a pair of chopsticks, and a sum of money equivalent to 100 kilos of rice (about 8 US dollars).[2] This meagre sum covered all expenses during the three months. It was accounted as follows: three months' board cost 75 kilos (25 kilos a month); this provided 15 kilos of rice for individual consumption, and an equivalent of 10 kilos of rice for vegetable and salt. The remaining 25 kilos covered stationery, lamp-oil and mimeographed documents.

Students were divided into groups of three, one in each group being a party member and in charge of the other two. Each group lived in one peasant's house and twice a day sent one of its members to the 'supply office' (the new term for collective kitchen) to collect food from the 'supply comrades' (cooks). He brought with him a bamboo basket and an earthenware pot, borrowed from the local people—the basket to carry the rice and the pot for vegetables. The food was of poor quality, the rice coming from public granaries being usually mouldy, and the diet as a whole suffered from a serious lack of proteins and vitamins. Meat was served only once a week, and even on these occasions the amount was infinitesimal. It was usually chopped up into minute pieces and mixed in with a huge dish of vegetables. The pieces were carefully counted and shared equally amongst the group. Everyone was subjected to the same diet, even those still rich enough to pay for more. Before the students arrived in the village, the local inhabitants received instructions forbidding them to sell any meat, eggs or other food-stuffs to the students. Only in cases of sickness or when absolutely essential to health could anyone obtain permission to buy a few pieces of pork or fish, and then only after application had been made through the group leader.

Students were not allowed to go beyond a certain limited area

[2] The kilo of rice served as a monetary unit, since, owing to a running inflation, the *piaster* was continuously falling and had no fixed purchasing power. Civil servants' salaries were fixed in kilos of rice, varying from 35 to 45 kilos a month. At the courses, students brought *piasters* with them and paid the management board whatever the current price for 100 kilos of rice happened to be. This varied greatly, depending on the market price at the time and the province in which the payment was made.

and were prevented throughout the whole course from having any contact with the outside world. They were permitted to write letters to their families (which were carefully censored), but could receive no letters from them in return. All incoming mail was held back and distributed at the end of the course. This was done to keep students free from any worry or outside distraction, so that they might devote their entire attention to their studies. One case is recorded of a student, a doctor, who was notified on leaving the camp at the end of a course that his wife had died two months earlier.

The routine of the course was military in character, and the timetable for the whole session was fixed beforehand. Reveille was at 6 a.m. followed by half-an-hour of gymnastics. There were classes from 7 to 11 a.m., lunch and rest from 11 a.m. to 1 p.m., classes again from 1 to 5 p.m., dinner and homework from 7 to 10 p.m. The last quarter-of-an-hour before going to bed was reserved for 'behaviour recollection'—a short review by the group of its individual behaviour during the day and slight self-criticism when necessary. Weekends were reserved for a bath in the stream and manual labour such as wood-cutting and digging trenches for use in case of air attack. Saturday evenings were reserved for entertainment. This was usually a performance of songs and dances given by the students themselves. On one course, a Russian film was shown, describing an episode in the Russo-German war.

III. TEACHING TECHNIQUE

A correctional training course consisted of classes in several subjects, all having the same ultimate aim. Each subject required about two weeks' study, representing approximately 150 working hours. The program was carried out with a painstaking attention to detail and divided into the following stages:

1. All students (usually about 500) were summoned to the conference hall and each given a mimeographed copy of the lesson. A party representative explained the lesson while the students took notes.

2. The students divided into their three-man groups and discussed among themselves the political terms used in the lesson, the better educated one in each group explaining the more diffi-

cult terms to the others. Then they discussed the meaning of the various passages in the text, and if no one in the group understood a particular passage, the group leader reported this to the teaching staff.

3. When all the reports had come in, the teaching staff would try to clarify the various problems before the assembled students. Sometimes the teaching staff would accept the students' suggestions for a change in the wording if this made the meaning of a passage clearer.

4. The students returned to their respective groups once more and began to discuss, paragraph by paragraph, the ideas contained in the text. Each in turn would express his own opinion regarding these ideas, and they were particularly encouraged to state quite openly whether or not they agreed with the party's view. If they disagreed, they were at liberty to raise an objection. As a rule, each student raised one or more objections, since if they did not they were suspected of hiding their own opinions. The stronger the objection, the more sincere the objector was considered to be. This was accounted very important in correctional training. As soon as one member in a group raised an objection, the others tried to explain to him the error of his judgment. If their efforts were in vain and the dissenter refused to change his 'erroneous' opinion, his mind was said to be 'blocked up' and the matter was reported to the teaching staff, who would then try to clear the blockage.

5. Once more the students gathered in the conference-hall to hear a representative of the party enumerate, one by one, all the objections sent to the teaching staff. He gave a brief reply to each objection. It was only during these occasions, listening to the long lists of objections (many of which were extremely violent), that one realised that the majority of the cadres and party members were excessively resentful against the party.

6. The students returned to their group and discussed these replies. If they were satisfied, then all was well. This was usually the case, but it sometimes happened that a student refused to accept the arguments and declared himself still unconvinced. One of the teaching staff was sent at once to the house where the unhappy student was staying; if all his efforts failed, then Truong

Chinh, secretary-general of the party, would himself come to the student. If he also was unsuccessful, then Ho Chi Minh would come in person and try his persuasive talents until, finally, the student accepted the rightness of the party's policy. No 'blocked-up' mind has ever been able to resist the persuasive power of Ho Chi Minh.

7. Meanwhile, the teaching staff proceeded to one or two 'demonstration parties'. For example, when students were having a lesson relating to colonialism, someone who had suffered imprisonment by the French was invited to describe the barbarous treatment he had received at their hands. Similarly, during a lesson concerning Land Reform, the whole class was taken to a nearby village to attend a 'denunciation party'. This was conducted at a huge meeting at which peasants denounced their landlords, accusing them of every sort of crime.

8. When the lesson had been completely understood and the party's view on that particular subject fully accepted, the whole class proceeded to what was called a 'preliminary' or 'partial confession'. In the light of all he had learned in the lesson in a particular subject, each student had to confess all his previous errors in regard to that subject. For instance, at the end of the lesson on colonialism, the students had to review their former attitude towards the French, and were urged to confess all they had previously done which might be considered profitable to the French. In the event of their never having served the colonial administration in any way, they had to confess any thoughts they might have entertained which ran counter to the attitude of a genuine patriot. There was, for example, the man who had been lost in admiration for the skill of a French pilot in manoeuvring his aircraft during a bombing attack. As a genuine patriot, he should have felt nothing but hatred towards the pilot, not admiration for his skill. To assist the students in their confessions and to jog their memories, the teaching team would read a long list of typical 'mistakes' already confessed during an earlier course. Model confessions, alleged to be those of eminent personalities, were also read to the class in order to inspire them.

9. After the individual confessions had been completed, the group leaders brought reports on them to the teaching staff, who

read them through, selecting the most interesting specimens. Those who made the most praiseworthy statements of errors were then invited to make a public confession before the assembled class. The students listened attentively to these discourses, interrupting from time to time with shouts of 'Down with —— !' but they were strictly forbidden to take any notes of the proceedings. There were students who admitted to having spied for the French and others who, amid uncontrolled sobbing, confessed to having committed adultery with their own sisters. Nobody could tell for certain whether they were sincere or whether they merely wished to impress the audience and to prove to the teaching staff that they were indeed changed beings, thanks to the instruction that they had received. On the whole, the prevalent impression was that the younger students were usually more sincere than the middle-aged ones.

10. After the teaching program had been completed, each student was asked, before he left, to write down his life-history and a general confession. Fifteen days were allowed for this. Each student was then given four thick copy-books (of sixty pages each) for these two tasks, which had to be written in duplicate.

The information to be included in these life-histories resembled that required by an employer from a would-be employee. The student had to give his full name, date and place of birth, details of his education, his occupation, knowledge of foreign languages, awards and decorations, and so on. But such information had to be given in greater detail than in the case of a job application. For instance, when describing his social origin he was asked to give details about the members of his 'three families' (his father's family, his mother's and that of his wife), back to the third generation. He was also asked to state what influence, good or bad, these people had had on his mind. Similarly, he had to write about his teachers, professors, schoolmates, office colleagues and friends, about the important books he had read, about their authors and the philosophies which had contributed to moulding his character and his way of thinking. Next, information was sought about his political inclinations and activities, emphasising any change of political standpoint and giving details of any such change. To conclude, the student was asked to answer the follow-

ing questions: What is your present occupation? How much do
you earn a month? What sort of property do you own? Are you
happily married? Do you have trouble with your wife (husband)?
Have you any financial worries? and other questions of this kind.

This life-history would enable any future reader to see at once
the circumstances and social background of the person in question
and to determine what sort of person he might be.

The general confession was the most tedious task of all, and
gave the students a good deal of trouble, even though they had
been prepared for it by repeated production of 'partial confessions'.
The difficulty lay not in the act of confessing itself, but in finding
enough mistakes, shortcomings and crimes to fill the required sixty
pages, and in proving that one had been converted to the truth
and was determined to break completely with the erroneous past.
It was a difficult task for an honest person who had nothing very
much in his past with which to reproach himself. The chief difficulty, however, lay in the social and educational background of
the confessor himself. It was, for instance, relatively easy for a
writer to invent his confession. He might first write a detailed
analysis of all his books and articles, openly acknowledging that
such and such passage in such and such a book was inspired by
imperialist or feudal ideas, and so forth. This was usually enough
to fill the entire sixty pages. Writers were, for the most part, city
dwellers and were not directly connected with 'landlordism'; thus
they ran little risk of being classified as landlords. At the time of
the correctional training program devised for the Land Reform
campaign, they were not particularly frightened and had no reason
for confessing to such sins as 'crimes towards the peasant'. What
writers and artists were expected to do was to produce a severe
self-criticism, followed by a *mea maxima culpa*, then a definite
repudiation of all their past works, even of their most brilliant
masterpieces. The final conclusion, of course, had to be a full
acceptance of the party's policy concerning Land Reform.

But for those students who came from a 'landlord' background,
the writing of the confession proved very difficult. They found
themselves on the horns of a dilemma: either they must confess
to all sorts of crimes towards the peasants, or else risk being
denounced by the latter when Land Reform reached their own

villages. On one side they were goaded by the unshakeable syllogism: 'Landlords are sinful, you are a landlord, so you are sinful,' and on the other side by the terrifying warning: 'If you refuse to confess your crimes, peasant comrades will denounce them on your behalf.'

A preliminary experiment in Land Reform had been launched in one or two localities before the correctional training course began. This experience had demonstrated to everyone that, during Land Reform, the peasants never denounced anyone of their free will (even had they done so, the party would have paid no attention), but only when they had been invited to do so on the orders of the party. Even the most simple-minded students realised, therefore, that correctional training was their last chance of redeeming themselves through confession of their mistakes, or at least of showing themselves capable of redemption. If they were successful in this, the party would not consider them to be incorrigible reactionaries, and so would not order the peasants in their own village to classify them as 'landlords'.

The question which eventually sprang to everyone's mind was: 'Since I can't remember committing any particular crimes, shall I invent a few?' Many of the students did, in fact, do precisely this, but were not always successful since, in order to prove one's sincerity, one had to confess to a crime that the party already had in mind for one. As soon as a student arrived at the camp, he was asked to fill in a form stating all the places in which he had lived and all the establishments where he had worked. The school authorities then sent letters and telegrams to all these places, requesting information regarding the student's behaviour and political attitude. Thus, in order to convince the party, the student must confess to a crime having some connection with what the party already had on its secret files. Another danger lay in the fact that one student may have been mentioned in the confession of another as being chief culprit in a particular incident. The main thing, therefore, was to discover what sort of crime would please the party most. It would be practically useless to confess to crime A if the party expected one to confess to crime B, which actually appeared on their records. But, at all events, there was little harm in confessing to such 'conventional' crimes as stealing from the peasants, or raping one or two peasant girls, because, as a rule, these sorts of crimes were attributed to the whole of the land-owning class, and also because of the well-kept promise that 'all confessed faults will be entirely forgiven'.

There were, however, quite a few students who, probably because of their 'petty bourgeois scruples' about inventing crimes, sat day after day writing vaguely of minor mistakes and short-comings instead of drawing up long lists of crimes. This was not what the party wanted and consequently, when Land Reform was carried out in their villages, these students, who had some connection with 'landlordism', were denounced as 'cruel and wicked landlords'.

The correctional training course was, in fact, a kind of purgatory where the almost, but not completely, purified minds had to purge themselves of all reactionary thoughts and thereby escape final condemnation by being classified as 'enemies of the people'. The fate of the latter and that of their families will be described in Chapters Fourteen and Fifteen.

TWELVE

The Five Lessons

The correctional training course of 1953-54 consisted of five lessons:

First lesson: The correct attitude of a student towards a correctional training course.

Second lesson: The History of the Vietnamese Revolution.

Third lesson: New circumstances, new tasks.

Fourth lesson: The correct behaviour of a cadre and a party member.

Fifth lesson: The Land Reform.

I. THE CORRECT ATTITUDE

This lesson dealt with the correct attitude of a student in a correctional training course. It recommended the student to cultivate a 'genuine devotion', which meant that he must make a real endeavour towards improving himself and changing his ideas through study, and not erect a misleading façade around himself with the intention of deceiving the party. He must also develop a true compassion for his group companions and an awareness that, in criticising a friend, his motivation should not be malice, but the hope of saving his friend from his sins. He must, in fact, adopt the attitude of a physician towards a patient. Thus, it was forbidden to resort to such methods (previously used in control-discussion sessions) as 'hat-cramming', 'hunt-the-criminal' and the like.

It was during this first lesson that the party gave the promise and the warning previously referred to in the matter of confessions: 'Confessed faults will be entirely forgiven' and 'It is entirely up to the individual whether he confesses or not, but if he doesn't, peasants will necessarily denounce his crimes for him'. The warning saved the party's representatives from having to use any other form of mental pressure, and allowed them to behave quite liberally throughout the course, since the threat of denunciation by the peasants constituted a Damoclean sword over every student's head. Under this terrifying threat, it is hardly surprising to find that every student tried to do his best to follow the party's advice and study hard. The more cunning appeared very reactionary to begin with, raising violent objections whenever invited to, and then seeming to become new persons after their lengthy confessions, thereby leaving no doubts about the enormous progress they had made during the correctional training course.

II. THE VIETNAMESE REVOLUTION

This lesson was concerned with the history of the Vietnamese Revolution viewed from the angle of the class-struggle. The party took great pains to explain the following points to the students:

1. Colonialism is thoroughly bad; everything that the French did in Vietnam was done only to serve their imperialist interests. The schools and universities that they built were merely to train sufficient Vietnamese to serve them. The railways they built were designed solely to transport their products, and their irrigation canals were intended to raise more taxes. Therefore it is the duty of everyone to fight the French and recover national independence.

2. During the eighty years of French rule, there had been ceaseless revolt and uprisings, but all of them had ended in failure. The reason for this was that they had been led by feudalists and petty-bourgeois intellectuals and did not command the support of the broad masses.

3. The Vietnamese Revolution had progressed steadily since the emergence of the Indochinese Communist Party in 1930, thanks to Marxist-Leninist doctrine and to good leadership which was the fruit of long experience in revolutionary organisation

throughout the world. Consequently, if one is a real patriot one will accept the Resistance Movement and the leadership of the Lao-Dong Party.

The main aim of this lesson was to persuade the students that to be communist meant to be patriotic, and that all patriots must be communists or must, at least, accept communist leadership.

III. NEW CIRCUMSTANCES, NEW TASKS

Taking a particular class as an example, the instructor for this lesson reviewed the current national and international situation. He fired the audience with enthusiasm by relating the most recent military and diplomatic successes (victory in Laos and recognition of the DRV by countries in the socialist camp). He explained the importance and the disinterested nature of both Soviet and Chinese aid, and compared the economic situations in the capitalist and communist camps, laying emphasis on Russia's strength and China's wealth. According to him, no capitalist company in Britain was rich enough to buy, for example, such an insignificant item as the amount of pig-hair collected by the Chinese Trade Office in one year. His detailed analysis of both the local and world situations led him to the conclusion that capitalism as a system would inevitably be destroyed and the French imperialists defeated in the very near future in spite of American military aid. But he stressed that, in order to face the new situation created by American intervention in Vietnamese affairs and the desperate efforts of the French to sabotage national unity, certain new tasks had fallen on the DRV's government, and there was need for yet more sacrifices from the masses to ensure complete victory. The most imperative of these tasks were:

1. The establishment of a people's democratic dictatorship, which was explained as 'democracy for the people and dictatorship for the enemies of the people'. The motives of this two-edged policy were expressed in these following terms: 'We must be democratic towards the people in order to be strong enough to be dictatorial towards the enemy, and we must be dictatorial towards the enemy so that we can defend the people's democracy.'

2. To consolidate national unity by means of a radical

elimination of all reactionary elements from the administrative machinery, and to achieve a greater participation by the proletariat in the political leadership.

3. A closer co-operation with, and a definite preference for, the socialist bloc, since without the valiant support of socialist countries the Vietnamese Revolution could not hope to succeed.

It is interesting to note that many objections were raised to this third proposition. Students argued that many countries, such as India and Indonesia, had won their independence without siding with either of the great power blocs. Consequently their neutralism rendered their position on the international chess-board very much stronger. When Ho Chi Minh came personally to persuade the more stubborn students, he condemned neutralism outright, describing it as 'political prostitution'. Talking on the same subject but before the whole audience, he said: 'As for those who continue to adopt a "middle-of-the-road" attitude, let me urge them to make a quick and definite choice: the fatherland or the enemy. I give my word that those who choose the French will be permitted to go over to the occupied zone without any difficulty. Exit visas will be delivered by local police bureaux whenever required.' Pausing for a little while, he added: 'There are two chairs. You are invited to sit on whichever you like, but please don't sit between the two for you risk falling down when the chairs move apart.'

IV. CORRECT BEHAVIOUR

The fourth lesson, dealing with the correct behaviour of cadres and party members, was unlike any of the others in the course. It was taught to party members and non-members in two separate classes. For non-members of the party, the lesson followed the lines of a book written by Ho Chi Minh in 1946 entitled *Rectification of Bad Working-Habits.*[1] This booklet contained a detailed list of all the bad habits prevalent among public servants during colonial rule, such as corruption, nepotism, sycophancy towards superiors, arrogance towards inferiors, and a 'mandarin attitude' towards

[1] *Sua Doi Le Loi Lam Viec* (Su That Publishing House, Hanoi, 1946). The booklet was signed XYZ, a frequent pen-name of Ho Chi Minh's.

the people, and so forth. It is, by the way, noteworthy that the
bad habits enumerated and violently combatted by Ho since 1946
had almost completely disappeared in the DRV by 1954. They then
reappeared after the establishment of the 'proletarian dictatorship'.
They continued to prevail under the Bao Dai régime in the French-
occupied zone, reaching their apogee under the Ngo Dinh Diem
régime in South Vietnam.

To bad habits of the colonial period was now added a further
list of new 'diseases' which first made their appearance during the
Resistance period. New names were given to them; for example:
rightist and *leftist deviations; opportunism; negativism* (doing
one's job through mere discipline or fear of punishment); *blanket-
wrapping attitude* (the 'wait and see' attitude); *romanticism* (lack
of realism); *subjectivism* (too much self-confidence); *loss of proletarian standpoint; loss of vigilance; liberty disease* (thirst for individual freedom); *sectarianism; bad-work-good-report; excess of
democracy* (behaving too democratically towards one's superiors);
dissatisfaction (with the régime), and many others.

The complete list was very long, and the extraordinary thing
was that all these 'diseases' were attributed solely to the landowning class. But they were contagious to party members, so these
latter also must be taught to combat them. In addition, they were
required to study a special chapter on the 'correct behaviour of a
party member towards non-party colleagues'. To the party members
it was explained that these 'diseases' were engendered in the main
by the petty-bourgeois mentality against which they must begin
a stubborn fight. This first was not mentioned to the non-party
cadres. (The author was not a party member and so knows no
further details concerning the special teachings dispensed by the
party to its members.)

Party members made their confessions apart, but attended the
public confessions made by non-party members. These confessions
were all concerned with the various 'diseases', the most remarkable
amongst them relating to 'regression'—a new term for adultery.
It was on these occasions that many people, in the best tradition
of Jean-Jacques Rousseau and with the verve of Françoise Sagan,
openly confessed to extra-marital love affairs with lady friends,
colleagues, cousins or even their own sisters. On one occasion, a

F

young man who was thought to be seriously afflicted with that particular 'disease' was invited to make a public confession. After enumerating his Casanova-like deeds with significant details which highly interested the whole audience, he ended by saying: 'Now, thanks to the party, I am fully aware of the enormity of my crimes, and am so ashamed that I dare not meet the eyes of one of my previous victims who is also here with us.' This unexpected bombshell caused an immediate flurry of confusion and indignation amongst the female group. It was later rumoured that the malicious confession was a nasty attempt to take revenge on a poor girl who had abandoned the young man for one of his colleagues, also present at the meeting. This anecdote goes to show that confessions were not always entirely motivated by a desire to purge the sinful soul.

Adultery, in fact, seemed to be widespread throughout the communist zone. It was tolerated to begin with, as the party wished the women to feel completely liberated from all 'feudal ties', including chastity and conjugal fidelity. Divorce was made easy. Dancing, which for centuries had been ignored by the Vietnamese, was enforced and in many places peasant women were asked to execute a few steps of some new dance before they were allowed to enter the market. The term 'Miss' was considered to be feudalistic and was banned from the Vietnamese vocabulary. Consequently, women of all ages, whether married or single, were addressed as 'comrade' (between party members) or 'sister', and they all used their maiden names. Mrs Le Van Hien who was, and still is today, President of the Women's Association, is called Sister Le Thi Xuyen (her maiden name). Teenagers were free to go together 'to seek a mutual understanding' without first obtaining the permission of their parents. One girl student at a control-discussion party was criticised as feudalist simply because she had refused to be photographed with a boy in her class when he had asked her to do so. It must be admitted, in all fairness, that despite some loose living amongst the young people, the party's policy of removing the age-old barriers between men and women, set up by the Confucian tradition, had some good results. Women in North Vietnam are today far less shy in society than their sisters in South Vietnam, not to speak of women in other Asian countries. But the communists must be blamed for their unavowed intention of favouring divorce, free unions and the like, not with the aim of achieving real emancipation, but simply to undermine the authority of the *pater-familias* so as to replace it with party control. For instance, young people under eighteen who wish to marry must still, under the law, ask the permission of their parents; but in practice this is unnecessary since there is no place on the marriage certificate reserved for the parents' signatures. On the other hand, in 1951 the party issued a regulation concerning party members on service in the administration or in the People's Army, stating that cadres of village level and soldiers must inform the party before they marry, that cadres of district and provincial levels and non-commissioned officers must obtain the party's agreement to their marriages, and that the marriage arrangements of high-ranking officials in the party and of officers in the People's Army are the party's affair. In fact, love was deprived of its social and emotional qualities and completely subordinated to political requirements.

To return to 'regression', or adultery: the fact that it was widespread was not solely due to the party's indulgence during the first years of the régime, but also to living conditions in a war-torn country, which encouraged cohabitation and promiscuity between men and women. Members of both sexes attended far too many meetings and evening classes, and public servants and students lived permanently in peasants' houses where the womenfolk were often left alone for long periods. This was because the male members of the family were away on 'citizen labour service' sometimes for months at a time. Peasants' houses were often used by travellers who were compelled to travel at night and were allowed to knock at any door and ask for hospitality. As a result, adultery was frequent between the man on citizen labour duty and the woman who took him into her house while her husband was away on citizen labour duty in another place. The situation reached a point at which many peasants refused to go on citizen labour duty, resorting to any excuse which would keep them at home so that they could protect their wives from the night-visitors. The party understood the real reason and from then on 'regression' was publicly criticised.

There were also many cases of bigamy, a problem for which

North Vietnamese legislators could find no suitable solution. Many people had lost touch with their wives after hasty flight from French attacks, and, to avoid loneliness during their period in the guerrilla zone, which they feared might well be indefinite, had married someone they met while in exile. Many cadres had also sent their wives to the occupied zone to seek some sort of financial support from their families living there, but large numbers of these petty-bourgeois ladies preferred not to return to the guerrilla zone. Such men were allowed to marry; when peace was restored, they found themselves with two wives, one living in the city, and the other, their 'Resistance wife', brought back from the guerrilla zone. There were also many eminent party members who wished to acquire wives who were their equals both socially and politically. This was the case, for example, with Hoang Minh Giam, Minister of Culture, Tran Huy Lieu, former Minister of Propaganda, and Dang Kim Giang, Minister of Munitions. It has been rumoured that these people had a very rough time over their confessions on this subject. Ho Chi Minh is reported to have spent many hours explaining to Tran Huy Lieu that it was wrong to have three wives, and particularly so when the one that he cherished most was a landowner, the widow of Pham Giao, a former reactionary who had been killed by the Vietminh in 1945.

It should be noted, however, that in the People's Army, the soldiers behaved quite differently and rarely committed any kind of 'regression'. The discipline in the army was very harsh, and for cases of rape the death sentence was liable to be imposed. The reason behind this excessive severity was the need to ensure irreproachable conduct by the army towards the population especially in the newly liberated areas, since it was hoped to win the latter over to the Resistance cause. It was the iron discipline of the communist soldier, in striking contrast to the behaviour of the French legionnaire, which assured the support of the population to the Revolution, and which consequently played an important part in the victory of the communists over the French.

The following anecdote offers just one example of the strict discipline imposed upon the communist soldiers. During the Tay-Bac campaign of 1950, the communist troops stationed in Son-La (a Vietnamese province inhabited by Thai tribes) were often teased by local girls who lived on the western slope of the Annamese Chain. Unlike Vietnamese girls, they are not bound by Confucian traditions and are consequently far less shy, being quite prepared to flirt with anyone who might visit their village. They soon discovered to their surprise and annoyance that the communist soldiers remained unmoved by their advances, and it was widely rumoured among them that Uncle Ho had had all his soldiers castrated before sending them to war.

It is interesting to note that, while prostitution was prohibited and all 'regression' severely punished, home leave was usually refused to those soldiers who were married. This was said to be necessary in order to maintain a strong fighting spirit amongst the soldiers, and it may well be true since this is the way in which fighting-cocks and racehorses used to be raised. Thus, loose living and ascetism were alternated and employed logically to serve the Revolution. This ability to employ different attitudes and different measures towards the various sections of the community illustrates better than anything else the way in which the communists have mastered the art of using all means to gain a single end.

V. INDOCTRINATION FOR LAND REFORM

As previously mentioned, the main aim of the 1953-54 correctional training course was to prepare the way psychologically for Land Reform by forcing the students to accept both the necessity for it, and also, and especially, the manner in which the party wanted to implement it. The party was, in fact, already omnipotent, but it refused to enforce the so-called reform by government regulations in the ordinary way, preferring to do so by 'giving a free hand to the masses', which meant mob violence. In this part of the course, therefore, the principal lessons were arranged in such an order that the students might be led from a natural, spontaneous patriotism to the final acceptance of Mao's technique of Land Reform. This ideological operation took the form of a multi-phased process of persuasion.

As an introduction, some of the points made in earlier stages of the course were re-emphasised. French colonialism is the most evil thing on earth; therefore, if one is a patriot, one's sacred duty is to fight the French aggressors. The nationalists have failed in their successive attempts because they could not mobilise the broad mass of the population. Now, thanks to the teachings of Uncle Ho and Uncle Mao—glorious disciples of Marx, Lenin and Stalin—we know how to win peasant comrades over to our side. Their participation in the struggle has brought about many important successes. They constitute at present the main force of the Resistance.

These points driven home, the Land Reform indoctrination proper began.

1. Peasant comrades are, by nature, utterly realistic. While they wholeheartedly join the fight and endure many sacrifices, they want to receive in return and without delay certain material and moral compensations. Thus, to sustain their efforts, we must encourage and comfort them by giving them sufficient land to till and full authority to 'shape their own destiny'.

2. The broad lines of the party's policy have been right, but nevertheless it committed a serious mistake when it accepted the landowning class into its ranks and regarded such people as one of the four partners of the people's democracy. The truth is now realised that far from being the friends of the people, they have been and will continue to be the mortal enemy of the people's democracy.

3. However, nobody, apart from peasant comrades, is in a position to recognise with accuracy who is landlord and how far each landlord is reactionary and criminal. Therefore peasant comrades are to have a free hand to denounce and punish them. As for the party, it would guide the 'struggle' but would not interfere.

It should be noted in this respect that such a technique of Land Reform, originally devised by Mao for China, was not in full accordance with the situation in Vietnam since, so far as the problem of landlordism was concerned, the two countries presented the following major differences:

(a) Feudalism was very strong in ancient China and remained so under the Kuomintang régime. Chinese landlords were, in general, warlords at the same time. Commanding their own army and taking the law into their own hands, they were entirely free to exploit and oppress the Chinese peasantry after the manner of the kings of old. Vietnam was, on the other hand, a country of 'Indonesian' background where the spirit of community, as well as significant vestiges of primitive communism, still prevailed. Communal lands, for instance, represented no less than 20 per cent of the total cultivated area; indeed, in a few districts, all the lands under cultivation were communal lands. Private ownership was undoubtedly unequal, but this inequality had nothing in common with Chinese inequalities of ownership. It seemed, furthermore, to be less excessive than in other countries. The following figures concerning the ownership-distribution of land in Vietnam before the Second World War are quite demonstrative.[2]

Ricefields	Tongking		Annam		Cochin China	
	Land-lords %	Land surface %	Land-lords %	Land surface %	Land-lords %	Land surface %
Above 50 Ha (123 acres)	0·10	20	0·13	10	2·46	45
From 5 to 50 Ha (12·3 to 123 acres)	8·35	20	6	15	25·77	37
Less than 5 Ha (12·3 acres)	90·88	40	93·80	50	71·73	15
Communal lands		20		25		3

(b) China was an independent country and Chinese land-lords enjoyed the protection of the Kuomintang government, whereas Vietnam was a colony ruled by foreign conquerors. Thus, although an exploiting class, the Vietnamese landlords were them-selves exploited and oppressed by the colonial administration. Being themselves victims of colonialism, they were in permanent

[2] The figures in this table were established by Y. Henri, in *Economie Agricole de l'Indochine* (Hanoi, 1932), and were reproduced in *Xa Thon Viet Nam*, an official publication of the DRV (Van Su Dia Publishing House, Hanoi, 1959) p. 62.

opposition to the French and did, in fact, constitute the main support of the Vietnamese Revolution, at least so far as financial contributions were concerned. This continued to be the case even during the Vietminh and the Resistance periods (*i.e.* up to the very moment when they suddenly ceased to be 'a pillar of the people's democracy' and became instead an 'enemy of the people').

(c) Although Confucianism had originated in China, its moral code had long since ceased to be observed in many parts of that country. The Vietnamese, on the other hand, although receiving Confucius' teachings at second hand, preserved what they were taught by their former conquerors in a purer form right up to the present day. In fact, China has been ruled for centuries by despotic emperors, cruel warlords and ruthless bandits, and the Chinese people lived, even after their 1911 Revolution, more or less in a state of anarchy. Vietnam, on the other hand, was ruled, almost continuously, from the royal government down to the villages, by a hierarchy of Confucian scholars, not by a pyramid of wealthy people.

(d) During the last eight decades, Vietnam has been a French colony and, consequently, the Vietnamese people were, by comparison with the Chinese, in closer contact with Western civilisation. Such a sudden and direct contact certainly produced many damaging effects on Vietnamese society, but, on the other hand, its positive aspects were no less important. Among these was a new respect for logic and reason; as a result of this, the Vietnamese, and particularly the Westernised intellectuals, tended to reject the purely arbitrary and the illogical. The proportion of the total population which could be described as intellectual was far higher in Vietnam than in China.

All these differences, combined with the numerous others in various fields, indicated a wide divergence between the Chinese and the Vietnamese pattern of society, and consequently, the Chinese technique of Land Reform was less suited to the Vietnamese problem than to China's. This criticism, of course, does not imply that Mao's technique was totally suited to the situation of his own country or to the mentality of his own people.

It was, therefore, quite evident that the leaders of the Lao-Dong

Party were faced with serious difficulties when they attempted to force Vietnam's Westernised intellectuals to accept the Chinese blueprint, or as some people said, to force the Chinese pill down the Vietnamese throat. Such an attempt was made during the fifth and last lesson of the 1953-54 correctional training course. Being something of a conjuring trick, it deserves particular notice and detailed analysis.

The main document studied in this lesson was the report presented by Truong Chinh, the secretary-general of the Lao-Dong Party at the time, to the First National Conference held from November 14 to November 23, 1953. This famous report was published in French and English in 1955 by the Ministry of Culture and Information of the DRV.[3]

Truong Chinh's main arguments as they are revealed in this report will provide readers with interesting details of the party's process of explanation, justification and persuasion. Subtitles have been added to each quoted paragraph with a view to summarising Truong Chinh's general idea and to translate into plain language what is hidden behind his process of 'double-talk'. This in substance is what he wrote:

> *The régime of exploitation.*
>   It is roughly true that the Vietnamese landlords, who represent less than 5 per cent of the population, together with foreign imperialists, own about 70 per cent of all the lands in Vietnam, while the peasants, who form about 90 per cent of the population, own only about 30 per cent of the lands.
>
> *If lands were fairly distributed, to what area would each farmer have a right?*
>   Over the whole country the total area of land given over to rice planting . . . is as high as 5 million hectares. If there are 5 million families in the country, then each family would be entitled to one hectare.
>
> *The Vietnamese landlords and the French imperialists are allies.*

[3] Truong Chinh, *Pour la réalisation de la réforme agraire* (Edition en langues étrangères, Hanoi, 1955).

Since the French domination, the Vietnamese landowning class has relied upon the imperialists to exploit
and oppress the peasants more than ever before.

Both are our enemies. We must destroy them.
The destruction of imperialism and feudalism is the
main objective of the Vietnamese Revolution for imperialism and feudalism *are the two principal enemies
of the Vietnamese people* [italics in the original text].
To overthrow imperialism . . . we must at the same time
overthrow feudalism. Conversely, in order to overthrow feudalism we must, at the same time, overthrow
imperialism.[4]

*To be anti-colonialist is not sufficient; one must also be
communist.*
The two tasks of the anti-imperialist and anti-feudalist
struggle are inseparable. We have to fight against the
tendency to isolate the anti-imperialist task from the
anti-feudalist one, and against considering the
imperialists as the principal enemy and the feudalists
the secondary one. [*'Anti-imperialist task' means the
anti-colonial war. 'Anti-feudal task' means liquidation of the landowning class.*]

A two-stage program.
Our land reform will be carried out in two stages :
    1. Reduction of land rent, in order to weaken the
economic position of the feudalists—a first step in the
overthrow of the feudalists' political authority.
    2. Land Reform, abolition of the feudalists' land-

---

[4] 'Feudalism' simply means 'land ownership'. The communists
use the term feudalism in place of land ownership with two
aims in view : to mislead Vietnamese landlords and to make
them unaware that their own turn would come after the
French had been disposed of, and, secondly, to make foreign
observers believe that land ownership in Vietnam had a
feudal character. The truth is that the feudal landlord ceased to
exist in Vietnam in 1883, when the Emperor Tu Duc confiscated all the feudal fields and turned them into communal
lands. Since then all landed properties, apart from some 'concessions' (waste-land given to some people for reclamation)
have been acquired by regular purchase.

ownership, liquidation of the feudalists' political authority.[5]

Is it true that the landlords are traitors?

As the war becomes daily more relentless, the feudal landowning class appears to be more and more reactionary. . . . Proof of this lies in the fact that during the present campaign for Land Rent Reduction, and in the course of receiving the testimony-accusations of the masses, we have discovered many instances of landlords carrying out espionage and organising intelligence networks for the enemy. They have also established bases in our rear for enemy commandos, directed various reactionary organisations whose aim is to sabotage our government policies—taxation, agrarian policy, labour mobilisation, etc. . . . Many of them have murdered cadres, set fire to peasants' houses, poisoned the wells, guided enemy aeroplanes to targets for their bombs and machine guns. [*'Testimony-accusation' means public denunciation for supposed crimes, such as those enumerated by Truong Chinh, which are evidently pure invention.*]

Our mistakes.

During these years we have cherished a one-sided conception of the national alliance. . . . We have often underestimated the magnitude of the anti-feudalist struggle, and failed to realise that an active anti-feudalist struggle fundamentally serves the anti-imperialist struggle and hastens its success.

Why should we not imitate Comrade Mao and wait until the end of the anti-French war?

We applied the experiences of the Chinese Revolution during the eight years of the Japanese War. However, the Chinese Revolution contented itself with land rent reduction, simply because the Chinese had to co-operate with Chiang Kai-shek's government in order to resist the Japanese aggression. That government represented the landowning class and the bureaucratic bourgeoisie. We, in our country, do not have this problem, there-

[5] This two-stage process will be described in Chapters Thirteen, Fourteen and Fifteen, dealing with the Land Reform.

fore there is no need for us to limit our agrarian policy
to land rent reduction.[6]

We shall correct our mistakes.

Our party is a Marxist-Leninist party which is accus-
tomed to practise criticism and self-criticism in order
to achieve progress. We admit our mistakes frankly
and are firmly resolved to correct them.

*To liquidate the landlords we must isolate them from the
peasantry.*

We must rely on poor and wage-earning peasants. . . .
We must also unite with the middle-level peasants.
. . . Now, to achieve this, we must have regard for
their interests, make them aware of their class-interests
and instil into them the spirit of the phrase: 'Poor
peasants, wage-earning peasants and middle-level
peasants are all brothers in the same family.'

As for the rich peasants, we must seek an understanding with them on the political level [*i.e. they are
not punished, but must remain quiet*]; on the economic
side, we must maintain intact their mode of agricultural exploitation. [*This was respected for one year
only.*]

The understanding with the rich peasants effectively isolates the landowning class—this move will
greatly facilitate its overthrow—and attracts the rich
peasants into the ranks of the Resistance, whilst, at
the same time, setting at ease the minds of the middle-
level peasants. If we ourselves place our full reliance
upon the poor and wage-earning peasants, and unite
with the middle-level peasants, it is with the aim of

---

[6] Land rent reduction here (as carried out in China in the pre-
1949 period) differs greatly from the Land Rent Reduction
campaign proposed by Truong Chinh, which is not land rent
reduction at all, but the first phase of the Land Reform. In
plain language this is what he wanted to say: 'Chinese landlords had the Kuomintang government to defend their
interests. Thus, it was not possible for Comrade Mao to liquidate them during this period of open alliance with Chiang
Kai-shek. As for Vietnamese landlords, although they
co-operate with us, they do not have any allied government
to defend them, therefore there is no need for us to postpone
their liquidation to a further date.'

liquidating, step by step, the régime of feudal exploitation. We do this in order to increase production and to
activate the Resistance.

Why do we proceed with two campaigns?
Land Rent Reduction is the first step and Land Reform
the second, in a single political process. We begin with
Land Rent Reduction in order to prepare the way for
Land Reform.

Why do we proceed in successive waves?
To execute the agrarian policy on at national scale, we
must wage war with the forces which oppose us. It is
the rules of warfare which decide the outcome. [*Land
Reform was carried out only in villages firmly controlled by the communists, not in areas bordering on
the French-occupied zones.*]
We must carry out Land Reform in stages, first in
the areas considered most suitable, and afterwards in
other areas, but not all at once. [*It was not carried out
in areas inhabited by ethnic minorities where the
population had not been sufficiently indoctrinated.*]

Don't panic! We shall discriminate.
The feudal landowning class is reactionary. However,
we have in our country at the moment three categories
of landlords:
1. Traitorous, reactionary, cruel and wicked landlords;
2. Ordinary landlords.
3. Landlords who have participated in the Resistance,
   among whom are a certain number of progressives.

You will be safe if you adhere to the party's policy.
Our behaviour will vary depending on the political
attitude of each category of landlords.

*If you are 'good' we shall not confiscate your property:
instead we shall buy it.*
After establishing the various categories of landlords,
and taking into account the different kinds of land, it
it advisable to use the following means to deprive the
imperialists and feudalists of their right to property:

1. Confiscation.
2. Requisition without compensation.
3. Buying on requisition [*a compulsory sale at a price fixed by the state*].

Truong Chinh's report was followed by the Agrarian Reform Law,[7] which laid down the method of application. Both report and law are masterpieces of communist official literature.

To return to the students perusing Truong Chinh's report: they proceeded to hold a detailed discussion on the report which lasted for more than ten days. Very few indeed of the participants in the correctional training course were convinced by Truong Chinh's arguments, for they contained too many obvious flaws. Nobody denied the fact that, hitherto, land had been unequally distributed in Vietnam—as in any non-communist country—or that there were landlords who exploited and oppressed the peasants. Nobody opposed the concept of land reform which would bring about a more equitable distribution of land. But they could not accept the extravagant figures relating to land distribution in Vietnam, invented by Truong Chinh to justify the violence of the two campaigns. He pretended that in Vietnam less than 5 per cent of the population were exploiting 90 per cent of it. He included among the 'exploited' about 2,000,000 city-dwellers who possessed no land, and a further 2,000,000 tribal people who were either nomadic or semi-nomadic, or not eligible for land tax because their jungle lands had not yet been surveyed. He also included the middle-level peasants, who formed the bulk of the landowning class (90.88 per cent in Tongking, 93.80 per cent in Annam and 71.73 per cent in Cochin China).[8] Truong Chinh claimed that the Vietnamese landlords, together with the imperialists, held in their grip about 70 per cent of the country's lands. This figure included all the communal lands, which represented about 20 per cent of the total lands and which, by traditional custom, were always

[7] Presidential Decree No. 197—SL, signed by President Ho Chi Minh, and voted by the National Assembly on December 4, 1953.
[8] Quoted from *Xa Thon Viet Nam* (Van Su Dia Publishing House, Hanoi, 1959).

equally distributed amongst the inhabitants of the village. But
how could Truong Chinh consider these communal lands as being
held in the grip of the landlords? He replied to this question when
it cropped up in a correctional training course by saying: 'These
lands are only common in theory, but in practice they have been
grabbed by the wicked exploiters of peasants. They have grabbed
these lands for themselves by cunning and trickery.' However, in
a later publication dealing with the land problem, the party
has been forced to admit that:

> ... the practice of communal lands has existed since ancient
> times, and the principle of equal distribution of these lands
> has become a deep-rooted tradition amongst the Vietnamese
> masses, which they have constantly fought to preserve. As
> long as this practice exists, the principle of equal shares can-
> not be abolished, for the landlords, even when they relied
> upon the colonial administration, could not appropriate the
> whole of these communal lands to share amongst themselves.[9]

Also, by adding 'together with the imperialists', Truong Chinh
embraced all the vast rubber, tea and coffee plantations owned, for
the most part, by French settlers who had created them out of
waste-lands in malaria-ridden areas. There was, beyond doubt, the
most barbarous exploitation of the Vietnamese coolies who cultivated these lands for the French, but these plantations which did
not exist before French colonisation cannot be said to have been
'grabbed' by the imperialists as Truong Chinh had claimed.

Truong Chinh's promise to give each Vietnamese one hectare
of ricefield was easily detected as so much cant. Although correct
in his calculation over the division of 5 million hectares of ricefields among 5 million families, he forebore to mention that 2·3
million of the 5 million hectares lay in the extreme south of Vietnam, not in the densely populated north where he intended carrying out the land reform. In order to give each farmer his promised
hectare, the party would have had to move at least half of the
population about a thousand miles to the south, and this was certainly not what the party had in mind.

[9] Ibid.

The purpose behind Truong Chinh's habit of referring to the Vietnamese landlords as feudalist was to confuse people and make them believe that there was a powerful feudalist element in Vietnam which needed to be crushed. When questioned about the use of the word, he replied vaguely that 'landownership originates from feudalism'. The students understood that Truong Chinh wished to give the landlords a bad name simply to 'hang' them, and they also realised that all the other crimes attributed to the landowning class were directed to the same purpose. After ten days of detailed discussion, it was obvious that Truong Chinh's report was designed merely to camouflage the party's sinister aim. This was the liquidation of the defenceless landowning class which had for years served the Resistance and had helped the Communist Party to secure and consolidate its power.

The debate on the report seemed to be as animated as those in previous lessons, but this time, at the end of the lesson, the whole class readily agreed with the party's teaching. They accepted, with less reluctance than they had shown in former classes, the necessity of Land Reform and the violent manner in which the party wished it to be carried out. The reason for such docility was simple. The students for the most part were themselves landlords, and they hoped that, by agreeing with the party, they would be classified as 'resistance' or 'ordinary' landlords, as defined in the report, when Land Reform eventually reached their own village. They had never committed any crimes against the peasants; as party activists and government officials, they had participated in the Resistance Movement. Therefore, their wisest course was to side with the party in its fight against the so-called traitorous and reactionary landlords, or at least to appear to do so. Thus, at the end of the lesson, everybody did his best to prove to the teaching team that he fully accepted Truong Chinh's explanation. As a result, this last lesson ended with a general feeling of enthusiasm and a thundering shout of 'Down with the landlords!'

Nonetheless, on their way home, the students could not but recollect that, when Ho Chi Minh came in person to address the course, he had used a striking allegory to elucidate his own policy: 'Imperialists are like tigers while landlords are like the bushes in which the tigers hide. Thus, in order to chase the tigers from our midst, we must necessarily destroy all the bushes at the same time.' Although they might be safe, their parents and relatives were now considered tigers and their family homes as the lairs of tigers, all marked down for destruction in the near future.

PART V

LAND REFORM

'To right a wrong, one should exceed the limit of the right.'

Mao Tse-tung *(Report on the Peasants' Movement in Hunan Province.)*

THIRTEEN

General Outlines of the Land Reform

The Land Reform was carried out in two successive campaigns: the Land Rent Reduction Campaign during the years 1953 and 1954; the Land Reform Campaign proper during the years 1954 and 1956.

The second campaign was interrupted in 1955 owing to the mass exodus of nearly a million people from North to South Vietnam. This took place during the 300-day period laid down by the Geneva Agreements to afford freedom of movement between the two zones. The communists temporarily halted the terror in order to avoid an even larger exodus. But after the closing of Haiphong, the last seaport through which people could escape, they at once resumed their campaign. This time, however, when carrying out the same policy in the newly liberated area, the densely populated Tongking Delta, they merged the two campaigns into one, and both the Land Rent Reduction and the Land Reform programs were accomplished by a single wave of terror.

These two campaigns had but one purpose, namely, the liquidation of the landowning class and the subsequent establishment of a proletarian dictatorship in the countryside. The technique used in both campaigns was almost exactly the same, the only notable difference being in the degree of violence and the nature of the wealth confiscated during each campaign from the same landlord. In plain language, the first campaign was intended to suppress the wealthier of the village bourgeoisie, who were described as the 'principal reactionaries', and to confiscate the ready money, jewels or any other precious objects they were suspected of having hidden away or entrusted to their relatives. The second campaign was aimed at the remainder of the village bourgeoisie, described as 'secondary reactionaries'. These latter constituted the main body of the landowning class; as they were relatively poorer, they were not suspected of having any hidden treasures. This second campaign also served as a 'legal' method of confiscating land, houses, furniture and the personal belongings of both categories of reactionaries: they were simply turned out of their homes completely empty-handed. The details of this technique of provoking waves of terror and of confiscating property during these two campaigns will be discussed in later chapters. But to understand how and why the liquidation of the landowning class was carried out in two separate stages, let us take the following example.

Let us suppose that in a certain village there are twenty-six families named A, B, C, D, and so on, in alphabetical order according to their degree of wealth, A being the richest and Z the poorest. At the start of the Land Rent Reduction campaign, the party taught the peasants how to classify the population into different social classes in accordance with the Population Classification Decree[1] which they had to study carefully for ten days. They could then classify the population of their village in the following manner:

A, B, C:	landlords
D, E, F:	rich peasants
G, H, I, J:	strong middle-level peasants
K, L, M, N:	average middle-level peasants
O, P, Q, R:	weak middle-level peasants
S, T, U, V:	poor peasants
and W, X, Y, Z:	wage-earning or landless peasants

[1] There are, in fact, two Population Classification Decrees: the 'provisional' Government Decree No. 239/B TTG, issued on March 5, 1953, and translated and quoted in *Conflict in Indo-China and International Repercussions*, edited by Allen B. Cole (Cornell University Press, Ithaca, 1956); and the 'definitive' Government Decree No. 472 TTG, issued on March 1, 1955, which incorporated a few additive clauses, all designed to give the appearance of more leniency.

The party then put into practice its famous slogan: 'Depend completely upon the poor and landless peasants, unite with the middle-level peasants, seek an understanding with the rich peasants[2] and liquidate the landlords.' It urged the people from G to Z to form a single alliance and to wage war against the unfortunate A, B and C, who were proclaimed as landlords. D, E and F, who came next in the general classification to the doomed A, B, C were not permitted to join this heroic fight, but their safety was guaranteed; and this is what was meant by the expression 'to seek an understanding with rich peasants'. These people were naturally overjoyed on learning that they were to be classified as rich peasants because they had been afraid that they would be considered landlords, since the dividing line between the two was too obscure and elastic for any degree of certainty.

Middle-level peasants on whom was bestowed the honour of siding with the poor and landless peasants (called 'home-force classes in the historical struggle') also rejoiced because they now felt secure under the new régime. Thus, to prove to the party that they fully merited this honour, they joined wholeheartedly in the fight against the luckless A, B and C. The outcome in practice was usually for A to be shot publicly, and B and C to receive varying terms of penal servitude. However, this was not the end of the affair for, about a year later, the party launched a second wave of terror—the Land Reform campaign proper. This time a new team of activists known as a 'land reform battalion' visited the same village and, after a brief survey of the situation, declared that the former classification made in the village had been wrongly drawn up.

'Our peasant comrades did not understand how to classify correctly,' they said, 'and in consequence they let too many real landlords slip through the net.' They ordered the peasants to study

---

[2] In 1953, this part of the slogan read: 'Let us isolate the rich peasant', but owing to the fear in which these lived (due to a general confusion between the 'political isolation' and the 'economic isolation', which will be discussed later) it was in 1954 toned down to: 'Let us seek an understanding with rich peasants'. This is quoted from the official translation, but the Vietnamese was *Lien-hiep phu-nong* which should, in fact, be translated as: 'Let us make an alliance with rich peasants.'

the Population Classification Decree once again, and urged them
to find more landlords. They said that according to the scientific
calculations made by 'our Chinese comrade advisers' who had
thoroughly investigated landownership in the villages (a flying
team of Chinese advisers was, in fact, moving rapidly from village
to village), a much greater number of exploiters should have been
found. The result of this was a new classification, and this time the
whole of D, E, F (rich peasants) and G, H, I, J (strong middle-level
peasants) became 'landlords', while K, L, M and N (average middle-
level peasants) became 'rich peasants' and so on. Thus, the total
number of newly found 'landlords' was about five times the number
of landlords found by the previous classification. Following an
order from the central committee, the minimum number to receive
the death sentence was raised from one to five per village. The
number of those who committed suicide, or who died from starvation because of the 'isolation policy' (to be explained later) increased in direct ratio. The total number of victims in this campaign has never been made public, but if we are to believe M.
Gérard Tongas, a French professor who remained in Hanoi up to
1959, and who claims to have accurate information: 'this in-
describable butchery resulted in one hundred thousand deaths.'[3]

So far, nobody has been able to assess accurately the exact number of deaths that occurred during these two 'sky-splitting and
earth-shaking campaigns'—the expression used officially to
describe the Land Reform; but according to refugees who reached
Saigon in 1957, the whole countryside of North Vietnam was
white with the turbans of mourners. (White is the Vietnamese
colour of mourning.) This does not seem to be an exaggeration,
since, apart from the number of people who were sentenced to
death by the Special People's Tribunal and publicly shot, there
still were people who died in jails and in concentration camps, and
those who committed suicide. As many again died in these institutions or by their own hand, but a far greater number of landlords' families—the majority of these being small children—died
from starvation owing to the 'isolation policy'. The staggering
size of the death roll could not have surprised the Vietnamese

---

[3] Gérard Tongas, L'enfer communiste du Nord Vietnam (Les
Nouvelles Editions Debress, Paris, 1960), p. 222.

communists for their maxim during the days of terror was: 'It is better to kill ten innocent people than to let one enemy escape.' These words were used in a speech delivered in Hanoi by Dr Nguyen Manh Tuong to the National Congress of the Fatherland Front in October 1956.[4]

These two campaigns were carried through in five successive waves, each one in a strategically placed area of a province, following the so-called 'technique of the oil-stain'. The pattern was something like this. The first wave was started in a few carefully selected villages in each province; these villages were chosen because they already contained among their inhabitants those who exploited and repressed the peasants to a considerable degree. The work of launching the campaign in these 'experimental spots' was carried out by a special team of cadres, carefully trained in China and having first-hand experience of the Chinese Land Reform. A great number of cadres from all parts of the province were sent to the chosen village to observe and to learn for themselves. After the first wave was over, these newly trained cadres, under the guidance of trained Vietnamese and Chinese advisers who remained nearby, launched the second wave in the surrounding area. Thus, like an oil-stain, the terror spread outwards over the whole district, and eventually over the entire province, so that by the end of the fifth wave the campaign had reached completion throughout all the territory under communist control. An exception was made in the case of the hilly country bordering the Laotian frontier which was inhabited by Thai tribes; this was done to avoid frightening the Laotians who have close ties with the Thais. Indeed up to the present time there has been no major reform in these areas where patriarchal authority is still respected. Again, in the Quang Tri province the Land Reform has been applied only mildly. This province lies close to the partition line dividing North and South Vietnam; here, excess lands were confiscated from the landlords and redistributed among the poor and landless peasants without any bloodshed. Such an easing of the general policy was

[4] Nguyen Manh Tuong, 'Concerning Mistakes Committed in Land Reform', quoted in full in the present author's *The New Class in North Vietnam* (Cong Dan Publishing Co., Saigon, 1958).

obviously intended to dispel any suspicions which might have
arisen in the minds of the non-communist population on the other
side of the border line. To quote Truong Chinh: 'In particular
areas, particular actions must be taken.'

Another point worthy of mention is that the government
seemingly stood aloof from these campaigns. Its attitude was that
the campaign was a people's affair, entirely carried out by peasants
in order to enhance their own political standing. This is clearly
what is meant by the phrase 'Let us give a free hand to the masses
in their struggle for Land Rent Reduction' or for 'Land Reform'.
The party disclaimed any responsibility, saying that it simply provided the peasants with advice and political guidance to help them
in their struggle. As for the army, it sent a few battalions, en-
camped nearby, to prevent any uprisings by the 'reactionaries' and
to lend the peasants a hand when necessary.

And now we will look at the way in which the Land Rent
Reduction campaign was carried out in one of North Vietnam's
ten thousand villages.

FOURTEEN

The Land Rent Reduction Campaign

Almost immediately after the 'Political Struggle' had died down, a group of cadres, trained secretly in China, came to the village disguised as peasants. Through the local party-cell, they made the acquaintance of a few landless peasants and asked for permission to live in their houses. Then they put into practice what is known as the 'Three Together System' (in Chinese *San Tong*), which means that they worked with their hosts (taking no payment), ate meals with them (whilst paying their own share), and slept with them in the same bed. When the host was married, as was usually the case, a girl cadre came and slept with the peasant's wife.

The cadres usually stayed from two to three months, and the peasants were very pleased to have them since they worked without accepting payment. They performed all manner of tasks, ploughing, harrowing or harvesting, according to the season; they cleaned the house or took care of the children, and the whole time they talked interminably. They demanded to know every detail in the lives of their hosts, showing particular interest and sympathy when they heard of any past misfortunes which the peasants had suffered. Before very long their hosts took them completely into their confidence and opened their hearts to them. The cadres went to great pains to show these simple-minded peasants where the cause of all their troubles lay. For instance, if a man's wife had left him for another, the cadre would explain: 'Had you not been exploited by the landlord you would have been well-off and could have afforded such things as would have pleased your wife. If that had been the case she would never have left you!' In short, according to the cadres, all the ills and misfortunes suffered by the peasantry were derived from its shameless exploitation at the hands of 'cruel and ruthless landlords, exploiters of peasants'. This was what they tried to instil into the minds of their hosts.

The next step was to make these peasants understand that there was only one way of improving their lives, namely, to side with the party and attack the despicable exploiters who were responsible for all the misery in the village. This intensive indoctrination went on for almost eighteen hours a day, until at last the formerly docile peasants were ripe for rebellion against their landlords. The converted peasant was called a 'root' and the operation just described was termed 'striking roots'.

At this stage, the cadre ceased all his own agitation in the village, and from then on remained inside the house where he was living. He acted only through his root whom he supported financially, employing him as a full-time secret agent. The root, whom we will call A, was urged to recruit B, and B in his turn would recruit C, and so on. This operation was called 'bead-stringing', and B, C and D etc... were called 'hard-core elements'. This system of enlistment (each root and hard-core element was allowed to introduce only one adherent) was specially designed to prevent the inadvertent recruitment of large numbers of 'reactionaries' and to avoid any traps which might eventually be set for them by local landlords. The root was also in charge of secret liaison with other cadres, posted in the nearby hamlets, for exchange of information provided by the hard-core elements. Every detail of village life, however insignificant, was thoroughly investigated; the landownership and the wealth of every villager, the kinship, political attitudes, past activities, and even the most secret love affairs of the villagers were examined. (Inquiries into these love affairs were aimed at one specific purpose: a woman who had been in love with some landlord when she was a young girl would be forced to state publicly that she had been 'raped' by the landlord in question.) Finally, after two or three months of this activity, the cadre had amassed sufficient information about the village assigned to him to make a personal report before a secret session of a provincial committee. There the cadre would decide, in consultation with the committee, upon the classification of the population of the village, his main preoccupation being who should be classed as landlords, and what 'crimes' should be imputed to each of these unfortunates.

It was then that the Land Reform Battalion came out into the open. The village administrative committee and the village branch of the party were immediately dissolved. The Battalion managed all the village affairs, appointed a new police guard composed entirely of hard-core elements, and ordered a blockade of the village. There are usually two gates in the dense bamboo hedge which surrounds every village in North Vietnam; these were closed, no one being allowed either to leave or enter without the permission from the all-powerful Battalion. The cadres now communicated with the higher authorities by means of a newly erected telephone line, and the sight of a line of bamboo poles supporting a telephone wire was enough to indicate to any passer-by that the terror was raging in that village to which the posts led. The wise avoided following the wires, for who knew what terrible fate might await them if they did.

Thus the campaign officially began, and was carried out in six successive stages, the final stage being the 'trial'.

STAGE ONE: POPULATION CLASSIFICATION

Peasants belonging to the 'home-force classes' (poor and landless peasants) were required to attend a special course in which they learnt how to classify the population into different classes, subclasses and categories. The documents they studied were the Population Classification Decree, explanatory texts relating to its practical application, and the 'norms of classification'. These norms were subject to variation from one province to another, and they have never been published. For instance, in one province the norms which determined the categories of middle peasants were:

(a) *strong middle-level peasants*: possessors of a cow, a pig and a poultry-yard;

(b) *average middle-level peasants*: possessors of a pig and a poultry-yard;

(c) *weak middle-level peasants*: possessors of a poultry-yard only.

But these norms varied, not only from province to province, but from stage to stage of the campaign.

After ten days of intensive study and 'democratic discussion', those attending the course voted a classification which, in most cases, was identical with that previously prepared by the cadres. There were inevitably differences of opinion, but eventually everyone was won over to the cadres' way of thinking. This was not surprising since the cadres showed themselves to be far better informed about the village and its inhabitants than were the villagers themselves.

STAGE TWO : CLASSIFICATION OF LANDLORDS

Immediately after the Land Reform Battalion came out in the open, but about ten days before the official list of landlords had been voted, those people who had been labelled as landlords by the cadres were arrested and their houses kept permanently under surveillance by hard-core elements. These landlords were now to be dealt with according to the classification determined for them.

In theory, and as stated by Truong Chinh in his speech (page 155), there were three main classes[1] of landlords : traitorous, ordinary and Resistance; and a fourth special class, that of 'democratic personalities', reserved exclusively for dignitaries of the royal court who had joined the communist government.

But in practice, the second and third classes simply did not exist. All the landlords found themselves classed as traitorous. As has been pointed out earlier, all landlords who remained in the communist zone up to 1953 had, whether they liked it or not, played some part in the Resistance, since communist policy up to then

[1] Although the official term used by Truong Chinh in his classification is *category*, we prefer to replace it here by the term *class*, reserving *category* for a subsequent subdivision which Truong Chinh did not mention. For instance, 'first class landlords' (traitorous, reactionary and cruel) are divisible into three categories : A, B and C (see next page).

was such that nobody could remain completely inactive. The young and able served in the army or in the administration on various administrative committees, village, district or provincial, and the elderly worked in puppet political organisations such as the Organisation of the Aged for National Salvation or the Vietnamese Alliance Front (*Lien-Viet*). Since all of them had lived seven years under the Resistance, they felt sure that they would be classed as 'Resistance landlords', or at least as 'ordinary landlords', and after searching self-examination they could not really see that they had committed any crime against the peasants. Certainly they had exploited the peasants to the extent of renting their lands to them and by hiring their labour very cheaply, but they reasoned that this was an inescapable feature of the former régime, and the communists had themselves condoned the practice for many years. They were greatly astonished and disillusioned, when the Land Reform reached their village, to find that they were all placed in class 1 and charged with crimes of every description. Even those who had served the DRV administration and had been decorated by Ho Chi Minh for their achievements were charged with deliberately penetrating the administrative and political structure of the country in order to sabotage the Revolution. No proof was required, and it was sufficient evidence for someone to have seen a landlord waving at a French aircraft, for instance, to condemn him as a spy working for the enemy.

This first class of landlord was subdivided into three categories, A, B and C. But those assigned to it were not told into which of the three subdivisions they had been classified. Nevertheless, if they were intelligent and noted the type of minatory language to which they were treated, it was not difficult for them to guess. For example, if the crowd shouted: 'Down with the traitorous, reactionary and cruel exploiter Chi' then it was certain that Chi was in category A. If, however, they shouted 'Down with the cruel exploiter Chi' he was category B, and if it was merely 'Down with the recalcitrant landlord Chi' then he was surely in category C. Each of these categories carried with it a different fate. Category A landlords were sent to a temporary jail set up in a nearby village, and the most 'dangerous' of them were kept in wooden cages like wild beasts. Category B landlords were sent on a type of brain-washing course especially devised for this class of land-lord ('rich but not very reactionary'). The main object of this course was to extract from them a confession stating to which of their relatives or friends they had entrusted their money, or where they had hidden their jewels. The course lasted some three to four weeks, during which time those forced to attend were prevented from sleeping and had to submit to the most barbarous treatment, so that by the end they were reduced to a mental state bordering on madness, and were ready to confess to almost anything. They were not only made to write a letter to their wives and children asking them to unearth hidden treasure and hand it over to the Peasants' Association, but they were required to draw up lists giving the names of all persons to whom they had lent money. These sums of money were collected at once, even if the landlord had made a false statement. Many tradesmen, having no direct connection with the Land Reform, were ruined by false declarations made against them by the landlords.

Category C landlords were held prisoner in a peasant's house in their own village, but they were moved from one house to another, always by night, and always escorted by police armed with naked swords. It should be stressed that this classification of landlords was anything but definite, and any landlord might be raised into a higher category or placed into a lower one at any time. His final category largely depended on his attitude during the campaign and whether he showed himself to be repentant, obedient or recalcitrant. Since this was made quite clear to the landlords, it rendered most of them very humble and obedient. But a fixed number of death sentences and terms of penal servitude had previously been stipulated by the party, so that however penitent they might prove themselves to be, many were executed to complete the quota. Nevertheless, humility was of some avail in many cases, and the Vietnamese, who had learnt how to be humble under the mandarins and the French, soon learnt that they must be even more so towards the communists.

STAGE THREE: EXTORTION OF MONEY AND VALUABLES

After the head of a family was arrested, his wife and children were called before the Peasants' Association and told that they must pay what was referred to as a 'debt'. Four or five years previously the government had issued a decree reducing land rent by 25 per cent. The Association now insisted that the arrested landlord had failed to comply with this decree, and demanded that he repay immediately all rent which he had received in excess of the stipulated amount. In point of fact, the majority of landlords had obeyed this law, but because their holdings were so small, they had never kept any accounts or records. In any case, to protest was useless, so that every landlord accepted the fact that he must pay back 'excess' land rent and tried his best to do so. This was paid to the Peasants' Association, a front behind which the Land Reform Battalion operated.

The order given to the landlord's wife and children was usually: 'Comrade peasants have calculated that you have taken from them an excess of X tons, Y kilos and Z grams of rice. [The amounts were very precise right up to the last gram.] And now they give you three days in which to discharge your debt; if by that time you have not paid the entire amount, beware!' The cadre would then hand the unfortunate woman a sheet of paper with the demand that she sign a statement promising to pay the full debt by a stated time and date (this was given to the exact minute). Then a stream of humiliating insults and abuse was hurled at the poor woman. A few details of this procedure are worth noting.

According to the cadres, the amount of the 'debt' was calculated on the individual declarations made by farmers, but in fact, little attention was paid to these, for they served simply to create a façade of legality. The 'debt' imposed on each landlord was based on the cadre's estimation of his private wealth, such as ready money and valuables—jewellery, ornamental vases, etc.—the object being to leave the landlord and his family with nothing save their lands, house and furniture, which would be confiscated at a later stage. That this was the intention became apparent when it was disclosed that the amount of the 'debt' was subject to subsequent variation, according to the resources and the goodwill of the 'debtor'.

If the landlord's wife paid off the whole amount within the time-limit, the cadre would inevitably tell her: 'We made a mis-

G

take in our calculations and find that your debt really amounts
to —— ' (the figure named was usually twice the amount of the
previous one). On the other hand, were she clever enough to pay
a substantial portion of the sum demanded within the time
allowed, and then, bewailing her poverty, beg for a little more time
in which to try to find the rest (thus proving both her willingness
and her financial incapacity), then the amount of her debt would
be lowered bit by bit. The cadre would say : 'We have revised our
calculations and now find your debt to be only —— ' (naming a
smaller sum). If, however, the poor woman paid nothing, or a very
small portion of the debt required, either through inability to pay
more, or through stubborn recalcitrance, then the fixed amount
would remain as it was with no reduction allowed. Her unfortunate husband in this case would be raised to a higher category.
That is what usually happened, since the amounts demanded by
the cadres were generally far beyond the means of most landlords
and their families.

After a landlord's wife, or his children, had been told to pay
the determined sum of money, in cash or in gold, his house was
sealed up, and the sale of even the smallest article forbidden. The
entire property—house, lands, buffaloes, personal belongings, dogs,
cats, everything—was declared people's property. Although the
amount of debt was calculated in kilos of rice, the payment was required in banknotes or jewels. Gold bracelets, earrings, wedding-
rings and pearls were all acceptable currency.

When the landlord's wife was slow in paying the debt, a section
of the village Peasants' Association was sent to her house to urge
her to be more speedy. They would ask her questions such as :
'Where have you put the pair of bracelets that you wore on your
wedding-day?' (this occasion might date back some twenty years);
or : 'How can you have spent the whole of the legacy left to your
mother by your maternal grandmother?' (this might have occurred
fifty years before).

A landlord's wife who could not produce any article of jewellery
was, together with her children, subjected to the most barbarous
treatment. She was often paraded through the streets carrying in
each hand a large piece of fresh cow dung, and wearing round her
neck a large placard bearing the inscription, 'I am a recalcitrant

landlord'. If she had a young baby, she would in all probability be incarcerated in another house and prevented from breast-feeding the child for a long period. If her children were older they would be arrested and kept in different places in the village, where they were threatened until they disclosed the places where their parents had hidden the supposed family treasure. These children were easily frightened and often disclosed some imaginary hiding place, whereupon the mother was at once given a pick and told to dig for it under the supervision of a group of hard-core elements. As a result of these 'mining' activities, which might last as long as a month, the peasants who were later moved into the landlords' houses found most of the floors dug up and pitted with large holes which they had no means of repairing.

STAGE FOUR: CRIME REVELATION

While this legalised form of robbery was going on, the peasants were made to attend a special course on 'Crimes Committed by the Landowning Class'. This was to teach them how the landlords had cheated, robbed, exploited and oppressed the peasants. At the end of the course, everyone attending had to make at least one accusation against his landlord. In order to refresh their memories, the cadres in charge of the course read a long list of typical crimes, believed to have been revealed by peasants in previous campaigns, or by Chinese peasants during the Land Reform in China. The result was that a number of peasants denounced the landlords for whom they had been working, inventing some crime with which to accuse them.

'Denouncers' could be roughly classed in three categories. In the first were people who were attracted by the promise of a reward either in kind or in the form of political privileges. The Battalion had openly promised that 'those who denounce most shall receive most' (meaning that they would receive a bigger share of the booty taken from the landlords in their village), and that 'he who is most vigilant in the present campaign will be recruited into the new party cell'.

Into the second category came those who wished only to protect themselves and avoid trouble. They denounced in order to appear faithful and obedient to the party. This category included people who had committed some offence for which they had not been punished, and children from landlords' families who deliberately denounced their parents. This they did at the request of the parents so as to save the entire family from destruction. On this particular subject the following passage quoted from *Thoi Moi*, a newspaper published in Hanoi (issue of May 8, 1957), is revealing:

Denounce as much as you can

... After the retreat of the Battalion, the daughter-in-law of [a certain lady] explained her position to the people of her village.

'I couldn't be so despicable as to denounce my own mother-in-law, so after the Battalion pronounced her a landowner, she and I discussed the matter all night. I wanted to go to the Battalion and protest, but my mother firmly advised against it. "I am almost eighty," she told me, "and cannot have much longer to live, so it doesn't matter very much if I am classed as a landowner. But if you protest you cannot avoid being *connected with landlordism*, and in that case we will both lose everything. Denounce me as much as you can and in so doing you will keep your land." '

In the third category were those who denounced through fear. Although the campaign was directed mainly against landlords, people from all walks of life were subjected to the same fate if they were found to have a 'landlord spirit', even though they did not possess so much as an acre of land. It was sufficient for them to have some connection with a landlord, and 'connection' was a very vague term which might mean family ties, friendship or mere acquaintance. The effect of this kind of terror at the time was shown in the following passage quoted from *Nhan Dan*, the party newspaper published in Hanoi (issue of June 2, 1956).

Fear of being convicted

... Mrs Ben went on: 'My neighbours and fellow-villagers are not ignorant of my situation. For generations we have lived in extreme poverty, and because of it we were reduced to living in the fields outside the village. We are old and make a living by netting prawns. When the Land Reform Battalion came to the village we entertained great hopes, and were eventually admitted into the Peasants' Association. A few days later my old Ben was elected a member of the Peasants' Assembly for the village. But then, I can't understand why, he came home in the middle of the session. He seemed in a trance, and neither ate nor slept for days. When I asked him what had happened, he replied vaguely: "I am ruined, irretrievably ruined. Try to find a way to save me or else I shall die." For months he did not attend the meetings but remained in bed, counting his fingers and repeating continuously: "In our family we have a son-in-law . . . and so-and-so . . . and so-and-so . . . who are all relatives of landlords, so we cannot avoid being classed as connected." '

Someone asked the old woman: 'And how about you?' She replied: 'Why do you expect me to feel differently? Only superhuman creatures would have no fear.'

Someone else said: 'You aren't the only one to get frightened; in my village a lot of people found themselves in the same situation.'

There were three varieties of 'connection' and each was treated differently.

1. Those who were believed to be 'closely connected' with landlords or were thought to have pro-landlord tendencies, were, like the landlords themselves, accused of some major crime—conspiracy, in most cases. They were then subjected to the 'isolation policy' which meant that they were outlawed and treated as lepers, boycotted economically, and very often kept as prisoners, with their wives and children, in their own houses, where they died of starvation.

2. People branded as 'moderately connected' were sent, together with their families, to some distant village, exchanging their houses and belongings with some other 'moderately connected' people who had also been exiled from their villages.

3. 'Slightly connected' people were simply expelled from the Peasants' Association which, after the downfall of the land-owning class, became the only means through which the peasants could hire buffaloes, borrow money in an emergency, or procure

seeds if they were short. In a society where everyone was equally poor, the Peasants' Association could mean life or death to the peasantry.

Despite all the cajolery and draconian coercion, however, a substantial number of peasants were courageous enough to refuse to denounce those labelled as landlords. For, though they lacked education, they had certain basic moral principles and in Vietnam, as everywhere else, denunciation of others to the authorities is looked upon with contempt. Moreover, the Buddhists believed in the principle of 'cause and effect', and were afraid that some disaster might befall them or their descendants if they deliberately harmed another. Revolt against this policy of denunciation was stimulated by Phung Quan in a poem, published during the Hundred Flowers period, which earned him years of exile.[2] After the Thought Reform Campaign of 1958, he was sent, along with other intellectuals who spoke against the régime, to the hilly and unhealthy region near the Chinese border to be 'taught' manual labour. As far as we know he is still there.

STAGE FIVE: DENUNCIATION SESSIONS

Following the completion of the lists of crimes to be attributed to each landlord, the denouncers were given a long and careful training to enable them to carry out their denunciations convincingly before a crowd and in the presence of the accused person. Denunciation sessions were, in fact, the keynote of the whole campaign, so they had to be prepared with the greatest possible care. Like actors rehearsing their parts constantly before the performance, the denuoncers practised their rôles so that they might play their parts perfectly and impart to the audience a feeling of sincerity and realism. The training was strictly secret, but the child of a

---

[2] The refrain of the poem ran as follows:
    Be truthful in your love,
    Be truthful in your hate,
    In spite of all cajoleries
    Never say that you hate when, in fact, you love.
    Even when threatened with a knife,
    Never say that you love when, in fact, you hate.
Published in the literary magazine, *Van Hoc* (No. 21, Hanoi, September 27, 1957.)

peasant household might frequently hear his father or mother repeating the same phrase over and over again during the course of the day, in order to memorise what he or she must say publicly. They even had to study gestures and actions under the guidance of a cadre who served as a kind of 'producer'. During the rehearsals, a dummy made of straw represented the landlord and was placed in the middle of the room; the denouncers stood in front of it one by one, and delivered the speeches that they had been learning by heart. When all the preparations were complete, the date of the denouncing was proclaimed.

Since there were three categories of landlords (A, B and C), there were three types of denunciation sessions.

Category A landlords were denounced before a crowd of ten to twenty thousand people, comprising the whole population of a 'multi-village', a new administrative unit consisting of from ten to fifteen villages.

Category B landlords were denounced before a crowd of perhaps one to two thousand people, representing the whole population of their own village, and the denunciation went on for two days. These landlords were accused of similar crimes, but of a slightly milder type than those of category A landlords.

Category C landlords were not present at their denunciation. They were kept apart and brought in only at the end of the session to listen to a list of all their alleged crimes previously reported by their tenants (the meeting was composed entirely of the peasants to whom they rented lands), and to say a few words acknowledging these 'crimes', and apologise for them. Finally, they were required to put their signatures to the minutes of the meeting. The party explained that this form of denunciation *in absentia* was a measure of clemency towards the 'secondary reactionaries' who were still believed to be capable of redemption. Hoping that, after this experience, they would change their attitude, the party did not want them to lose too much face before their fellow villagers. In fact, the landlords in this category were, for the most part, landlords-cum-tradesmen and usually lived in towns, coming only occasionally to the villages where they were landowners. Thus, it is not difficult to understand the reasons for this type of denunciation *in absentia*. Since these landlords never lived in the same villages as their tenants, the latter could know nothing of their private lives and could not have suffered ill-treatment at their hands, so that it was impossible for them to make any of the accusations sound convincing. The party was afraid that, under these circumstances, the denouncers might falter in their accusations if the accused were present. It was reckoned they would have more self-confidence if the meeting were private; any hesitancy or stumbling on their part would not result in any loss of prestige either for them or for the party. There had, indeed, been some acutely embarrassing occasions when the accused land-lords had burst out laughing.

Attendance at a denunciation session for Category A landlords was compulsory for the whole population of the multi-village, ex-ceptions being made for one adult only in each family, who was allowed to remain at home in order to look after the fire and the small children.

The meeting was composed of separate groups. 'Middle-level peasants' and 'poor and landless peasants' attended in groups repre-senting the Peasants' Association to which they belonged. 'Rich peasants' had to form a separate group and walk apart, while land-lords and the members of their families who were compelled to attend the party were scattered amongst the crowd, each one entrusted to a different peasants' cell. They were subjected to a thorough search and then placed in the centre of the group where a vigilant eye was kept upon them. Every cell was subdivided into sections each of which carried a jar of water and a water-pipe (they smoked a very strong Laotian tobacco in the water-pipe) for the communal use of the whole section, because, once they were in position, nobody would be allowed to move about. Each village formed a procession, the villagers carrying placards and waving flags and the small children beating drums. The captive landlords marching among the crowd were forced to imitate the other peasants, shouting the same slogans and shaking their fists at intervals.

The proceedings were always held in the open air, usually on a football ground or preferably on the slope of a hill. A special space, demarcated by a whitewashed line, was allocated to each village. The peasants sat on the ground facing the tribune before which people came to make their denunciations. This was a three-storey construction made of timber and bamboo. On the stage floor sat fourteen clerks, all but one of them poor peasants, the exception being a middle-level peasant who could read and write. The second stage was occupied by a presidium of seven presidents, again all poor peasants, and among them one woman whose rôle was that of a police-chief. (The author noticed the same phenomenon at five successive denunciation sessions which he attended. It seemed to him that this was intended to enhance the political prestige of women in the eyes of the crowd.) She commanded the village guards, and at intervals of about five minutes barked orders at the landlord appearing before the tribune. These were usually commands to stand up, kneel down, raise both arms horizontally or vertically, and so on. On the top stage of the tribune stood three huge portraits, Ho Chi Minh in the middle, flanked by Malenkov on the right and Mao Tse-tung on the left, and all decorated with the flags of their respective countries. On either side of the tribune were enormous placards bearing such slogans as: 'Let us give a free hand to the masses in their struggle for Rent Reduction' and 'Down with the traitorous, reactionary landlords and exploiters of peasants'.

During the war with the French, such mass sessions were always held at night to avoid French bombing, and the gathering was surrounded by a circle of lighted bamboo torches. Naked flames puthering out huge columns of smoke into a cloudy sky gave to the scene something of an infernal aspect—a nightmarish scene suggesting to the Vietnamese mind that the pictures in Buddhist temples depicting the fearful punishment of damned souls in Hell had become a reality.

The tribune was lit by electricity, sometimes provided by a generator but more usually by small bicycle dynamos. The bicycles were fixed behind the tribune and were pedalled continuously. Also behind this screen stood members of the Land Reform Battalion who directed the presidium in a low voice. Very often a Chinese adviser dressed in Vietnamese clothing was among them.

The chairman of the presidium opened the meeting by declaring briefly, but with great solemnity, that the peasants had been the main force behind the Revolution and the War of Inde-

pendence and that, thanks to the guidance of the party, they were
now the real masters of the country. Their most urgent task at
present was to overthrow their principal enemy, the traitorous
and reactionary landlords who for thousands of years had exploited
and oppressed them and who were still working as spies for the
colonialists. The woman acting as police-chief then stood up and
shouted an order to the village guards, commanding them to bring
forward the landlord who was to be denounced. A chorus of
thousands of voices immediately commenced to shout: 'Down
with the traitorous, reactionary ——,' yelling out the name of the
landlord concerned. The wretched victim then made his entrance,
crawling animal fashion on his hands and knees. He was dragged
on to a small earthen platform about a yard square and a yard
high in front of the tribune. Facing him was a similar platform reserved for those who would come, one by one, to denounce him.
If the person to be denounced was a Catholic priest or a
Buddhist monk, an order was given to remove his robe before he
was ill-treated in any way.

The chairman called for volunteers; a sea of hands rose in answer.
After a quick glance at his paper, he called a name. The man
chosen climbed up on the platform and pointed a finger at the
accused asking: 'Do you remember who I am?' and without waiting for a reply he continued: 'I am —— who has served you for
—— years.' A short autobiography followed, lasting for several
minutes. Since the greater part of the audience came from other
villages, they could not possibly know the denouncer or anything
about him, so, copying the practice of the Vietnamese and Chinese
theatre where each actor, upon making his first appearance on the
stage, always announces 'I am ——', giving the name of the
character he is playing, the denouncer announced himself. He
then reeled off at top speed all the wrongs that the landlord in
question had inflicted upon himself and his family—perhaps he
had beaten him, raped his wife or killed his children—and all that
he had witnessed in the way of traitorous activities on the part
of the accused. He might, for instance, have seen him waving at
a French aircraft, or have been urged by the landlord to join a
reactionary organisation. Denouncers were free to use the most
insulting and vulgar terms when speaking to the accused with the

twofold purpose of destroying the prestige of the landlord and of making the peasants' own speeches sound more natural. The landlord was not allowed to reply to the accusation or to defend himself; he might only say 'yes' or 'no'. Each time he said 'no', the immediate reaction from the crowd was a thunderous roar of 'Down with the traitorous ———'. At intervals of about five minutes he was ordered either to kneel down, stand up, raise his arms, kneel down again and so on. Each denouncer was allotted about fifteen minutes in which to make his accusations; after four of them had been heard, the landlord was led before the 'secretaries' to sign a report drawn up by them.

The denunciation of an A type landlord lasted for three consecutive days or nights. On the first, which was reserved for 'debts of sweat', the peasants related how they had been unjustly exploited or robbed. The accusations on the second day or night, reserved for 'debts of happiness', dealt with the way the peasants had been beaten or their wives raped. On the final day or night, devoted to 'debts of blood', the luckless landlord would be accused of sundry murders and counter-revolutionary activities. If the landlord persistently said 'no' during the first day, the charges brought against him on the following day were generally graver. Finally, if he proved himself to be recalcitrant, refusing to admit to any crime, he would be charged with countless murders and spying activities, and then shot before the assembled crowd. But if he were prudent and answered with a meek 'yes' to all the accusations, including those of murder, rape and sabotage, his punishment was likely to be less severe. There were, of course, some landlords who had previously been condemned by the party, and for these the death sentence was a foregone conclusion. It would be true to say that the party was not anxious to kill too many, at least in the first stage of the campaign—perhaps one landlord in each village—but if the victims proved to be recalcitrant, many might be shot. Its purpose was, after all, to prove to the population that the party, acting through the Peasants' Association, was all-powerful. If the accused admitted to the various charges, this was all to the good as far as the party was concerned, for the denouncers would appear to be truthful and reliable, but if too many denied the accusations, a substantial number of spectators might be inclined to the view that the charges were merely invented and groundless. In the latter case, the party was often obliged by means of threats to force the victim to change his attitude, or even to shoot him in order to safeguard its own prestige. As a result, many landlords were shot during the first wave of the campaign because they persisted in affirming their innocence. Their deaths, however, served as a lesson for the victims of the second wave, who submissively admitted all charges against them. Gradually, the Vietnamese people began to realise that the whole process was but a tragi-comedy, in which the denouncer and the denounced had to play the parts ascribed to them by the all-powerful party.

The various crimes attributed to the landlords were much the same in every province. The most common were that they had hanged a peasant from a tree, forced another to lick a spittoon or to eat human excrement or cow dung, burned down houses, drowned small children, put poison in the village well, thrown stones at peasants' meetings, killed and raped, etc. The following passage published in *Nhan Dan* (the party newspaper) on February 2, 1956, will give the reader some idea of the nature of these accusations.

> At Nghia-Khe village, in the district of Bac-Ninh, landlords urged small children to steal documents and to throw stones at peasant meetings. In Lieu-Son, they persuaded a small child to set fire to a peasant's house. More cruelly, they gave a poisoned cake to some children in Lieu-Ha, almost killing them. In Van-Truong, they urged young Suu, aged thirteen, to persuade two other small girls to join her in committing suicide by jumping together into a pond; this was to create confusion in the village. In Duc-phong (Ha-Tinh province), they distributed playing cards amongst the children, so that the latter, absorbed in their game, allowed the buffaloes to ruin the crops.

It is interesting to note that the raping of women was a crime reserved for landlords and those who enjoyed a certain moral prestige in the community, such as Catholic priests, Buddhist monks and in particular scholars of the Confucian school. As a rule, the more respectable the landlord's appearance (if, for example, he had a white beard or a bald head), the greater was his moral crime. It was quite common in such cases to see the accused's own daughter or daughter-in-law stand before the tribune and announce publicly that he had raped her. Similarly, the more patriotic a landlord was known to be, the more he would be charged with anti-patriotic activities.

Since accuracy was not demanded, any of the deaths which had occurred in the village over the past few years might be attributed to the landlord in question. Nguyen Dinh Phap of Nghe-An province, planter and member of the National Assembly, was accused of thirty-five murders simply because that number of coolies had died of malaria in his plantation. During a denunciation session held for Le Trong Nhi, a nationalist leader of the 1907-8 movement who had spent nine years on Poulo Condore prison island, a woman confronted him with the words: 'Did you know that my son was not fathered by my husband, but by you? You came to my house during my husband's absence and slept with me. It was then that my son was begotten.' Nhi was then seventy-five, the woman about sixty, and her son in his forties. Some villagers made a rapid calculation and found that at the date the woman's son was conceived, Nhi was languishing in a French jail, a thousand miles away.

There were several landlords who acted courageously and calmly throughout their ordeal, retaining their dignity the whole time. One old lady in Nghe-An province said neither 'yes' nor 'no', but repeated continuously: 'Please, shoot me!' In Thanh-hoa province, a denouncer, asking his customary question: 'Do you remember who I am?' received the cool reply: 'Indeed, I do. You are the one who stole a chicken from my poultry-yard last year.' But after such an incident the chairman would close the meeting abruptly, postponing it for a week or two. When it was resumed, the recalcitrant landlord was more subdued and the 'chicken thief' was not called again. Landlords who were brought to these denunciation sessions were quite well fed during the three days of the meeting. They received generous portions of chicken, beefsteak, and other nourishing foods, and tea and coffee to drink. The purpose behind this generosity seems to have been to ensure that the victim had enough strength to withstand three days, or three nights, in the open, and to execute all the movements demanded by the woman police-chief without collapsing. After the three days of the denunciation session were over, the landlords were sent to jail to await the Special People's Tribunal's decision on their future.

During the two campaigns, a local paper called *Forest Leaves* was issued in each province (crimes committed by the landowning class were said to be as numerous as forest leaves), in which detailed descriptions of the various denunciation sessions were published. All cadres working in the government offices were compelled to go at one time or another to a village to watch the procedure of the Land Reform Campaign. The purpose was to endow them with a profound understanding of the party's policy, which was claimed to be 'in perfect accordance with reason and emotion'. These cadres practised the 'three together system' with local peasants, but they attended simply as observers and had no authority to interfere in the business. Their presence, however, had a beneficial effect; in the villages where they were, the campaign was better conducted and, on the whole, landlords were less severely punished. This was because the party wished to impress the cadres with the rightness of its policy. As a result, landlords in the villages visited by these observers considered themselves fortunate and looked upon them as 'guardian angels'.

STAGE SIX: THE TRIALS

A few days after the denunciation session, a Special People's Tribunal came to the village to try those recently denounced by the peasants. There was one mobile tribunal for each district, and it was composed entirely of peasants who knew nothing of law or jurisprudence. There was a judge and a public prosecutor, but no one to act for the defendant, because, in practice, the accused was not permitted to defend himself; the 'act of denunciation' which he had signed earlier was taken to serve as his testimony. The jury comprised the same peasants who had formed the presidium in the denunciation session. Sentences imposed by the tribunal varied from the death penalty to five years' hard labour, with the confiscation of part or the whole of the prisoner's property. Partial confiscation meant little since everything he owned would be confiscated later on when the Land Reform campaign was set under way in earnest.

Those unfortunates who were sentenced to death were shot immediately after sentence had been passed. Before the tribunal began, a hole was dug nearby to receive the bodies of the victims. At the very beginning of the campaign, the condemned were allowed to say a few words before execution but after one of them had shouted: 'Long live President Ho! Long life to the Lao-Dong Party!' just before he was shot, this 'bourgeois' practice was abandoned. From then on, a cadre stood behind the accused, ready as soon as the sentence had been passed to thrust a piece of cloth into his mouth and drag him away. What made the fate of these landlords the more terrible was that those who formed the firing-squad knew little about shooting, being for the most part village guards handling a gun for the first time. Consequently, it frequently happened that the victims were buried alive. The grave was then levelled over and a tree or shrub planted on it. A huge parade was organised on the occasion of a landlord's execution, with small children beating drums and the adults shouting the usual slogans. The crowd had to clap their hands when the victims fell down.

Those who had witnessed the whole process from the start were put in mind of the cat-and-mouse image; as a cat plays with a mouse before finally killing it, so the party seemed to have played with the landlord during the three days of the denunciation session before finally striking him down. The landlord was a scapegoat to satisfy the cruel instincts of a few fanatics and to strike terror into the heart of the whole population.

To complete the picture of the Land Rent Reduction campaign, a few words must be said about the famous 'policy of isolation' which was responsible for a number of deaths, probably ten times greater than that ordered by the Special People's Tribunals.

THE POLICY OF ISOLATION

As soon as a man had been labelled as 'landlord', he and his family were boycotted and shunned by their fellow human beings. Like leprous dogs, they became creatures at whom children were encouraged to throw stones. Nobody was permitted to talk to them or to have any contact with them. For more than a year, from the beginning of the first campaign to the end of the second, members of landlords' families were prevented from working. In consequence the majority of them died of starvation, children and old people first, and eventually the others.

This appalling measure, rigorously applied, was devised to wipe out forever the race of 'exploiters' in the countryside. As has been said earlier, no official report states the numbers of people who died from starvation owing to this policy, but one thing is certain: the larger part of the landowning class died in this manner. Nguyen Manh Tuong, in his speech to the National Congress of the Fatherland Front in Hanoi in 1956, stated simply: 'While destroying the landowning class, we condemned numberless old people and children to a horrible death.' In another passage of the same speech he said:

> The responsibility is that of the guilty person alone, not of his wife and children and relatives. It would be unjust, and unnecessary disturbance would be created in the social order, if we were to compel the relatives of a guilty person to share his responsibility with him. None of the Western countries has proceeded in such a manner for four hundred years. Responsibility before the law is always individual. Aged persons are often pardoned and not sent to jail, and adolescents benefit from more indulgent measures.[3]

It would seem that Ho Chi Minh was engaging in genocide. On the whole, Hitler and Eichmann were less hypocritical than Ho and Mao since, by ordering the Jews to the gas-chamber, the Nazi leaders at least accepted full responsibility for their crimes. The Vietnamese and Chinese leaders, on the other hand, preferred to watch the landowning class die a 'natural' death, for which nobody would appear directly responsible.

[3] Nguyen Manh Tuong; 'Concerning Mistakes Committed in Land Reform', quoted in full in the present author's *The New Class in North Vietnam*.

There was a callous deprivation of medical assistance. Dr Tuong aptly summarised the situation when he said:

> When a patient enters a hospital for urgent treatment, the first question to be answered is 'To what social class does he belong?' To give medical treatment to a landlord would inevitably entail the loss of one's political standpoint. If, however, one allowed him to die, then one would preserve one's standpoint.[4]

Such landlords as miraculously survived up to the Rectification of Errors movement, which followed directly after the de-Stalinisation campaign in Europe, were those who had been succoured by humanitarian neighbours. These neighbours threw balls of rice, medicines and other necessities over the landlords' wall during the hours of darkness.

[4] *Ibid.*

FIFTEEN

The Land Reform Campaign Proper

Despite its almost unbelievable violence, the Land Rent Reduction campaign was but a mild preliminary to the Land Reform proper which followed it. As has been said earlier, the Land Rent Reduction campaign was aimed at liquidating a relatively small section of the landowning class, economically the richest and, in Marxist political terminology, the most reactionary. The annihilation of these 'ringleaders' was no more than a precautionary measure aimed at clearing the countryside of all potential resistance to the party's policy regarding land collectivisation and the establishment of a proletarian dictatorship.

In the manner of their application both campaigns followed the pattern of the 'spreading oil-stain'. In each village, Land Reform was carried out one year after the Land Rent Reduction campaign had been completed. One reason for this year of respite was the necessity of reorganising the village economically as well as politically. During the first campaign, peasants had spent too much time in meetings and processions, and rice cultivation had been neglected in consequence. In fact, villages where the Land Rent Reduction had been enforced looked as though a typhoon had swept through them, most of the hedges being down and the straw roofs of the peasants' huts unrepaired. Dogs, pigs and even cows wandered about the village unattended. People were still suffering from the effects of the terror which they had lived through and seemed to have lost all incentive to work. For genera-

tions these people had worked hard to improve their economic and
social condition in order to have something to leave to their children, but it was suddenly brought home to them that to acquire
more than others was to commit some sort of crime. So they felt
no urge to work or to produce more than was absolutely essential.
To counteract this general sluggishness, the party resorted to
'socialist emulation', but the task of converting the peasants to
this new way of thinking required time. A minimum of one year
was therefore necessary to make them realise that they must still
work hard, indeed harder than before. They were exhorted to
repair their houses, cattlesheds and hedges; they were organised
into groups to dig canals, build roads and to prepare against
drought and flood. Orders from the Peasants' Association tended
to replace private or individual initiative, and the collectivist pattern of life gradually took the place of the old pattern.

This intervening year also saw the reorganisation of the administrative committee and the party's branch in each village,
since both of these bodies had been disbanded after the start of
the Land Rent Reduction campaign. All former cadres and party
members who were in any way connected with the landowning
class were omitted from the new bodies, no matter how vigilant
and faithful they might have been. The village administrative
committee was recruited entirely from poor and landless peasants
regardless of the fact that many of them were quite illiterate. The
same changes occurred in the reorganisation of the party branch.

To be admitted to the new cells, one was required to have no
connection at all with the landowning class, and to have proved
oneself sufficiently vigilant during the Rent Reduction campaign.
As a result, only a few of the former members were readmitted,
and the new branch was comprised mostly of newly recruited
members selected from among hard-core elements who had maintained their political standpoint throughout the campaign. A dis-
tinction was made between the 'old members' and the 'new members', and not unnaturally conflict arose between them. The outcome of all this was that, during the Land Reform campaign, the
new members denounced the old ones as landlords and had them
sent to jail. A great number of these veterans were shot as reactionaries, while twelve thousand others were sentenced to

various terms of imprisonment (official figure admitted by *Nhan Dan*). These latter were released three years later during the Rectification of Errors campaign. But during their absence their houses and property and even their wives were confiscated. Since this was lated declared to be an 'error', it will be discussed in Chapter Sixteen on 'Rectification of Errors'.

One question which arises is: Why were party members, held in high regard during the first campaign, treated so badly during the second one? The reasons for such an abrupt change seem to be as follows:

1. Land Reform developed into a vast purge on a national scale, from which the party itself was not excluded. Party members were submitted to the same ordeal of public denunciation as other members of society. In effect, the poor and landless peasants—and they alone—were entrusted with the task of purging the whole of the population including the rank and file of the party itself. That party members were spared in the first campaign, but not in the second, was simply a question of tactics: each one in his turn.

2. Almost the whole of the 'old' party members were of bourgeois and feudal background, so it is not difficult to understand why they, too, were finally classed as landlords when the party wanted to acquire a proletarian rank and file.

3. The clash between the old and the new party members probably arose from the fact that, during their ten years of power (1945-55), old party members had formed a new class and, despite their proletarian viewpoint, were often far from gentle in their treatment of the proletariat itself. It might be said that during the second campaign they paid for the way in which they had misused their authority during the period prior to the first. The following passages quoted from *Cuu Quoc*, the official newspaper of the Fatherland Front, published in Hanoi, will help the reader to understand why the workers hated their 'liberators' as much as they did.

A cadre, wishing to cross the Gianh river during a bad storm, asked the ferrymen to take him across. They explained that it was too dangerous to cross just then, but the cadre insisted, shouting 'I am an Executive Commissar. My life is of more importance than yours!' Using his authority, he compelled them to take him across. However, when they reached the middle of the river the wind was so strong and and the waves so high that the boat rolled heavily, causing the terrified cadre to order the ferrymen to turn back. They returned only to be scolded later by the cadre for having heeded him. *(Issue of July 22,1956.)*

Minh was a party member who became manager of a factory previously owned by a Frenchman, but he and his wife came to regard the factory as their own property. Several times during the course of the afternoon, dressed in his pyjamas and accompanied by his wife, Minh would tour the factory inspecting one section after another. Sometimes his wife walked around by herself and always with a proprietorial air which offended the workers. At the end of the day when they finished work, they would see Minh and his wife watching them from a window on the first floor and would whisper amongst themselves that Minh was no different from their former French employer. The same number of chickens were killed, wines and spirits were more plentiful than ever, and from time to time Minh or his wife called a young apprentice upstairs to clean the floor or to sweep away the orange and banana peels. Through the window eggshells were dropped with the same regularity as before.
(Issue of September 8, 1956.)

4. The party had fixed the number of landlords to be denounced in the Land Reform campaign excessively high—five times greater than in the first campaign—so that if old members were to be spared, the required number simply could not be achieved.

The second campaign therefore provoked increased internal conflict between the old members, the majority of whom were petty bourgeois, landlords and rich peasants (all attracted to communism for reasons other than class interest), and the new members comprising poor and landless peasants along with a few bad characters and hooligans. The sole ambition of the new members seems to have been to reduce all other social strata to their own level. This was precisely the party's aim, since open conflict was necessary for the carrying out of a general purge, without which the party would not be able to move from its anti-colonial position to an anti-feudal one. This is proved by the fact that, although in-numerable veteran members were jailed or executed, the party never once interfered in their favour. It was only at the end of the campaign that General Vo Nguyen Giap, on behalf of the party, declared the whole campaign to be an error and promised rectifica-tion.

As in the Land Rent Reduction campaign, Land Reform began with a classification, or reclassification, of the village population, continued with denunciations and ended with trials and execu-tions. The same techniques for provoking and spreading terror were used, the only difference being that the victims in the second campaign were much more numerous. The number of death sen-tences was fixed at a minimum of five per village. The impression was widespread that the number of suicides was also far greater in the later campaign owing to the fact that the newly-discovered landlords experienced an overwhelming sense of shame at being thus classified, since only a year earlier they had themselves fiercely denounced those classified as landlords in the previous campaign. The number of deaths from starvation caused by the 'isolation policy' also seems to have been higher, since rich and middle-level peasants found it more difficult to survive the isolation period than did the true landlords. Psychologically, the true land-lords were better prepared to face the situation. Many of them knew in advance what to expect and were thus, in some measure, ready for their terrible ordeal. Materially also, true landlords had more in their favour, for most of them—or members of their families—were engaged in other trades which remained unaffected by the law. Most true landlords had relatives or friends who were tradesmen or public servants (these were not directly affected by Land Reform) who could, in one way or another, provide them with some financial help. The newly-discovered landlords, on the other hand, were people who had never been out of their villages and had no occupation other than rice cultivation. They were better off than the average villager only by dint of hard work and thriftiness. They had no other source of material help and, there-fore, very little chance of surviving.

The programmes of the two campaigns differed in only one respect. Expropriation was occasional during the first campaign,

but it was universally practised during the second, at the end of
which land was redistributed.

EXPROPRIATION

During the first campaign some attempt was made to justify the
confiscation of wealth. It was a form of punishment meted out by
the Special People's Tribunal to those 'ringleaders' whose alleged
criminal deeds merited such a penalty. Other landlords, whose
property was not ordered to be confiscated, retained full legal
ownership of all they possessed. They were, however, forbidden to
sell even the smallest of their possessions. Every item had been
recorded at the very start of the campaign, and the owner was held
responsible for any subsequent loss or damage. From that time on
the landlord's garden, for instance, remained his legal property,
but the fruit on the trees already belonged to the 'people'. Many
landlords were, in fact, badly maltreated simply because, like Adam
and Eve, they could not resist the 'forbidden fruit'. The same
absurd measure was applied to the ricefields. Landlords continued
to own them in theory, but all rent paid for the land went directly
to the Peasants' Association. This state of affairs lasted for a year
until the advent of Land Reform proper, when it was declared that
all properties would be requisitioned. According to a law (Decree
No. 197-SL, Chapter II, Art. 4, issued on December 19, 1953), 'only
lands, livestock and agricultural implements will be liable for
requisition' and 'all other property will be exempt'. But, in the
event, the landlord and his family were simply told to vacate their
house and leave all their possessions behind.

Expropriation, which had been used as a punishment for a few
landlords during the first campaign, was applied to the entire
landowning class during the second, when it was treated as a
measure necessary to ensure the transition from a property-owning
to a socialist society. It should be recalled in this respect that,
according to the Land Reform Law, there were three different forms
of expropriation:

> 1. *Confiscation* of lands and properties of 'French
> colonialists, and other imperialist aggressors, and of Viet-

namese traitors, reactionaries and cruel bullies'. Confiscation, which was to be total for the first group, might be total or partial for the second group (Vietnamese traitors and the rest), according to the gravity of their offences.

2. *Requisition without indemnity* concerning the property belonging to the second group which had not been confiscated. This meant that expropriation was to be total, one way or another, for the second as well as for the first group.

3. *Requisition with indemnity* concerning non-reactionary landlords. The compensating indemnities were to be equal to the value of the average annual production of the land expropriated and were to be paid in the form of special grants of national stock at an annual interest rate of $1\frac{1}{2}$ per cent. The capital, fixed at the value of one single year's production, was to be reimbursed at the end of ten years. But since there was great reluctance, to put it mildly, to classify any landlord as 'non-reactionary', this third form of expropriation existed only on paper and found no application during the two successive campaigns.

Only two years later, on the occasion of the Rectification of Errors campaign, many of these persons were reclassified as 'ordinary' or 'resistance' landlords, or even as middle-level or poor peasants, and were thus given back their lands and houses but not the furniture, which had been distributed long ago to poor peasants. When back from jail and allowed to resume possession of their former houses, these 'rehabilitated' persons usually found a roof supported by a few bare pillars. The poor peasants who had been allowed to live in them for one or two years had dismantled doors, windows and wooden walls so as to use them as firewood. They had also chopped down all the trees in the garden and sold them before they were ordered to move away. For all these losses, victims of 'errors' received no compensation or indemnity, only a few words of consolation.

As for the famous $1\frac{1}{2}$ per cent interest, no landlord has been courageous enough, up to the present moment, to ask for payment. All of them knew that, if they did, they would prove by that very fact that they still possessed the 'landlordist spirit' and would not merit a reclassification into another social class (as provided by the Population Classification Decree) after a five-year period of hard work. Thus, by a kind of discreet understanding, both the victims and the party passed over this well specified clause in silence. As for the reimbursement of the capital, promised to be effected at the end of ten years (*i.e.* from 1964 to 1966), we still have a few more years to see whether the government of the DRV will honour its engagement or not, and to observe, after ten years of collectivism and intense re-education, whether or not there still are people stubborn enough to ask for such a payment.

Thus, the three forms of expropriation provided for by the law were reduced in practice to two only, *i.e.* confiscation, and requisition without indemnity—the latter being exactly equivalent to confiscation. In actual fact, all those people who had been classified as 'landlords', either rightly or wrongly, had to leave their houses utterly empty-handed, except for a few rags. Like everything else, these two forms of expropriation were carried out with much ritual and ceremony to impress the masses. To give readers a fair view of such a ceremony, we reproduce here a press article from *Cuu Quoc*, No. 2741, of January 1, 1956:

> Peasants from Thuong village poured into Phong's house like waves upon the seashore. There was a great deal of flag-waving and drum-beating to the accompaniment of the usual shouts of 'Down with ——' and 'Long live ——'. In the centre of the courtyard were ploughs, spades, watering cans, sickles, scythes, baskets, saucepans, copper trays and basins, etc, all neatly arranged. Surrounding the courtyard were camelia and peony plants, red with blooms. A hardcore comrade summoned Phong's wife and, on behalf of the Peasants' Association, declared that her entire possessions were to be confiscated. The peasants gathered round in a circle, their shouts, increasing in violence, went on and on. The comrade explained to the woman that her father and grandfather had done no manual work, and that her property was the fruit of exploitation and usury, and was now to belong to the peasants. The comrade then solemnly declared the confiscation of her twenty-four mau [twenty acres] of ricefield and all her property. All clapped their hands, shouting: 'Long live President Ho!' and 'Welcome to the policy of confiscation and requisition, with or without compensation, of the party and the government.' Whereupon groups of boys

and girls carried out baskets of rice and two buffaloes were brought in. Clapping and shouting commenced once again.

The people carried all the belongings away on their back or slung from a pole on their shoulders, beating drums all the time.

EXHIBITIONS

As soon as the confiscation ceremony was over, an exhibition of the confiscated personal belongings of the landlord was organised. To illustrate the sharp contrast in living standards between peasant and landlord, the personal effects of the two social classes were exhibited side by side. In one half of the room such things as silk cloths, European hats, walking sticks, leather shoes, ivory pipes, copper spittoons, photograph albums (in which many photographs of high-ranking cadres were usually found) were displayed; while in the other half were a tattered skirt, a few rags and some earthenware pots and the like, representing the poverty of the Vietnamese peasant. Sometimes two contrasting meals were also shown: that of the landlord, consisting of chicken, fish, roast pork and wine, and that of the peasant, consisting of poor-quality rice, a few vegetables and a tiny bowl of evil-smelling soya sauce.

In 1954, a few weeks after the communists had returned to Hanoi, an exhibition of this kind was held in Hang Dau Square in the centre of the city. The object of this was undoubtedly to prove to the people the necessity for Land Reform and the benefits which would accrue from it, and to win them over to the cause of the proletarian revolution. This exhibition was quickly closed, however, after some visitors had offered the opinion that, if such was the way a landlord lived, then his standard of living was lower than that of a Hanoi factory worker. This is quite true, for in any underdeveloped country there exists a vast difference in wealth and possessions between the more or less Westernised towns and the surrounding countryside where people still live as their ancestors have done for centuries. The contrast was particularly striking in Vietnam, where war had dragged on for almost a decade. The communist-controlled zone had been cut off from the civilised world and subjected to daily bombing, while the occupied towns, where the French Corps Expeditionnaire spent a large portion of the

French budget, were well supplied with goods of all kinds, imported from France or supplied by the American Aid missions. Thus, living standards in these towns tended to be exceptionally, if artificially, high. In contrast, the people in the communist-controlled zone, deprived of all modern commodities, gradually reverted to a medieval pattern of life. The so-called landlords of the Resistance areas, although better off than the average village dweller, had nothing which would arouse the envy of the city dweller. But the class struggle had to be carried through, despite universal poverty; these landlords, branded as 'vile oppressors' and 'servants of colonialism', must forfeit their lands, houses and personal possessions so that these might be given to the poorer peasants.

APPORTIONMENT OF LAND AND OTHER PROPERTIES

Before a fair assessment can be made of the results achieved by Land Reform, two factors need to be known : first, how much land was confiscated and from how many landlords? Secondly, to how many people was this land given, and how much did each receive? The task of finding this information is not easy, the principal difficulty arising from the lack of data. The DRV authorities have never stated the number of dispossessed landlords in any of their official publications. The probable reason for this is that the number of people classified as landlords was so enormous that, if it were published, then the more intelligent would realise that the proportion of the population classified as 'enemies of the people' was fantastically high.

As for the lands, not all the confiscated holdings belonged to the landowning class. Many were, in fact, communal lands cultivated in turn by the peasants resident in the village to which they belonged. However, on the pretext that these lands had, for the most part, been usurped by 'exploiters', the communists confiscated them, distributed them to poor peasants, theoretically as private property, and then grouped the whole as the collective property of the co-operatives. Again, the DRV authority has not stated how much of the expropriated lands belonged to private landlords and how much was simply communal land taken from the community. But it was well established in the Bulletin Econo-

mique de l'Indochine, 1938, reproduced in a recent Hanoi official publication,[1] that communal lands represented as much as 20 per cent of all cultivated land in Tongking and 25 per cent in Annam. It was a characteristic feature of Vietnamese agriculture, and in this respect the following passage quoted from the same communist source speaks for itself:

> In some localities, communal lands comprised a very high proportion of the whole. In Xuan-Truong [Nam-Dinh province], for example, communal lands represented 77.5 per cent of the total cultivated lands in the district. But in other localities they reached smaller proportions: 59 per cent in Tien-Hai district [Thai-Binh province], 42.5 per cent in Khoai-Chau district [Hung-Yen province], 46 per cent in Ly-Nhan district [Ha-Nam province]. . . . In Quang-Tri province, for instance, there was more communal than private land, and in Trieu Phong district all the land under cultivation was communal. Each adult in this latter district received on average three *mau* [about two and a half acres].[2]

Communal land had existed in Vietnam for a very long time and is probably a survival from an early form of communism. But now these lands were added to those taken from the landlords, the Communist Party redistributing them to the peasants to demonstrate the advantages of its Land Reform. It would seem, however, that half of these advantages accrued from primitive communism and only the remaining half can be attributed to 'Marxist communism'.

Nguyen Hong Phong (in *Xa Thon Viet-Nam*, p. 69) admits the existence of 240,000 *ha* of communal land in Tongking, and 200,000 *ha* in Annam. Since the territory of the DRV covers the whole of Tongking and the northern half of Annam, one presumes that the total area of communal land confiscated during Land Reform was 240,000 plus 200,000 divided by two, *i.e.* 340,000 *ha*.

The Hanoi government has never disclosed the total area affected by Land Reform, publishing only partial results in various different

[1] Nguyen Hong Phong: *Xa Thon Viet-Nam*, Hanoi, 1959.
[2] *Ibid.*

localities. Moreover, after the first apportionment there were repeated 'rectifications', and in many cases lands and houses already
given to poor peasants were taken back and given to their former
owners, who were said to have been wrongly classified as landlords. All this makes the problem more complex, and one cannot
be sure, even if one analyses all the official documents available, of
the exact amount of land confiscated and reapportioned. The following figures, however, were published in 1957 by a Soviet
expert, V. P. Karamichev, in the Moscow publication *Ekonimika
Sel'kogo Khozyaistva* (Breeding and Rural Economy) [Vol. 5]:

> The Land Reform campaign accomplished the confiscation of
> 702,000 hectares (1,734,642 acres) of land, 1,846,000 agri-
> cultural implements, 107,000 animals and 22,000 tons of
> food. All have been redistributed amongst 1,500,000 families
> of wage-earners and poor peasants.

If Karamichev's figures are correct, then each family would
receive about one acre of land, one agricultural implement and one-
thirteenth of an animal. It has to be realised that under the heading
of 'agricultural implements' came such things as baskets, sickles and
scythes, as well as saucepans, copper trays, and so forth. Dogs, cats
and goats were included with cows and buffaloes in the category
of 'animals'.

But there are reasons to believe that Karamichev's figures are
somewhat exaggerated, since the most optimistic of the partial
results published in the Hanoi press lay claim to a far more modest
figure. For instance, a communiqué of the Land Reform Committee,
relating to the Hanoi suburban areas, the richest in North Vietnam,
states:

> The toiling peasants have confiscated or requisitioned from
> the landowning class 20,482 *mau* [18,220 acres] of ricefields,
> 511 animals, 6,156 agricultural implements, 1,032 houses and
> 346,903 kilos [763,187 lb] of foodstuffs. They have also
> compelled landlords to pay back as excess of land-rent 155,069
> kilos [341,142 lb] of paddy and 6,429,950 *dong* [approxi-
> mately $1,000]. All these have been shared between 24,690
> peasant and worker families, comprising in all 98,113 people.

On average, each landless peasant receives 2 *sao*, 9 *thuoc* [0.205 acres]; each poor peasant receives 2 *sao*, 8 *thuoc* [0.200 acres]; and each middle-level peasant receives 2 *sao*, 13 *thuoc* [0.270 acres].[3]

An analysis of these figures shows that each person would receive, over and above his piece of land: 1/17th of an agricultural implement; 1/95th of a house; 1/192nd of an animal; 11 lb of foodstuff; and 65 *dong* (about $0.01).

A careful study of the foregoing text enables the following conclusions to be drawn about expropriation and redistribution.

1. According to the Land Reform Law (Title II, Chapters one and two),[4] property other than lands, livestock and agricultural implements was confiscated only from traitors and reactionaries. This implies that the 1,032 houses mentioned in the communiqué must have belonged to traitors and reactionaries. If we suppose that one reactionary had lived in each of these houses (there is every justification for doing so, since the Vietnamese term *nha-cua* used in the text simply means a dwelling place or a residence), then we can obtain some idea of the number of reactionaries. This represents about 4 per cent of the total number of landowning, peasant and worker families, a figure so high that it suggests that the whole of the landowning class was classified as reactionary and treacherous.

2. If the number of confiscated animals, agricultural implements, food, together with the area of confiscated land and the amount of confiscated money, are divided by the number of landlords, then the average landlord appears to have possessed 1.8 acres, half a farm animal, six agricultural implements, 1,100 lb of food and $1.00 as his total possessions. This is hardly indicative of great wealth.

3. The fact that middle-level peasants could receive a bigger share than the poor and landless ones, makes it clear that all these epithets (landless, poor and middle-level) had no connection with the respective material status of the various persons so categorised. These three categories were, in fact, equally—or almost equally—poor and should have been grouped together as poor peasants. But

[3] Quoted from *Nhan Dan*, No. 740, Hanoi, March 13, 1956.
[4] See Allan B. Cole, ed., *Conflict in Indo-China and International Repercussions*.

since real middle-level peasants had been classified as rich peasants
or landlords, it was necessary to choose some poor peasants and
call them middle-level ones.

4. If the total amount of food and money confiscated is divided
by the number of peasants, then each person received 11 lb of food
(probably paddy, maize and sweet potatoes) and $0.01. Assuming
that each person needs one pound of food a day, each then received enough food and money to last him for about ten days. But
this is a theoretical calculation. In actual practice, things were
slightly different, since a sizeable portion of the confiscated amount
of food and money had already been spent by the Peasants' Association under various forms, including a festivity in honour of the
'brilliant victory against feudalism'. In a village where we stayed
during this 'sky-splitting and earth-shaking campaign', a poor
peasant received about 5 lb of paddy, while a middle-level peasant
was given a sum just sufficient to buy a packet of local cigarettes.
Many people were, in fact, criticised for having spent the whole
sum in buying delicacies for themselves and for their children.
This was the reward for six months of continual studying, discussing, marching, flag-waving and shouting, at the cost of the
lives of nearly half a million people. One is forced to the conclusion
that, apart from the one acre of land which each peasant family
received (and half of this land was formerly communal anyway),
the confiscated property distributed amongst the peasants was
practically insignificant.

A ricefield is very precious in the delta of Tongking, particularly
in the outskirts of Hanoi, where prices ran as high as $100 for
one acre; it was, therefore, something of an achievement to give
each peasant such a fortune. Poor peasants were naturally very
happy to receive a gift of land, but their frenzied enthusiasm
quickly faded when they realised what was to come. When the
newly-acquired portion of land was added to the area they already
possessed, their income from the produce increased in proportion.
Consequently, the progressive agricultural tax now imposed on
them was two or three times higher than the tax they had previously paid. The situation was aggravated by the fact that these
lands confiscated from landlords had been previously taxed on the
basis of an excessively high 'average production', with the

deliberate purpose of ruining the landlords. These lands were now distributed to poor peasants, that is, to those who had voted such exaggerated figures and who now, in consequence, had to bear the results of their previous well intentioned misdeeds. The end-result was that they had to pay the government as much as they used to pay the landlords.

A few months after this land had been distributed, the whole of their private property was collectivised, which meant that they owned no land of their own, but had to work from dawn to dusk to earn the maximum salary permissible—ten *marks*. This represented the equivalent of three pounds of rice a day. Out of the twenty *marks* obtained daily by the peasant and his wife, one or two had to be paid to some woman in the hamlet who served them as baby-tender and another *mark* to the neighbour who went shopping for them. The system is still in force and will probably last until the commune-system is installed in North Vietnam.

Like all communist actions, the distribution of land was carried out with great ceremony. There were the usual huge meetings, processions, long speeches, slogans, flags and drums. Each peasant received a 'Certificate of Private Ownership' and a wooden placard on which his name was inscribed in neat lettering. This was placed in the middle of the land allotted to him. Inevitably, noisy disputes arose among the peasants as to who should have which piece of land, but on the whole these were settled without much difficulty, for there was enough land to satisfy everybody.

The allotment of houses, farm animals and particularly of furniture, was quite another matter. In many cases, party cadres were stretched to the limits of their ingenuity to sort things out to everyone's satisfaction and to prevent open feuds. The following extract from the party's newspaper vividly illustrates the scenes which took place.

The Cupboard

In D.M. village, the meeting called for the allotment of property acquired in the struggle lasted from early morning until late in the evening, with nothing settled. At dinner-time, everyone ran home for a hurried meal and rushed back to the assembly room again. Even the children went to the

meeting with their mothers and, when overcome with weari-
ness, slept on some wooden planks there. Buffaloes, cows and
houses were dealt with, and there remained only the distribution of the objects more difficult to share out. It was hard to
reach agreement on any point; everyone was in need and all
goods to be shared were in great demand. The arguments
were endless, but the object which created the most difficulty
was a cupboard. Mrs Tru and Mrs Du were equally poor and
needy and both desperately wanted to possess the cupboard.
It quickly became obvious to everyone that neither of them
wanted the other to have it. At the end of a long argument
Mrs Tru said: 'I have been trying to explain to you all afternoon how I am placed, and I've given you scores of good
reasons why I want the cupboard, but you positively refuse to
understand. I've never met anyone as covetous as you.'
Whereupon Mrs Du, red with anger, exclaimed: 'How dare
you call me covetous! Do you despise wealth so much yourself? You have a room and a lock already, yet you still long
for a cupboard!' . . . After this scene, the cadre in charge
called a meeting of hard-core elements; after a discussion, he
told them to go and appeal to the 'revolutionary spirit' of the
two women. So Comrade Bao [a girl hard-core] called first
on Mrs Tru, but as soon as Mrs Tru set eyes on her she said:
'I know why you've come: to make me change my mind. But
I tell you it's no good, it can't be changed. I'll never surrender
the cupboard to Du. . . . I worked as a servant for Xoe [the
lady from whom the cupboard had been confiscated] for over
ten years and suffered a lot at her hand. Now that the struggle
has brought us so many of her belongings. I haven't had a
single thing yet. Did you notice that right from the start I
gave way every time to those in greater need than myself?
The only thing I really want is that cupboard. You see, I live
in an isolated spot outside the village and have to attend
meetings every night. While I am out my mind is never at
ease, because I am afraid that I might be robbed while the
house is empty. If I had a cupboard to lock everything away
in, I would feel much easier in mind.'

'Yesterday,' replied Comrade Bao, 'everyone remarked on
your unselfishness—the way you stood aside for those poorer
than yourself. I can see that the question of the cupboard is
important to you, and you're right when you say that your

H

house is isolated. I know, too, that you are frequently out.
. . . Our misfortune is that there are not enough goods to
satisfy everyone. How much easier it would be if there was a
cupboard for each of you, instead of only one. As it is, Mrs
Du wants that cupboard too.'

Mrs Tru replied calmly : 'Both she and her husband are
as healthy and strong as elephants. If they go on living as
idly as before, they will be in that tumble-down shack of
theirs till the end of their days. But I have worked hard as a
servant in the Xoe family for more than ten years. Every day
I saw her opening and shutting the cupboard, and always
hoped that one day I would own a cupboard like that myself.
Now, thanks to the leadership of the party, the struggle has
been won and I have a chance of getting the cupboard; I'll
not be satisfied until I have it.'

'That is very understandable,' said Bao, 'but remember
that the cupboard was made by peasant sweat and tears. Now
it's communal property and doesn't belong to the Xoe family
any more. The comrade peasants have succeeded in taking
the ricefields, houses and furniture from the landowning
class only through a united effort; individual effort can never
be as successful. If everyone were to claim all his former
master's belongings for himself, there would no longer be
unity and mutual understanding in our ranks.'

That evening Mrs Tru let it be known that she had with-
drawn her claim to the cupboard.

(Nhan Dan, May 20, 1956)

The above article has been quoted at some length, for it provides
a truthful picture of one important aspect of the Land Reform. It
also reveals a psychological factor very prevalent among the masses
in underdeveloped countries, and one which leads them to give
their support to communism. Only in communism do they discern
any hope of obtaining the object of their desires. For the sake of
some tawdry possession such as this cheap wardrobe, they are prepared to back the communists despite any hardship and dangers
which this may entail.

SIXTEEN

Rectification of Errors

As soon as Land Reform was completed (by 1956) and the so-called peasants' authority well established in the villages, the party quite unexpectedly admitted to having made many serious mistakes during the two previous campaigns when the 'masses' had been 'given a free hand'. Accordingly, the communists promised to correct all these mistakes which, in their own words, had had a devastating effect on the party's prestige and the well-being of the people. So a 'Rectification of Errors' campaign was launched, beginning with the resignation of both Truong Chinh, secretary-general of the party, and Ho Viet Thang, vice-minister in charge of Land Reform.

Vo Nguyen Giap, as the party's spokesman, read a long list of errors to the 10th Congress of the Party Central Committee. This ran:

> '(a) While carrying out their anti-feudal task, our cadres have underestimated or, worse still, have denied all anti-imperialist achievements, and have separated the Land Reform and the Revolution. Worst of all, in some areas they have even made the two mutually exclusive.
>
> '(b) We have failed to realise the necessity of uniting with the middle-level peasants, and we should have concluded some form of alliance with the rich peasants, whom we treated in the same manner as the landlords.
>
> '(c) We attacked the landowning families indiscriminately,

according no consideration to those who had served the Revolution and to those families with sons in the army. We
showed no indulgence towards landlords who participated in
the Resistance, treating their children in the same way as we
treated the children of other landlords.

'(d) We made too many deviations and executed too many
honest people. We attacked on too large a front and, seeing
enemies everywhere, resorted to terror, which became far too
widespread.

'(e) Whilst carrying out our Land Reform program we
failed to respect the principles of freedom of faith and worship
in many areas.

'(f) In regions inhabited by minority tribes we have attacked tribal chiefs too strongly, thus injuring, instead of
respecting, local customs and manners.

'(g) When reorganising the party, we paid too much importance to the notion of social class instead of adhering
firmly to political qualifications alone. Instead of recognising
education to be the first essential, we resorted exclusively to
organisational measures such as disciplinary punishments,
expulsion from the party, executions, dissolution of party
branches and cells. Worse still, torture came to be regarded
as a normal practice during party reorganisation.'[1]

This confession, together with the spectacular removal of those
responsible for the movement, has led many outside observers to
believe that the confessed errors were genuine mistakes, and that
there was a sincere effort on the part of the North Vietnamese
leaders to correct them. A few even have gone so far as to conclude
that the whole process had been a complete failure. This was far
from true, for the so-called Rectification of Errors campaign was
only another bluff to be added to an already long list.

Rectification of Errors was indeed an integral part of the well
planned process of Land Reform and, as such, it had been conceived long before as a necessary conclusion to Land Reform. The
reader will recall that, right from the very beginning, in 1953, the
party had engaged in the so-called Political Struggle (described as
First Wave of Terror in Chapter Seven) to pave the way for Land
Reform, i.e. to move step by step from a normal situation to that

[1] Nhan Dan, No. 970 (October 31, 1956).

of terror. This time the process was reversed. After three years of sustained violence, the party wished to return to a normal situation as smoothly as possible. They did this by resorting to the Rectification of Errors campaign. It was inevitable that the party should suffer a certain loss of prestige but it was prepared to accept this small sacrifice.

There is no doubt that when Mao and his theoreticians devised their techniques for Land Reform, they deliberately planned an excess of violence because they believed it to be necessary to ensure success. According to their calculations, this excess would be corrected by a process of reversal called 'Rectification'. Convincing proof of this is to be found as early as 1926, when Mao clearly stated that 'to right a wrong one should exceed the limit of the right'.[2] Mao's attitude was later adopted by Ho, who carefully explained to a restricted number of party cadres the basic strategy of his policy. 'To straighten a curved piece of bamboo,' he said, 'one must bend it in the opposite direction, holding it in that position for a while. Then, when the hand is removed it will slowly straighten itself.'

Evidently, both Ho and Mao anticipated a strong public reaction against their Land Reform policy and concluded that only a deliberate excess of terror would annihilate that reaction. To understand why this excess was thought to be indispensable, one must first understand the purpose for which the two leaders carried out their Land Reform.

In the first place, Land Reform did not consist solely of confiscation and redistribution of land. If that had been its only object, then government regulations alone would have sufficed. Prior to Land Reform a number of landlords of their own free will had offered their lands to the state. The offers were rejected or, in some cases, accepted for a few years, after which the lands were returned to the former owners on the pretext that 'no citizen should be deprived of his normal means of livelihood'. The truth was that the landlords were required to remain landlords until the time came for them to become scapegoats. It was immaterial, after all,

[2] Mao Tse-tung: 'Report of an Investigation into the Peasants' Movement in Hunan Province', in *Selected Works* (Lawrence and Wishart, London, 4 vols., 1954-56).

who owned the lands since these could have been confiscated by the dictatorial government whenever it wished. The true purpose behind Land Reform was this:

1. Confiscation and redistribution were only transitional stages before the ultimate aim—collectivisation of the land. In order to compel the entire peasantry to accept without rancour the collective pattern of life, communist leaders felt it necessary to 'kill the spirit of ownership' which had existed in the mind of every peasant for centuries. To achieve this aim, they applied an ancient Chinese maxim which says: 'Kill just one and frighten ten thousand others.' In the circumstances, it might have read: 'Kill a few landlords in every village and frighten the whole population.' This explains why a minimum 'quota' of death sentences was fixed for every village, even in those villages in which all the land was communal. 'Fright' was achieved rapidly, and the people of North Vietnam coined a new maxim, which was on everyone's lips: 'Take your water from the river, buy your rice from the market, go to hospital in case of illness and be buried in a public cemetery after death.' (This expression is much more epigrammatic in the Vietnamese language.) It meant that the wise man would take care never to possess anything of his own throughout his whole life.

2. In forcing them to denounce and kill landlords, the party wanted to make the peasants share in the blood-guilt. Thus, those who had directly or indirectly participated in the massacre, being morally and politically compromised, were forced to side with the party through fear of retaliation. Unable to side with their former masters in a revolt against the new masters, they had to accept whatever fate the party had in store for them. The guilt-complex which haunted the peasants' minds after the massacre of about 5 per cent of the total population has been euphemistically described in official communist literature as 'the peasant's consciousness of being master of his own fate'.

3. Land Reform, in the political sense of the word, means a radical shift from the anti-imperialist to the anti-feudalist standpoint or, in other words, from the anti-colonialist war against the French to the mass slaughter of local landlords. In changing the aim of its fight, the party felt it essential not only to purge all

nationalist elements from the Resistance, but also to throw over-
board any party members (and there were many) in whom there
was the least suspicion of unorthodoxy. It believed that a purge as
drastic as this could not be carried out if decisions concerning the
fate of each individual were left to the upper classes, for nepotism
was still widespread and many would be bound to slip through
the net. In the party's view, the purge must be implemented from
the bottom up, that is, from the village level, since nobody could
better assess a man's political attitude than his fellow villagers.
'The people are clear-sighted,' they said; and among the people
'only the poor and lesser peasants are trustworthy.' The logical
result of this argument was that 'the masses should be given a
free hand to carry out Land Reform'. Although the masses would
inevitably abuse it and resort to indiscriminate accusations, the
party nevertheless concluded, after due consideration, that such a
method was the best that could be devised, since a complete
success could not be ensured without excess. To quote Nguyen
Manh Tuong, the sacred principle applied to Land Reform was:
'It is better to kill ten innocent people than to let one enemy
escape.'[3]

Thus the party recommended an excess of violence and turned
a blind eye to all the abuses they knew to be the inescapable consequences of the 'free hand' policy. Hundreds and thousands of
people were unjustly killed, jailed or starved to death without the
all-powerful party raising a finger to help any of them. According
to the law, anyone sentenced to death had the right to appeal to
the President of the Republic for clemency, but the stark truth is
that Ho Chi Minh did not pardon one single person, not even
loyal party members who, at the moment of their execution by
firing squads, still shouted: 'Long live Ho Chi Minh.' In March
1956, Ho did, however, order the temporary postponement of all
capital punishment, but this was a consequence of the far-reaching
de-Stalinisation campaign started in Moscow on the occasion of
the Soviet Party's Twentieth Congress. Those fortunate people
whose executions were postponed, and who were later released

---

[3] Nguyen Manh Tuong: 'Concerning Mistakes Committed in
Land Reform', quoted by Hoang Van Chi in *The New Class in
North Vietnam*.

from jail, owed their lives, indirectly, to Nikita Khrushchev—not at all to Ho Chi Minh.

A further proof that this policy of violence was deliberate is to be found by comparing Giap's speech with Truong Chinh's, previously discussed in Chapter Twelve. The point that stands out clearly is that all the so-called mistakes listed by Giap derived directly from the failure to apply basic principles which Truong Chinh enunciated and which he promised would be carefully respected during the process of Land Reform. In the event, the party made numbers of wild promises it did not keep. Only when the campaign was all over did it express regret for its failure to honour this or that promise. Truong Chinh was the hand which bent Ho's bamboo shoot, and Giap the hand which released it. Rectification of Errors represents the bamboo's resuming its normal straightness, the resumption of a more or less normal life.

The first step was the release of all landlords and party members who were still in the prisons or concentration camps. The total number of prisoners has never been disclosed, but Giap mentioned in his speech that among those released were 12,000 party members. Not unnaturally, it was these communists who suffered most in the party's jails. Ngo Duc Mau, a veteran communist who had ten years' experience of French jails, gave the following description of his sufferings in a communist prison:

> When we were in our dark, damp cells we would comfort each other . . . for there is a vast difference between the imperialist jail and our own. In an imperialist jail I suffered only physical pains, my mind being comforted and at peace. . . . But how was I treated in this place? I was trampled underfoot both physically and mentally. Those around me considered me to be an enemy, a traitor and a spy, and no one understood my situation.

The same communist also disclosed that it was his own 'comrades' who had tortured him, forbidding him to speak in his own defence:

> A comrade from my province [Ha-Tinh] brought purely imaginary charges against me, transforming all my past

achievements into crimes. I was not allowed to speak in my own defence. They tortured me day and night in order to force me to admit to crimes which I had never even thought of, let alone committed. (*Nhan Dan*, October 30, 1956.)

These prisoners were told that they had been imprisoned through an unfortunate error and would be released before long. However, a month before they were allowed to leave the camps or prisons, they were made to attend a special course entitled 'Preparation for Going Home'. This required them to study and discuss, under the guidance of a party representative, such thorny subjects as Giap's long list of errors, the party's attitude of self-criticism, the eternal rightness of the Marxist-Leninist doctrine, and the 'correct attitude towards those who had made false denunciations'. They were assured that they would be rehabilitated as free and honest citizens, and that they would recover all their rights and their unjustly confiscated property. They were also urged to forget their recent misfortunes and to renew their faith in the party, serving it as faithfully as they had done in the past. But the essential point for them to remember was that they should not take any retaliatory action against the authors of their misfortunes.

Orders were then given to village authorities to arrange for a delegation to be sent to the jails to welcome the prisoners and take them home. As might be imagined, there were many pathetic scenes when they returned to their villages and became reunited with their families. *Nhan Dan* described the case of Tan, one typical of countless others:

Tan belonged to a middle-level peasant family which had tilled the soil for three generations. He joined the Revolution when it first began [1945] and, after training and acquiring the necessary experience, he was admitted to the party. In 1947 his village fell under French occupation and, in his capacity as secretary of the village cell and president of the village committee, he led his villagers in a fight against the French. Frequently during enemy searches he was forced to remain hungry for long periods in underground hide-outs. Sometimes he was obliged to run away, but immediately the French had gone, he returned and rebuilt the village organisation, carrying out guerrilla warfare until final victory [1954]. After the truce, in accordance with his orders from higher authority, he prepared to carry out an attack against feudalism [Land Reform]. However, not only was he not allowed to participate in the attack, but was classified as a cruel landlord and a reactionary. He was accordingly denounced and tried before the People's Tribunal.

During the Rectification of Errors campaign, Tan was told that the case against him had all been a mistake and that very soon he would be released. Then:

> Tan counted on his fingers . . . eight months in jail awaiting execution, one month more attending the course: in all he had been absent from home for nine months. . . . When Tan entered the courtyard of his brother's house, he went first to the tumbledown kitchen in which his family had lived since the day his property had been confiscated. He was forced to bend double to get into the kitchen, which was coated in soot. A bamboo bed occupied about half the room, and the whole place was in complete disorder. . . . Tan was heartbroken to see this evidence of the wretched plight of his wife and children during his months in jail, but he made a great effort to remain calm and waved to his sister who still wept bitterly. 'Don't cry,' he said, 'tears and resentment are superfluous, they only increase our suffering.' He then entered his brother's house where there was great rejoicing. During the evening people came in groups to talk about the mistakes that had been made during Land Reform. They recalled how the villagers had been compelled to denounce and torture one another, to sever all family ties and to suppress all human feelings. There was sorrow in every heart.
>
> (Nhan Dan, November 14, 1956.)

The next step following the release of the prisoners was the restoration of their confiscated property, or such of it as was still recoverable. Their furniture was never returned as it had been divided amongst the villagers who, in many cases, had sold goods and chattels to others. Houses, gardens and ponds were usually all that remained to return to, but even these were in a sorry state because the poor peasants, to whom they had been given, lacked the means to maintain them properly. And, as we have already mentioned, trees and fences were pulled down for timber and fire-wood and cattle slaughtered for sale as meat.

In spite of all damage inflicted on their property, those allowed to return were always thankful to do so. The thought of returning to the place where they had been born and to the home of their ancestors, was sufficient compensation. Distress was more in evidence amongst those ordered to leave the house which they had been told would always be theirs.

The third step was to effect the return of wives who had been separated from their husbands. There were cases of 'voluntary' separation through fear of 'connection' or because of dissension between the two families as a result of mutual denunciation. But in the majority of cases where the women were young and good-looking (as a racial characteristic most Vietnamese women appear youthful and attractive at a relatively advanced age) they were forced into marriage with 'new' party members after their husbands had been sent to jail. A large number of these unfortunate women had been 'married' to their new husbands for two or three years when their former husbands were released from jail, and many of them had borne children, so the problem of returning them to their first and lawful husbands was a difficult one. The problem was solved by a special memorandum of the Ministry of Justice, issued on April 19, 1957. Since this document is unique, and will provide the reader with a better understanding of the seriousness of the situation, it is given here in its entirety.

DEMOCRATIC REPUBLIC OF VIETNAM

Ministry of Justice

MEMORANDUM

Concerning cases where husbands and wives
have been separated during Land Reform

During the recent Land Rent Reduction and Land Reform campaign, there have been numerous cases where husbands and wives have been separated owing to the following circumstances :

> Either the husband or wife, or either his or her family, has been rightly or wrongly classified as landlord or reactionary;
>
> or there were 'denunciations' between husband and wife, or between their respective families.

These separations, occurring in many areas, have had a serious effect upon the spirit of unity in the countryside. They are the result of errors committed during Land Reform. Thus a solution to this problem must be part of the Rectification of Errors campaign, and in this respect the Ministry of Justice issues the following regulations :

(a) In the case of a husband and wife who have been separated but neither has remarried, the cadres must explain to them that their separation was the result of an error in Land Reform policy and advise them to resume their conjugal life, especially when they have small children.

(b) In the case of a husband and wife who have been separated and where one partner has remarried, the following alternative is to be considered :

(i) If the wife and her new husband have no children, she should, provided she is willing, be permitted to return to her former husband, and the cadre must explain the position to the new husband. However, should the wife prefer to remain with her new husband, the cadres must explain the situation to the former husband so that he will accept divorce. But if there were children of the first marriage the question of divorce must be approached more cautiously.[4]

(ii) Where the husband has a new wife and wishes to return to his first one but finds the latter unwilling, divorce must be allowed. On the other hand, should she be prepared to go back to her former husband and should it be permitted by local morals and manners, some ami-

---

[4] This clause concerns 'confiscated wives'. Note that it is more favourable towards new husbands than to the rightful one. Note also that what is referred to as 'second marriage' in the text has nothing legal in it, for all these unions were without marriage certificates. Only the first marriages were lawful.

cable solution should be reached between the trio concerned.[5]

(c) Where the husband and wife have both remarried,
divorce should be granted so that each may remain with his
or her new partner.

(d)   In cases of bigamy, divorce should be granted to
concubines who had abandoned their husbands as the result
of 'denunciations'. But should they wish to return to their
former husbands through mutual love, or because of their
children, they must be allowed to do so.[6]

There have been no official statistics concerning the total number of separated husbands and wives, but the mere fact that a
special memorandum had to be issued to deal with the problem
indicates that the number was high. A great many widows who
had been forced into marrying new party members after the execution of their husbands were not mentioned in the memorandum.
Similarly, large numbers of landlords' daughters, against their
will, had married poor peasants, and these also were not mentioned in the memorandum, since according to the party they were
not subject to any rectification.

The fact that the party had for years ignored the countless
indignities heaped on these unfortunate females is more revealing
of the party's true attitude towards women than all the many
declarations it has made on this subject. Like land, houses and
furniture, they were disposable property, and as such were subject
to reapportionment.

The party's leaders were confident that these measures of rectification—the release of prisoners, the posthumous reinstatement
of executed party members, the return of confiscated property and
wives—would be sufficient to overcome any feeling of ill-will towards them amongst the population and to normalise the situation. The party was quite confident of its control over the population whose capacity for revolt had been completely annihilated by

[5] This meant that where non-Christians were concerned
bigamy would be the best solution.
[6] This memorandum, signed by Tran Cong Tuong as vice-
minister of Justice, and dated April 19, 1957, was published in
Ha-Noi Hang Ngay, Hanoi, June 16, 1957.

the brutal policy of terror. But they had overlooked one or two factors which eventually gave rise to violent uprisings. This time when the bent bamboo was released, it sprang back with a greater force than had been anticipated. Peasants in some areas and intellectuals in the capital began to revolt against the régime.

SEVENTEEN

Revolts and Repressions

THE PEASANTS

Not unnaturally, the 'new' party members were far from pleased at the release of the 'old' members from prison and at their subsequent rehabilitation. They foresaw that the probable result would be the loss of their own prestige and the collapse of their authority. The party's official paper described their distress in the following terms.

> Generally speaking, our 'new' comrades are afraid that, once the 'old' party members are released from jail, they will unite and fight against the 'new' party members. They predict retaliation by the 'old' members since there can be no love lost between the two groups. This attitude is entirely wrong and can do no good. In meetings called to discuss 'how best to welcome old comrades', their talk is of how to oppose them.   (*Nhan Dan*, November 21, 1956.)

All this was true, and in many areas 'old' party members were simply killed by the 'new' as soon as they returned to their own villages. The following affair which was brought before the Tribunal of the Third Zone exemplifies the situation clearly.

> Vu Van Tien was formerly president of Lo-Giang village. During Land Reform he was classified as a cruel landlord but, on his release from jail, was reclassified as a middle-level

peasant. However, only three days after his release he was killed by Hien, political commissar and member of the village branch committee. Hien acted in complicity with deputy police chiefs Thung and Duc, chief of the village guard Tu, and with Ho, Xuyen, Soan, Thiep, Xe, That, Dan and Thu, all village guards. . . . At 10 p.m. on January 28, 1957, Hien called the group together at Thung's house to plan the murder. Afterwards he posted his confederates at different places on the road along which Tien was known to be coming. As he passed by, Hien himself shot him. Tien dropped to the ground immediately whereupon the whole group fell upon him, butchering him with swords and knives and finally, Xuyen, with his light machine-gun fired six more bullets into the unfortunate victim. When it was over, Hien ordered the others to return to their former positions so that they might kill any other members of Tien's family who came along.   (*Thoi Moi*, March 14, 1957.)

This affair, which was only one of many reported in the Hanoi press at that time, showed unmistakably that the poor peasants who had become 'new comrades' were not at all inclined to relinquish the 'free hand' that the party had allowed them three years before. Faced with this situation, the old party members were forced to act in self-defence, and on many occasions resorted to open retaliation. Secure in their rehabilitation and emboldened by the support and sympathy of the villagers, they began apprehending those who had accused them falsely and carried out on these the very crimes they had been accused of. Thus the slanderers fell victim to the crimes of which they had previously accused others. The most typical form of vengeance consisted in capturing former denunciators and forcing excrement into their mouths. This was because during Land Reform, many hard-cores, following suggestions put forward by the party, had stated that landlords had forced them to eat excrement. There were also many cases of lynching watched by large crowds, and instances of slanderers having their mouths split or their tongues cut out. This kind of punishment was considered by the Vietnamese to be the most appropriate for calumniators, since similar scenes were depicted on pagoda walls as pictorial descriptions of the fate reserved for calumniators in the next world, according to Buddhist belief.

There was so much retaliation all over the country that, on December 1, 1956, the Ministry of Justice was obliged to issue a special memorandum in an attempt to remedy the rapidly deteriorating situation. One passage in the memorandum issued by Nguyen Van Huong, vice-minister of Justice, read like a call to arms.

> The interest of the state, the life and property of the people have been violated, in many instances, very seriously. In some areas there is no regard for the Law, while in others it is openly flouted. This grave situation is greatly damaging the moral and material life of the population as well as the prestige of the government. (*Cuu Quoc*, December 2, 1956.)

New party members, in an effort to defend themselves before public opinion, openly blamed the party for their misdeeds thereby greatly damaging its prestige. The following passage quoted from *Hoc Tap*, the organ for ideological indoctrination of party members, sums up this peculiar situation:

> When referring to mistakes made during Land Reform, many of our comrades blamed other comrades who were responsible for the carrying out of the Land Reform program. They have even accused the party; and always these accusations have been made in a public place such as theatre, train or public garden . . . they have discussed these mistakes in a completely irresponsible manner. There are many comrades who took an active part in Land Reform, either as team-chiefs or group-committee members, who have openly declared before the public that they acted under pressure from higher authorities. Their only crime, they persisted, lay in the fact that, although they had been aware that the whole policy was wrong, they had lacked the courage to protest.
>   (*Hoc Tap*, Hanoi, No. 10, October 1956.)

It should be understood that, while trying to please the old members by repairing some of the moral and material damage inflicted upon them earlier, the party never ceased to protect the new. The party felt that the latter, having a proletarian background, should

I

be sustained no matter what the cost. This policy was primarily dictated by the necessity of maintaining, if only as a façade, a certain number of 'proletarians' in the leadership of the so-called proletarian dictatorship. For more practical reasons, the proletarian group inside the party was very necessary : since its members acted as watch-dogs for the régime, it was a convenient weapon with which to repress any anti-party movement.

During the three years of their authority in the villages, the new members had forfeited all respect from the general public through their countless misdeeds. But, since they were uneducated and acted mainly on natural impulses, the party considered they were more easily managed and more reliable than the non-proletarian elements who had joined the party because of their ideals. The latter had been very useful to the party and to the Revolution but, as idealists, they were subject to ideological deviations. The proletarians, on the other hand, were without ideology and their interest was purely selfish. So long as their newly acquired privileges were respected, they would remain obedient to the party. Even if they should become dissatisfied they would be unable to create serious trouble by themselves. Thus, after the rehabilitation of the old party members, the party had two different groups in its ranks whose respective qualities and shortcomings were complementary. Not unnaturally, therefore, the party leaders were anxious to impose a policy of peaceful co-existence and compulsory co-operation between the two mutually hostile groups. This was precisely the object of the Rectification of Errors campaign. While recovering the services of the old members, the party hoped to make them accept the existence of the new.

This was not easily acomplished, particularly since enmity had been deliberately created between them. Despite patient efforts at reconciliation, the gulf between them widened; it was most apparent in areas where, prior to Land Reform, the party's organisation had been strongest. This was the case in Nghe-An province, the native province of Ho Chi Minh and the very cradle of Vietnamese Communism. According to the official organ of the party, it was in Nghe-An that the party met with the most serious kind of trouble :

Nghe-An is the province in which party organisations existed as early as 1930. But it is in the same province that the most serious mistakes have been made, and the greatest number of party members have been executed during Land Reform. During Rectification of Errors, this province once more failed in its responsibilities, particularly in that of controlling the ill-feeling towards 'new' party members. . . . Such an erroneous attitude on the part of the provincial committee naturally affected that of the district and village committees. In some villages, 'new' members have been arrested and brought before a crowd for public denunciation, while in others, hard-core elements have been beaten at village meetings.   (*Nhan Dan*, November 21, 1956.)

Village organisations and party cells were once more re-organised, but this time it was the new party members who were expelled. The article quoted above gave the following statistics for the whole Nghe-An province.

Number of 'proletarians' admitted to the village committees after Land Reform	1,839
Number of these expelled from the same committees on the occasion of Rectification of Errors	1,162
Number of new party members among the expelled group	900

In fact, Rectification of Errors became a purge of new party members who had previously purged old ones so that they might replace them. Because of the conflict within the party and the effort to prevent open fights, the pattern of party life was completely altered. An article in *Thoi Moi* included the following description of a party meeting:

People sat about quietly, their chins resting on their knees. On one side of the room sat the girls, their heads resting on one another's shoulders, all of them looking very tired. On the opposite side sat comrade Su, cutting his nails with a penknife. The chairman of the meeting could arouse no interest among his audience, and only a few members expressed their views since many had long since fallen asleep, their regular snoring broken by an occasional shriek as though the subconscious mind uttered some hidden grievance.   (*Thoi Moi*, May 8, 1957.)

This meeting evidently took place in a village where the differences between the two groups were not too serious, for the people, though apathetic, made some response to the party's appeal for a reconciliation of the two opposing groups. In other villages the atmosphere was far more explosive, and bloody fights were frequent between old and new members. Although both sides were ordered to stand together under the party flag, each regarded the other as an irreconcilable enemy. The following description of another meeting is quoted from a long report on the Rectification of Errors in the villages published in a series of articles in *Thoi Moi* under the title 'After the Stormy Days'.

> Tang [a 'new' just out of hospital after treatment for a head wound inflicted by old party members] sat quietly leaning his back against the wall, his arms resting on his knees. The black kerchief on his head could not hide completely the white bandage. . . . Opposite him sat Lan, Kiet and Ton with the other old members. . . . Women members huddled together in a corner twittering like sparrows and occasionally pinching one another and giggling. Discussions were carried on in a lifeless, uninterested manner, interrupted from time to time by the arrival of a newcomer. Men and women who, the day before, had looked upon each other as enemies and thrown stones at one another, now sat together under the Hammer and Sickle flag. It was probably the first time since the Land Rent Reduction campaign that they thought of each other as 'comrades', and it was also the first time that they had raised their hands in a common salute to the party flag.[1]

The party's inability to control its members had two direct results: a general disregard for party policy and, in a few cases,

[1] 'After the Stormy Days', a series of articles reporting on Rectification of Errors in the villages, *Thoi Moi*, April 5 to 19, 1957.

open revolt. Many peasants willingly gave up the land they had received during Land Reform to the landlords who had owned it previously without waiting for regulations concerning the matter. But more serious was the sudden disappearance of the hatred between rich and poor which the party had carefully fostered during the preceding years. Landlords and farmers resumed their former goodwill towards each other and the community spirit which was traditional in the Vietnamese villages. This is well demonstrated in the following extract from a Hanoi paper.

> My friend was present at a card party where landlords and farmers sat together with no sign of hostility towards each other. One of the landlords, on picking a certain card, patted the farmer sitting next to him, saying: 'If only I had drawn this card earlier, what would have happened?' This scene typifies what was happening in the villages immediately after the inception of Rectification of Errors. Card parties such as this were invariably accompanied by banquets for which pigs, chickens and dogs were slaughtered. The players continued their card games all night long, and obliged the vendors of food to remain awake and serve them.
>
> (*Thoi Moi*, May 12, 1957)

In many villages there was an atmosphere of festivity where rich and poor alike rejoiced at the prospect of having all previous 'errors' rectified, and a normal way of life restored to the community. But this was not quite what the party intended. Its idea was to restrict 'rectification' to a limited number of specified errors, while maintaining mutual hatred and suspicion between various classes of society. The authority given to new party members was also to be upheld.

In some areas public anger, aggravated by bitter despair, led to open revolt. There were reports from several areas (Bac-Ninh, Nam-Dinh, for example) of peasant uprisings, but according to the official sources 'serious trouble was avoided by the tact of soldiers and cadres'. This simply meant that, in troubled areas, three soldiers were permanently billeted in every peasant house. In November 1956, however, the official press admitted that there had been an armed revolt in the Quynh-Luu district of Nghe-An province. The whole story was told later to press correspondents by a group of defeated rebels who managed to escape by boat into South Vietnam. They reported that twenty thousand peasants, armed only with sticks and other crude weapons, had fought against a whole division of regular troops.

There is no real possibility of a successful uprising against the new régime. One fact alone makes it virtually impossible. After Land Reform, blacksmiths, who travelled from village to village repairing agricultural implements for the peasants, were formed into groups and concentrated in certain areas where they worked under the direct control of the Trade Office. Their entire production, down to the sale and distribution of even the smallest article, is now controlled the state. It is obvious that, under these circumstances, the secret production of weapons is well-nigh impossible. Moreover, the blacksmiths who once forged weapons for the communists find themselves forbidden to do this now by the same communists, who are well versed in matters of revolution and consequently know very well how to prevent revolts against their own rule.

THE INTELLECTUALS

While peasants in the villages were fighting against the party cadres and the People's Army, intellectuals in the cities were not inactive. Through their writings they made a courageous attack on the party's leaders and, strange as it may seem, it was their efforts that met with most success. Although their successes were quite ephemeral, they made a lasting impression upon the Vietnamese mind. The participants in this revolt were exclusively intellectuals who had played an active part in the Resistance war and had returned from the guerrilla zone a year or two previously. It is well known that during their period of active service they suffered considerable hardship and discomfort. Living deep in the jungle, many of them contracted malaria, amoebic dysentery and other unpleasant tropical diseases which, after nine years without treatment, often became chronic. They were badly paid and had practically nothing to eat but cassava roots and the bamboo shoots which they collected in the forest. Many of them were fully aware that by supporting the Vietminh government they were working against their own interests. They realised that they could expect no brilliant future under the new régime; this became all too obvious after the arrival of the Chinese advisers in 1950, particularly after Land Reform, when the party placed its confidence almost entirely in 'poor peasants'. The intellectuals often described themselves as the 'concubines of the régime', indicating that the party had 'flirted' with them without any intention of marrying them. 'Marriage' was an honour apparently reserved for peasants and workers. The difference between the 'one who shares the warm blanket and the one who lies in the cold', as a Vietnamese expression puts it, was emphasised by Nguyen Manh Tuong in this extract from his speech:

> Intellectuals who joined the Resistance . . . were bitterly disillusioned when they realised that the party had no confidence in them, despite the many sacrifices they had made for the party. Have they been too demanding? Have they asked to be made ministers or ambassadors? No, they haven't. The majority of the intellectuals are not ambitious and would willingly give these positions to politicians and party members. They simply wish to give the benefit of their qualifications and experience to the service of the people, and to safeguard their honour and freedom of thought which they believe to be essential to the dignity of the intellectual.[2]

Phan Khoi, a veteran journalist, sought to clarify the position of the intellectuals in another way. He asked his friends to chew some locally made sweets while drinking their coffee (there was no refined sugar in the communist zone). 'The sweets represent patriotism,' he explained to his friends, 'they serve to offset the bitterness of the coffee, which may be likened to party leadership, while allowing us to enjoy the aroma of the coffee which is comparable to the dignity of the intellectuals.'

Among the many humiliations endured for years by the intel-

[2] Nguyen Manh Tuong, 'Concerning Mistakes Committed in Land Reform', quoted by Hoang Van Chi in *The New Class in North Vietnam.*

lectuals was the insulting arrogance of party cadres, whose attitude
is depicted by an anonymous writer in the following poem:

> *The Blustering Leader*
> As yet unskilled in arts and letters,
> He tried, nevertheless, to teach and criticise,
> Quoting parrot-fashion, half-understood passages from books.
> His heart is dry as firewood,
> And his criticism smells as bad as burned rice.
> When questioned, and being unable to reply,
> He beats his chest and waves the party in his hands,
> Attempting to intimidate his audience.[3]

This kind of intellectual oppression was accompanied by a score
of other spiteful actions, and the constant tyranny had a terrifying
effect upon the victim's mind. Another poet has described it vividly
in an open letter to his immediate superior:

> One night, in a dream, I felt your hands, with their long-
> nailed fingers, seize my neck and drag me into a dark pit.
> Another night, I dreamt you were a raven which grasped
> me in its talons and carried me away, rather as the eagle
> carries away the princess in the fairy tale. I uttered inarticu-
> late sounds, and ground my teeth during those terrible
> nightmares.[4]

The sudden decline of both their social and material standing
after the communist régime was well established was another
factor which led the intellectuals to rebellion. The following passage from the 'Report on Writers and Artists' read by Hoang Hue
before the National Congress of Arts and Letters of 1956, may
provide the reader with some idea of the living conditions of
'Resistance intellectuals' in Hanoi, after their return from the
guerrilla zone:

> Everyone knows that our living standards are deplorable.
> The truth of this is, unhappily, so obvious as to make even

[3] *Van Hoc* (literary magazine published in Hanoi), No. 24,
October 10, 1957.
[4] Tran Le Van, 'Letter to a Former Friend', in *Giai Pham Mua
Thu*, No. 2, October 1956.

the most simple-minded person stop and think. It is true to say that there are many writers who cannot afford so much as a cup of coffee when they have been working late into the night. Moreover, there are poets who have not enough money to buy themselves a cigarette; there is the case of the playwright who was obliged to pawn his watch in order to buy food for himself while finishing his play, but even after the play was published he had not the means with which to recover it. Huu Loan tells us that his one desire is to own an oil lamp so that he might work at night in the one room where he lives with his wife and children.[5]

The situation was aggravated by the fact that another group, acting as 'cadres in Arts and Letters', was living in contrasting affluence. This, according to the same report, was how this favoured section lived:

> They wear red neckties, leather shoes, and spend their time delivering speeches and attending banquets, where they eat in a very coarse and ill-mannered way. Having eaten, they pack their suitcases and depart elsewhere—gone with the wind.[6]

The truth of the report has been confirmed by Nguyen Tuan, a 'cadre in Arts and Letters' who, on returning from Helsinki where he attended a World Peace Conference, had the audacity to boast of the princely life he led abroad. He described:

> three meals a day, consisting of tasty and nourishing food. Dinner was very formal, served on beautiful china and crystal, with snow-white napkins, while an orchestra played. We were waited upon by women as beautiful as princesses in a fairy tale.[7]

The great difference between the two groups, both in political stature and material conditions, formed an 'antagonistic contradiction' between them (this conforms with Marxist theories) and not, as Mao claimed in his *New Democracy*, a so-called 'non-antagonistic contradiction'. Rebellion against such social and political injustice

[5] *Giai Pham Mua Thu*, No. 2, October 1956.
[6] *Ibid.*
[7] Article in *Van Hoc*, No. 1, May 10, 1957.

was only a matter of time, and the opportunity came when the de-Stalinisation campaign was launched in Moscow in 1956 by Nikita Khrushchev. The Soviet leader's speech produced a chain-reaction which reached North Vietnam only a month later. The Minh Duc publishing house, which had published communist official documents in the guerrilla zone, lost no time in publishing *Giai Pham*[8] (Selection of Belles Lettres), which included an attack on the national leader, Ho Chi Minh. It was thinly disguised as an innocuous poem by Le Dat about a lime-pot, a vessel to be found in every household and used by betel-chewers. The poem ended:

> People who live too long
> Are like lime-pots.
> The longer they live
> The worse they grow
> And the narrower they become.

The insides of lime-pots do indeed become narrower owing to the carbonatation of the lime; in time they become quite unserviceable and have to be replaced. But the process is very slow and a family might have the same lime-pot for more than a generation. There is always one in some corner of every Vietnamese living-room. It is witness to all the family events: births, marriages and deaths and other special events. Many superstitious people believe that the pot possesses a soul and refer to it as 'Mr Lime-pot'; and when it is of no further use, place it under some ancient tree and pay it reverence. By drawing a parallel between ageing people and lime-pots, Le Dat was undoubtedly attacking the personality-cult, the adulation of leaders who had ceased to benefit their country despite notable achievements in the past. The poem was immediately recognised as an attack on the ageing Ho Chi Minh, whose patriotism was obviously waning as he grew older. The man who

---

[8] There were, in all, four issues of *Giai Pham*: the first, bearing simply this title, without any reference to season, came out in March 1956. It is convenient to call it the spring issue. The second, entitled *Giai Pham Mua Thu*, No. I, or summer issue, appeared in August 1956. The third, No. II, or autumn issue, came out in October, and the fourth, No. III (which was, unfortunately, the last), appeared in December as the winter issue.

had begun his revolutionary career as a patriot, even calling himself Nguyen the Patriot, had finally allied himself with the 'Big Brothers' rather than with his own people.

The party at once recognised the implications of the poem and, not long after it was published, the publication was seized and one of its most frequent contributors (Tran Dan) put in prison. North Vietnamese leaders were, at that time (March 1956), reluctant to follow Moscow in the de-Stalinisation policy. Land Reform was still in full swing in the Tongking delta, and the party considered it ill-advised to introduce any 'liberal' measure before the program was completed. It was important that full terror be maintained for a few more months. Thus, it was not until August that the 'personality-cult' was officially denounced. Meanwhile, the Polish workers had rebelled in Poznan (June 28, 1956) and Mao had begun his 'Hundred Flowers' campaign. These things increased the already tense situation in North Vietnam. When, after a delay of five months, Rectification of Errors was finally announced, the intellectuals in Hanoi had reached the end of their patience and were ready to launch an all-out attack against the régime.

Giai Pham Mua Thu, reappearing in a new guise, carried in its summer issue of August 29, 1956, a poem which ended with a call addressed to the whole nation:

> You, who defeated invaders
> And did not bow down
> Under colonial domination,
> Why do you bear with these villains
> Who shame our Fatherland?

The response was immediate. All writers and artists of talent, young and old, whether party members or not, joined in the fight. A week later there appeared *Nhan Van* (Humanities), a weekly paper serving as mouthpiece for the opposition. Oddly enough, the chief editor was Nguyen Huu Dang, a communist of long standing who had at one time been Minister of Culture. The contributors who submitted the most violent articles belonged to a group of young writers who were all party members. But the writer whose style and sound argument far surpassed all others was Phan Khoi, a septuagenarian writer whose knowledge of the Vietnamese,

Chinese and French languages was outstanding. Grandson of Hoang Dieu, the governor of Hanoi, who hanged himself when the city was captured by the French in 1883, Phan Khoi had participated in the Scholars' Movement of 1907, of which he was, after 1947, the sole survivor. Phan Khoi was also the sole Confucian scholar of note who survived the Land Reform, almost all such scholars having been ruthlessly liquidated during that campaign. Thus, this earlier offspring of a brilliant, disappearing race became, during the last years of his life, a lonely fighter making a last attempt to defend Confucianism against the merciless attack of Marxism.

During his forty years in journalism, Phan Khoi was known to be extremely outspoken and a virulent polemicist. Now he boldly attacked the 'leadership in Arts and Letters', going on, in company with younger writers, to accuse the party of nepotism, despotism, corruption and oppression. The very dogma of Marxism was repeatedly rejected and the sincerity of the party's leaders called in question. University students joined in the fight and issued their review, *Dat Moi* (New Land), in which they accused the party cadres of monopolising the 'bourgeois' girl students. All forms of literary composition were employed: poems, short stories, sketches, rapportage, fiction and editorial comment. Finally, Dr Tuong, a lawyer representing this group of intellectuals, delivered a speech to the National Congress of the Fatherland Front in Hanoi on October 30, 1956, in which he vehemently condemned the whole régime.

These writings are rich in information, revealing all aspects of the communist régime in North Vietnam. At the same time they are beautifully written and well deserve the title, borrowed from the Chinese, of 'the Hundred Flowers'. They are masterpieces of Vietnamese literature. By comparison with the 'flowers' blooming at that time in other communist countries, the Vietnamese species are, if anything, even more valuable and significant. This is probably due to the fact that Vietnamese writers have combined the literary traditions of both their former rulers (the French and the Chinese) with the humour which is characteristic of the Vietnamese race. Ten years of compulsory Marxist studies and political indoctrination must also have taught them how to reinforce their arguments, particularly in criticism of communist policy. Truong Tuu, a self-taught writer, gave an example of this when he attacked the party's policy in a series of articles published in *Van Hoc*, basing his arguments on many of the writings of Marx and Lenin which he quoted from memory without giving references. It took a full three months for the party to be in a position to reply to his attack; without references, they could not be sure whether or not Marx and Lenin had written the passages cited by Truong Tuu. The whole series of articles was sent by officials of the party to Moscow with a request for verification and a draft reply.

There is not room in this book, unfortunately, to reproduce any of these excellent works in full. Readers who would like to study them in detail should refer to the White Paper entitled *The Hundred Flowers Blooming in North Vietnam*, published in its original version by the 'Front for the Defence of Cultural Freedom' in Saigon in 1958.[9] Part of this has been translated by the present author and included in his *New Class in North Vietnam*, published by Cong Dan, Saigon, 1958. The following outline of some of the most outstanding pieces will give the reader a general idea of the character of this short-lived flowering of free literary expression in North Vietnam.

1. *The Giants* by Tran Duy. This is a legend which tells the story of a group of giants created by God for the purpose of helping mankind to fight the devils. But, though they fought the devils bravely, the giants had, by an oversight, been created without hearts; consequently they caused tremendous havoc among the men they had been sent to help. Without realising what they were doing, they trampled over and killed more men than devils. The meaning behind this legend is not hard to detect. God represents Marx and the giants are the communist leaders; the havoc created by them is an allusion to the massacres occurring during Land Reform. (Tran Duy, *Giai Pham Mua Thu*, No. 2, autumn issue, October 1956.)

2. *The Robot Poet*, by Nhu Mai, is a vision of the future rather in the manner of George Orwell's *1984*, in which the

[9] *Tram Hoa Dua No*, published by Mat Tran Bao Ve Tu Do Van Hoa, Saigon, 1959.

author predicts the creation of robots to replace the rebellious poets. These machines are capable of producing 'more than 8,ooo verses per second at the touch of a button'. Describing the poetry produced, the author writes: 'Each poem starts: *"The happy age . . ."*, then continues with such expressions as *"Red Flag"* . . . *"Drum beating"* . . . *"Workers' hands"*, finishing every time with *"Be enthusiastic . . . Go ahead".'* (Nhu Mai, *Nhan Van*, No. 5, Hanoi, November 30, 1956.)

3. *I Seek You Forever* is a poem by Ta Huu Thien in which he looks at girls of every walk of life and expresses sorrow at not being able to marry any of them, because the indoctrination of all young people has caused them to lose all capacity for love and personal feelings. (Ta Huu Thien, *Tram Hoa*, Hanoi, January 6, 1957.)

4. *The Old Horse* by Phung Cung. This is the story of a magnificent racehorse which was used as a draught animal in the Queen's service. The horse was overfed and lacked its former daily training, with the result that, when returned to the racecourse, it was left far behind by all the other runners. The story is a dig at 'cadres in Arts and Letters', whose talents fade when they attain privileged positions. (Phung Cung, *Nhan Van*, No. 4, Hanoi, November 5, 1956.)

This period of relative freedom of expression, during which communism was attacked in almost the same way as the Church had been attacked by Voltaire two centuries earlier, was unfortunately not destined to last more than three months. At first, the DRV's leaders hesitated over the best course to adopt, and temporarily relaxed their control. They had to decide between continued toleration, which they knew in the end would mean the collapse of their system, and further repressive measures, which would be contrary to the line agreed on at the Twentieth Congress of the Soviet Communist Party. But after Khrushchev smashed the Hungarian revolt in October 1956, they regained confidence. The peasants' uprising in Nghe-An and the revolt of the intellectuals in Hanoi were firmly suppressed. Unrest among the workers was similarly put down.

The struggle between the party and the opposition can be divided into three stages, each lasting about a month. During the first stage, the opposition attacked 'sycophants' and 'cadres in Arts and Letters', exposed cases of corruption and nepotism and so forth. In this first stage, the party did not retaliate. On the contrary, one or two official publications joined with the opposition in denouncing mistakes which they attributed to minor officials and low-ranking cadres.

During the second stage, the opposition turned their attack upon certain party leaders. This time, the party counter-attacked by publishing a series of articles written by one or two pro-party intellectuals. Their arguments were, naturally, extremely weak and made little impression. On one point concerning the Leninist conception of Arts and Letters, Hoang Xuan Nhi, a university professor defending the party, was utterly defeated by one of his own pupils. The latter refuted all Nhi's arguments, quoting Lenin to support his case, and then went on to say: 'Either Mr Nhi has failed to understand Lenin's writings or he merely uses them to sustain his fallacious arguments. In either case he lacks intellectual honesty. . . . I would like to suggest to Mr Nhi that he study harder and think more, so that he might preserve the natural honesty which characterises an intellectual.'[10] Nhi remained silent and the party abandoned the fight, since it had no apologist capable of confounding the arguments put forward.

During the third stage, the opposition began to criticise the party's policy as a whole, and this time the party resorted to illegal ways of defending itself. The purchase of newsprint was forbidden to opposition newspapers, and bookshops found selling these papers got into serious trouble with the police. Party cadres went from house to house advising people against reading these papers, and finally the trade union ordered its printing workers not to print Nhan Van. But meanwhile dissatisfaction was growing among the population. Workers from South Vietnam attacked the police station in Hanoi, and students in Moc village openly rebelled and barricaded the road between Hanoi and Hadong. When the sixth edition of Nhan Van was being prepared, in which the people of Hanoi were called on to demonstrate in the streets against the régime, the party closed the paper and arrested those responsible for its publication. The opposition was thus

[10] Bui Quang Doai, 'Hoang Xuan Nhi's Humanism', Nhan Van, No. 4, November 5, 1956.

silenced and at the same time the party accused its opponents of being spies and saboteurs and the like. It immediately started a national campaign of 'Thought Reform', accompanied by the usual individual confessions. Some months later the 'Reform by Manual Labour' campaign was launched.

In theory all intellectuals, whether pro- or anti-party, were forced to join the movement and accept manual work either in the factories or on the land. In practice, pro-party intellectuals were sent to factories in the large towns such as Hanoi or Haiphong, where they enjoyed a fairly comfortable life; after a while they were told that they had fulfilled their task and were allowed to return home. On the other hand, former members of the opposition group and those connected with it were sent to remote villages in the malaria-ridden highlands, where they were made to work under the control of minority tribesmen. Thus many of the intellectuals who had lived in the jungle during the Resistance found themselves back there after a brief interval of two years. But there was a notable difference. During the Resistance period they had enjoyed the support and sympathy of the local inhabitants, but this time they were treated more as political prisoners. The minority tribes inhabiting the area had been well indoctrinated by the communists in 1941, when the first Vietminh guerrilla bases were established in their country, and again during the Resistance period. Since they were culturally backward, they accepted the teaching of the communist leaders far more readily than did the Vietnamese living in the delta. (It is significant that Ho Chi Minh's bodyguard is composed almost entirely of soldiers recruited from minority tribes.) Having sent the anti-party intellectuals to live amongst these tribesmen, the party could rest assured that escape was virtually impossible. Moreover, there was very little chance that the rebellious intellectuals might convert the tribespeople to their way of thinking, since most of the latter spoke no Vietnamese.

A member of the group, the poet Yen Lan, wrote the following passage in a letter to the magazine *Van Hoc*, describing the place where he had been sent:

On arrival here, I noticed a scarcity of children in relation to the number of adults, for infant mortality in this area is excessively high. A great many of the inhabitants have legs which are so swollen that they resemble those of elephants...

(*Van Hoc*, No. 9, August 16, 1958)

Another letter from Hoang Chuong, an actor regrouped from the South, gives a further description of the kind of work the intellectuals were required to do:

We live about three kilometres from the fields where we work. We make a great effort to rise very early in the morning in order to avoid carrying manure to the field in the glaring sun. We carry it on our shoulders [by means of a pole], and Thu, a Hanoi girl, who previously knew little of how to carry anything in this manner, is now able to carry up to twenty kilos [36 lb]. (*Ibid.*)

Many of these unfortunate intellectuals never returned home and have not been heard of again. The ones who were eventually allowed to rejoin their families were given jobs other than teaching, writing or painting. A large number of them are reported to have committed suicide. After the coup, the party from time to time reorganised the leadership in the Association of Arts and Letters, with the result that there is now no trace of either art or literature in the controlled press. At present, literary magazines published in Hanoi are normally in two sections, the first containing a few unsavoury articles by party cadres, while the second is reserved exclusively for short stories and the like, translated from other communist literature.

EIGHTEEN

Resumption of Collectivisation

Following the suppression of the peasant uprising in Nghe-An and the intellectuals' revolt in Hanoi, the party returned to its former policy in order to complete the setting up of a collectivist pattern of life. Tremendous efforts have been made in the country-side to organise co-operative farms, to fight against flood and drought, and to dig canals and build roads. Peasants work in teams, less for themselves than for the communist State. When the bell rings at six each morning, they set out to work in the fields, returning home for lunch, followed by classes, at 11 a.m. Then back to the fields at 1 p.m., where they remain until six in the evening. During the evening they must attend meetings for the purpose of reporting on one another's work and receiving orders for the following day. When the rice is harvested, the crop is immediately divided by the co-operative, which collects it into four parts. The first is for tax payment, the second for sale to the Trade Office at requisitioned prices, the third pays off debts owing to the National Bank and other State agencies, and the fourth is divided among the co-operative's members. Consequently everyone is undernourished, but no one is actually starving. It is significant that production per unit is continually decreasing, and this must spring from the fact that the peasants, having no incentive for individual profit, have grown careless about their work, particu-larly when it comes to replanting the rice and keeping water in the ricefields. The result of such negligence is that the rice does not get sufficient water to ensure normal growth and fructification. Communist leaders in China and Vietnam are faced with a problem not shared by other communist countries, in that rice, being a wet crop, cannot easily be adapted to the communist pattern of life.[1]

In the few towns remaining, the DRV authorities have successfully achieved the ruin of the urban bourgeoisie by a series of measures, the most important of which are:

1. A *special tax imposed on goods 'remaining in store'*. A few days after the communist take-over in Hanoi, a huge army of cadres was sent to all the shops to list all goods 'remaining in store' and impose on them a special tax called the 'remaining-in-store tax'. The amount, which largely exceeded the price of the goods, was demanded without delay for payment in 'Indochinese banknotes'.

2. *The changing of banknotes*. The government ordered the entire population to exchange its banknotes for newly-issued currency. But they only received a small amount of the new money in return. The same measure was applied to gold and silver articles.

3. *The formation of [so-called] State and Private Joint Enterprises*, where the former owners were kept on as managers. The result of this system has been so effective that an article in *To Quoc* of February 1960 boasted that 'our former private entrepeneurs are at present outwardly almost identical to comrade workers'.

All these measures have been described in detail by Gérard Tongas, who was living in Hanoi at the time, in his book, *L'Enfer Communiste au Nord Vietnam*.

Collectivisation has, therefore, been completed. But one point deserves particular attention. *People's communes* have not yet been introduced into North Vietnam. This is significant, for from the Land Reform campaign up to the introduction of co-operatives (passing through the various forms of 'mutual-aid teams'), the DRV has always followed Red China step by step, about two years behind. Although Ton Duc Thang, chairman of the North Vietnam National Assembly, stated in Peking in 1956 that 'the China

[1] See Hoang Van Chi, 'Collectivisation and Rice Production', *The China Quarterly* (London), No. 9, January-March 1962.

of today is the Vietnam of tomorrow', Vietnam is still marking time in the 'co-operative' stage, six years after China has enforced the people's communes. It would seem that this cautious attitude has been advised by Khrushchev, who does not approve of the system of people's communes.

It should be noted in passing that while communist orthodoxy preaches workers' and peasants' communes without recommending any form of military training for commune members, Mao makes his communes a form of military colony. It seems that he has been influenced not only by Lenin, but also by T'sao T'sao, the Chinese dictator who planted military-agrarian colonies throughout China in the third century AD.[2] Two facts corroborate this impression: first, during the Yenan period, Mao's soldiers had their own 'agricultural bases'; and secondly, Mao has never ceased, over the last thirty years, to defend and rehabilitate T'sao T'sao, whom traditional Chinese writers have described as a villainous character.

It is likely that this refusal to follow Mao in his biggest 'leap forward' has saved North Vietnam from China's terrible disaster of an exceptional and unprecedentedly widespread famine. There are, nonetheless, close similarities in the food situation in the two countries. To use a simple image, one might say that, while China has boldly 'leapt' straight into famine, North Vietnam is 'walking' slowly but surely to the same goal. The following extract from the Hanoi press leaves no doubt that North Vietnam is already in the grip of a severe food shortage:

> ... Each time they [workers of a certain spinning mill] wish to buy their ration of rice, they are obliged to take half a day's leave from the mill. Sometimes, when the crowds waiting to buy their rice are too great, the workers are forced to take several of these half-day leaves in succession before they can get their ration.   (Thoi Moi, September 7, 1961)

There has been a similar decline in the production of animal foodstuffs. According to Nhan Dan, May 7, 1962, the consumption of meat per capita in 1961 was 6.2 kilos [13¼ lb] and of cotton

---

[2] See L. Carrington Goodrich, A Short History of the Chinese People, third edition, Harper Brothers, New York, p. 58.

cloth 4.8 metres [approximately 15½ feet]. Thus, if these figures
are correct, the average Vietnamese would have eaten 17 grams
[or slightly more than half an ounce] of meat a day and have
worn a single suit of pyjamas all the year round. But according
to French soldiers who returned to France in December 1962,
having deserted to the Vietminh during the war, these ration
allowances are available only to town dwellers, not to peasants.

Such a situation is, in the last analysis, the predictable consequence of the two Land Reform campaigns followed by almost a
decade of forced collectivisation.

Mao's program of gradual communisation can be summed up in
nine stages, as follows:

1. *Agricultural Tax* campaign: ruin of the landed bourgeoisie.
2. *Political Struggle* campaign: nationwide political purge.
3. *Land Rent Reduction* campaign ⎫
4. *Land Reform* campaign proper   ⎬ Land Reform
5. *Seasonal Mutual-aid teams*   ⎭
6. *Year-round Mutual-aid teams*   ⎫
7. *Co-operatives: first stage*   ⎬ Land Collectivisation
8. *Co-operatives: second stage.*   ⎭
9. *Communes*

In the program for co-operatives, the first stage permits peasants
to be paid a small sum proportional to the land-surface they have
pooled in the co-operative; in the second stage, they are paid solely
on the basis of their individual work. This second stage leads into
the final stage of the process of land collectivisation: the commune,
i.e. peasants living together in agro-military camps.

Each stage in the campaign is initiated about one year after the
implementation of the preceding stage. It is prepared by a
're-education course' and may be followed by a 'rectification of
errors' campaign. The intensity of the re-education and rectification depends largely on the severity by which the stage they are
associated with is implemented. The whole process, accordingly,
takes about ten years to be fulfilled.

The fact that North Vietnam is still marking time in the co-
operative stage, reaching the second phase only in 1962, consti-

tutes an anomalous variation of Mao's program. This may be the result of two intervening factors: pressure from Moscow, and cautious concern not to reveal the régime as totally communist before South Vietnam is 'liberated'. We may therefore assume that the present situation will not last long, particularly since North Vietnam is now openly siding with Peking in the Sino-Soviet dispute. Provided a second Dien Bien Phu victory can be scored in South Vietnam, the DRV's leaders will then be in a position to pass on to the final stage of the Chinese program, that of the popular communes.

As this book goes to press, the situation in South Vietnam is becoming increasingly complex. The mass uprising of Buddhist monks in Hué and Saigon has produced a new challenge to the Diem régime, the consequences of which, at the time of writing, it is not possible to assess. But one thing appears clear: Buddhism, whose philosophy of tolerance made it seem a dormant force which no politician need take account of, now seems likely to play a decisive rôle in the future reunification of Vietnam.

*

The story I have related is that of a small nation which has heroically resisted assimilation by China for two thousand years; a nation which has scored the most brilliant victory in the modern history of anti-colonialism. Its escape from foreign domination of one kind has, however, been followed by foreign domination of a different kind. Its intelligentsia lacks cultural self-confidence, while its political leaders are ever willing to neglect, and indeed to betray, the national cause.

The result is what we have seen. The country is partitioned into two conflicting halves led by two mutually antagonistic governments. The North is enduring the painful experience of Maoism, while the South, in a fit of reaction, has slipped back into medievalism. In both zones people are unfree, and the democratically-minded elements are mouldering impotently either in concentration camps or in self-imposed exile.

'Every people gets the régime it merits,' said Engels. But in this particular case the Vietnamese are not alone to blame for the régimes under which they live. The Allies supported the Vietminh during the Second World War and provided the communists with their opportunity to emerge as a government. The same powers are still, at present, supporting a highly reactionary government in the South, thus making a propaganda gift to communist subversion.

Is it too much to hope that such a disastrous policy, due either to gross miscalculation or to sheer stupidity, will be reversed, so as to invalidate, just for once, the communist dictum according to which 'capitalists and imperialists' invariably side with feudalists and reactionaries? What is needed is a change in Western policy towards the régime in South Vietnam such as will give Vietnamese patriots the opportunity—lacking these last hundred years—of participating constructively in national affairs and permit the Vietnamese people to resume effectively their historic rôle as the defenders of the gateway to South-East Asia.

RECOMMENDED FURTHER READING

Vietnamese History and Culture

JOSEPH BUTTINGER: *The Smaller Dragon*. Frederick A. Praeger, New York, 1958; Stevens and Sons, London, 1958.

PIERRE HUARD and MAURICE DURAND: *Connaissance du Vietnam*. Imprimerie Nationale, Paris, 1956.

The War in Indochina

ALLAN B. COLE (editor): *Conflict in Indochina and International Repercussions*. Cornell University Press, Ithaca, New York.

BERNARD B. FALL: *Street Without Joy—Indochina at War 1946-63*. Third revised edition, Stackpole, Harrisburg, Pa., 1963; Pall Mall Press, London, 1963.

VO NGUYEN GIAP: *People's War, People's Army*. Frederick A. Praeger, New York, 1962; London, 1963.

ELLEN J. HAMMER: *The Struggle for Indochina*. Stanford University Press, 1954.

DONALD LANCASTER: *The Emancipation of French Indochina*. Oxford University Press, 1961.

PAUL MUS: *Vietnam—Sociologie d'une Guerre*. Editions du Seuil, Paris, 1952.

North Vietnam

BERNARD B. FALL: *The Viet Minh Régime*. First edition: Institute of Pacific Relations with Cornell University Press, 1954; second revised edition: Institute of Pacific Relations, 1956.

BERNARD B. FALL: *The Two Vietnams—A Political and Military History*. Frederick A. Praeger, New York, 1963; Pall Mall Press, London, 1963.

P. J. HONEY (editor): 'North Vietnam Today'. *The China Quarterly* (London), No. 9, January-March 1962; Frederick A. Praeger, New York, 1962.

GERARD TONGAS: *L'Enfer Communiste au Nord Vietnam*. Les Nouvelles Editions Debresse, Paris, 1960. An English translation is in preparation by Frederick A. Praeger, New York and Pall Mall Press, London.

South Vietnam

ROBERT SCIGLIANO: *South Vietnam: Nation Under Stress*. Houghton Mifflin, Boston, 1963.

Index

Agrarian Reform Law, 156
Agricultural Tax, 75-83, 205
Annam, 124, 149, 156, 202
Annamese Chain, 3, 4, 12, 64, 147
Annamese Communist Party, 47
Arts and Letters, 'leadership' in, 231, 234, 237, 239
Association of Revolutionary Youth, *see* Thanh-Nien

Bach Lien, 37
Bac-Ninh, province, 124, 186, 227
Bai Xay, 15
Bangkok, 17, 41, 47
Bao Dai, Emperor, 26, 35, 60, 61n., 143
Bazin, René, 23-4
Behaviour, correct, 139, 142-7
Berlin: Anti-Imperialist League, 47
Bigamy, 145-6, 219
Blum, Léon, 39
Borodin, Michael, 45-6
Brimmel, J. H., 26
British Intelligence Service, 50, 59
Buddha, Buddhism, 7, 117, 180, 183, 184, 187, 223, 244

Cachin, Marcel, 39
Cambodia, 4, 6, 10, 12-13, 49, 68, 84
Cameroons, 13
Canton, 14, 17-19, 40-4, 49, 110, 124
Champa kingdom, 6

Chaigneau, M., ix
Chang Tso-lin, 109
Chiang Kai-shek, 45-6, 61, 104, 109, 125, 153, 154n
Chi Chi-yu, 8
China, Chinese: communist methods 48-50, 57, 68, 92, 98-9, 103-4, 109, 119-23, 122, 124, 167, 169, 241-4; culture of, in Vietnam, 6-8, 15; dynasties and rulers, 4-5, 150; in Malaya and Indonesia, 5-6; military support for Vietnam, 63-4, 109, 125; People's Republic proclaimed, 63; threat from, 3-5, 14, 40-4; train and educate Vietnamese, 17-19, 25-6, 63, 112; troops disarm Japanese, 60
Chou En-lai, 110
Chungking, 125
Citizen-labour, 94, 98, 145
Co Am village, 25
Cochin China, 8, 10-13, 17, 23, 53, 149, 156
Cole, Allan B., 164n., 204n.
Communal lands, 201-4
Communist movement in Vietnam: beginnings, 14, 29ff., 41-53; collapse (1927), 47; Mao's program for, 243; reasons for success of, 67-8; six principal movements, 41; special techniques, 119-23;

three rival parties, 47, 49;
triumph of, 54-72; voluntarily disbanded (1945), 30, 61 (see also
Marxism)
Compradorist bourgeoisie, 103, 111
Confucianism, 7, 8, 15-16, 20, 43,
102, 112, 144, 147, 150, 186, 234
Control-discussion, 117-23; special
techniques of, 119-21, 139
Corneille, Pierre, 112
Correctional Training, 117, 122,
124-38 147, 151, 156-7; confessions
in, 136, 140, 143-4; five lessons of,
139-58; life-histories in, 135-6; list
of 'diseases', 143; organisation of
course, 129-35; three kinds, 126-7
Cuu Quoc newspaper, 76, 194, 199,
223

Dabezies, Pierre, 26n.
Daily Worker, 50
Dai-Viet Quoc-Dan Dang, 61
Dalat, 62
Dang Kim Giang, 146
Dang Lao-Dong, see Lao Dong
Dang Thai Mai, 54
Dang Van Huong, 95
Dang Van Viet, 96
Dat Moi, 234
Democratic Party, 69-70
Denunciation sessions, 180-8
De Tham, 15
Dien Bien Phu, 54n., 64-6, 102, 244
Divorce, 144-5, 218-19

Echo du Vietnam, 40n.
Education, 15-19, 68, 122 (see also
Correctional training)
Eichmann, 190
'Enemies of the people', 138, 150,
201
Engels, Friedrich, 244
Escoffier, Auguste, 38
Exhibitions, 200-1
Expropriation, 197-200

Fall, Bernard, 50n., 77
Fatherland Front (To-quoc), 70,
167, 190, 194, 234, 241
Feudalism, meaning of, 152n., 158

Fontainebleau Conferences, 32, 62
Forest Leaves, 188
Formosa, 12
France, French: conquests in Far
East, 6, 8-14; in Vietnam, 9ff., 59-
71, 98-9, 104-6, 109, 134-5, 140,
146-8, 200-1, 214-15; resistance
movements against, 14-26; revolt
planned against Japanese, 60;
plantations of, 157; Popular Front
Govt., 53, 55; recognises Republic
of Vietnam, 62, 68; southern
zone blockaded, 84-5 (see also
Resistance War)

Geneva Agreements, 65, 68, 106,
163
Giai Pham Mua Thu, 230n., 231n.,
232-3, 235
Gia Long, Emperor, ix, 11
Gianh River, 194
Giap, see Vo Nguyen Giap

Hadong, 237
Haiphong, 32, 163
Ham Nghi, Emperor, 15
Ha-Nam province, 202
Han culture, 3-5, 8
Han-hwa process, 5
Hankow, 46
Hanoi, 4, 8, 11, 30-2, 37, 43, 54-5,
59, 60, 124-6, 167, 190, 194, 202-5,
230-6, 239-41; Collège du Protec-
torat, 24n., exhibition at, 200;
intellectuals of, q.v.; May Day
celebrations, 55; police station
attacked, 237; university, 16, 22,
105; Viet-Nam Hotel, 23
Ha-Tinh province, 32, 214
Helsinki, 231
Hien, Lord, 8
Himalayas, 3-4
Hitler, Adolf, 190
Hoang Dieu, 234
Hoang Hue, 230
Hoang Huu Nam, see Phan Boi
Hoang Minh Giam, 146
Hoang Xuan Nhi, 237
Ho Chi Minh (Nguyen Ai Quoc), 6,
29-40, 109, 224, 238; question of

identity, 31-2; personality and training, 33-4; family of, 35-8; various names of, 36, 42; in London, 38; activities in Paris, 37-9, 62; joins Socialist party, 39; in Moscow, 40, 44-7, 51, 58, 110; in China, 40, 42-6, 58-9, 71; in Siam, 47-8; in Hong Kong, 18-19, 48-51; disappearance of, 50-1; becomes President of Vietnam, 31, 60-1; attacks French, 62-3, 69; in reign of terror, 97-9, 125-6, 130, 134, 142, 146, 148, 158, 173, 183, 189-90, 211, 213-14; book on *Rectification*, 142-3; attacked by intellectuals, 232-3 (*see also* Nguyen Ai Quoc)
Hoc Tap, 223
Hong Kong, 17-19, 34n., 48-51
Ho Tung Mau, 46, 59
Ho Viet Thang, 209
Hué, 20, 244
Hunan, 49, 52, 98, 122
Hundred Flowers movement, 111, 113, 180, 233-6
Hundred Yuëh, 5
Hung-Yen province, 202
Huu Loan, 231

India, 3, 142
Indochina: Communist Party, 30n., 47, 49, 50, 52, 58, 61, 69, 140; Communist Union, 47; French Union of, 10-14, 20, 54, 75
Intellectuals' revolt, 228-40
Inukai, *see* Ki T. Inukai
Isolation policy, 166, 179, 189-91, 196

Japan, Japanese: culture and qualities, 7-8, 17, 33-4; Military Academy, 17; occupation of Vietnam, 10, 20, 56-60, 67, 69; surrender of, 60, 67; war with China, 153

Karamichev, V. P., 203
Khrushchev, Nikita, 214, 232, 236, 242
Khublai Khan, 4

Kim-Liên village, 36
Ki Tsuyoshi Inukai, 5, 17
Kuomintang, 19, 23, 33, 40, 42, 45, 46, 50, 59, 61, 63, 67, 75, 104, 109, 125, 148-9

Labour Party, *see* Lao Dong
Lacouture, Jean, 51n.
Lam Duc Thu, 18-19, 46
Land Reform campaign, 34, 41, 72, 95, 98, 112, 134, 136-8, 147-208, 227; campaign proper, 163, 165, 192-208; deaths in, 166, 189-90, 213; distribution table, 149; divergence from China's, 148-51; indoctrination for, 147-8; landlord classification, 166, 172-4, 181; report on, 151-8; true purpose of, 212-13
Land Rent Reduction campaign, 152-5, 163-4, 168-92; denouncers in, 177, 222; six stages of, 171-89; trials in, 188-9
Lang Son, 17, 20, 71, 96
Lao Dong Party, 30n., 69, 71, 141, 150-1, 189
Laos, 4, 12-13, 47, 49, 68, 141, 167; French in, 10; invaded by Siamese, 13; provinces annexed to Vietnam, 13
Lao-tse, 117
League of East-Asian Peoples, 17
League of Human Rights, 16, 37
Leang-tche doctrine, 7, 8
Le Dat, 232
Le Du, 5
Lenin, Nikolai, 39-40, 48, 118, 148, 235, 237, 242
Le Thanh Khoi, 24, 25n.
Le Trong Nhi, 187
Le Van Hien, Mrs, 144
Lien-Viet Front, 69, 70, 173
Literature, 234-9
Lo-Giang village, 221
Lo Kwei-po, 63-5
Long March, The, 110, 124
Luang Prabang, 64-5
Lu Han, 25

MacMahon Line, 3

Madagascar, 60
Mai Ngoc Ngon, 37
Malaya, 5
Malenkov, Georgi, 183
Manufactures and trade, 84-5
Mao Tse-tung, 6, 12, 25, 41, 48, 50,
    52, 58, 62-3, 71, 110-12, 125, 183,
    190, 211, 233, 242; communist
    tactics of, 72, 99-100, 103-4, 122,
    127, 147-8, 150, 153; New Demo-
    cracy, 231; nine-stage program,
    243-4; system of taxes, 75
Marriage, 145, 217-19
Marty, Louis, 54n.
Marxism, 22, 24, 33, 39-40, 43-4, 53,
    55, 97, 111-15, 128, 148, 202, 215,
    231, 234-5; program of indoctrina-
    tion, 113-17
Medical care, 83, 191
Meiji Revolution, 7
Mekong River, 10, 12, 64
Mendès-France government, 65
Moc village, 237
Monarchist movement, 14-15
Montaigne, Michel de, 111
Montesquieu, Baron de, 15
Moscow, 40-1, 44-55, 58, 110, 116,
    127, 213, 232-3, 235
Moutet, Marius, 39, 62
Mus, Paul, 34

Nam-Dinh province, 202, 227
Nanking, 61, 126
'National bourgeoisie', 103
National Front, names of, 70
Nationalist movement, 14-26; Quoc-
    Dan Dang, 14, 20-6, 29-30, 44-5,
    61, 148
Nehru, Pandit, 4
Nghe-An province, 32-4, 36, 50, 92,
    187; conflict in, 224-5, 228, 236
Nghe-An Soviets, 41, 47-52
Ngo Dinh Diem, 35, 61n., 66n., 68,
    143
Ngo Duc Mau, 214
Ngo Tu Ha, 30n.
Ngu-Xa movement, 61
Nguyen overlordship, 11
Nguyen Ai Quoc, 6, 18-20, 39, 51;
    becomes Ho Chi Minh (q.v.),
    31-2, 59

Nguyen Cong Vien, see Lam Duc
    Thu
Nguyen Dinh Phap, 187
Nguyen Hai Than, 35, 61
Nguyen Hong Phong, 202
Nguyen Huu Dang, 233
Nguyen Khanh Toan, 51-2, 58-9,
    125
Nguyen Manh Tuong, 167, 190-1,
    213, 229
Nguyen Ngoc Bich, ix
Nguyen Sinh Huy (Tat Sac), 36-8
Nguyen Son, 58, 124-6
Nguyen Tat Dat, 37
Nguyen Thai Hoc, 22-5
Nguyen The Truyen, 38-9
Nguyen Thi Giang, 25
Nguyen Thuong Huyen, 18n.
Nguyen Ton Hoan, 61n.
Nguyen Truong To, 8
Nguyen Tuan, 231
Nguyen Van Huong, 223
Nguyen Van Huyen, 59
Nhan Dan newspaper, 194, 242; ex-
    tracts from, 178, 186, 204, 208,
    210, 215-16. 221. 225, 236; suppres-
    sion of, 237
Nhan Van, 233
Nhu Mai: The Robot Poet, 235-6
Noulens, Hilaire, 47

Organisation of the Aged, 173
Orwell, George, 235
Overseas Workers' Union, 38

Pan-Asian movement (Dong Du),
    14, 17-20
Paria, Le, 38
Paris, 22n., 32, 37-9, 41, 55, 61-2,
    65, 111
Pathet Lao, 13
Peasants' Association, 84, 174-6,
    179-81, 185, 193, 197, 205
Peasant uprisings, 50, 227-8, 240
Peking, 41, 63, 71, 116, 118, 122,
    125, 127
Peng Teh-huai, 124
Pham Giao, 146
Pham Huy Co, 61n.
Pham Van Dong, 43

Phan Boi Chau, 17-21, 35, 45, 60n.
Phan Chu Trinh, 16, 21, 37-8
Phan Dinh Phung, 15
Phan Khoi, 229, 233-4
Phan Quang Dan, 61
Phan Tu Nghia, 22n.
Phung Cung: *The Old Horse*, 236
Phung Quan, 180
'Political struggle', 90-101, 110, 169, 210
Populaire, Le, 39
Popular communes, 241-4
Popular Front, 41, 52-6
Population Classification Decree, 164-6, 171-2, 198
Potsdam Agreement, 60
Poulo Condore prison, 24, 36-7, 53, 187
Poznan, revolt in, 233
Private Schools and Scholars' movement, 14-17, 36-7, 234
Procès de la Colonisation Française, 38
'Proletarian dictatorship', 143

Quang Nam province, 11, 16
Quang-Ngai, 34
Quang Tri province, 167, 202
Quoc Dan Dong (VNQDD), *see* Nationalist movement

Rassemblement, newspaper, 55
'Rectification of errors', 72, 80-1, 95, 98, 126, 191, 194, 198, 209-20, 225-7, 233; list of errors, 209-10, 215; Memorandum re husbands and wives, 217-19; object of, 224
Red River, 10, 64
'Regression' (adultery), 143-7
Reform by manual labour, 238
Resistance War (1946-54), 41, 62-8, 71, 101, 112
Romance of the Three Kingdoms, 110
Rousseau, J.-J., 15, 143

Sagan, Françoise, 143
Saigon, 36-8, 39n., 54, 59n., 235; British landing in, 60; Buddhist uprising, 244

Saint-Just, Louis Antoine de, 34, 36
Salan, General, 32
Scholars' movement, *see* Private Schools
Shanghai, 16, 18, 41, 48, 104, 110
Siam, Siamese, 13, 47-8
Singapore, 5, 17, 50
Sinn Fein, 21
Socialist Party, 69-70
Song Ma delta, 65
Son-La province, 146
Soviet Russia, 12, 68, 243
Special People's Tribunal, 166, 188-9, 197
Stalin, Josef, 44, 48, 52, 125, 148, 191, 213, 232-3
Students' Movement, 21, 43, 124
Sun Tzu, 66
Sun Yat-sen, 5, 17, 23, 42, 46

Ta Huu Thien: *I Seek You Forever*, 236
Tan-Viet Party, 47, 54
Tassigny, De Lattre de, 65
Taxes, 75-89, 241
Tay-Bac campaign, 146
Tay Son brothers, 11
Thai Binh province, 19, 202
Thai-Ha suburb, 37
Thailand, 4, 47n.
Thai-Nguyen, 17, 67
Thai tribes, 167
Thakhek, 64
Thanh-Hoa province, 65-6, 105, 187
Thanh-Nien (Assoc. of Revolutionary Young Comrades), 18-19, 29, 41-7; newspaper of, 44
Thoi Moi newspaper, 81, 178, 222, 225-7, 242
Thorez, Maurice, 52
Thought Reform, 72, 109-59, 180, 238
Three Together system (*San Tong*), 169
Tibet, 4, 10, 12
Tin Tuc newspaper, 55
Tokyo, 5, 17
Ton Duc Thang, 241
Tongas, Gérard, 166, 241
Tongking, 10-13, 23, 66, 124, 149, 156, 163, 202, 205

Tong Oanh, 18n.
To Quoc, see Fatherland Front
Tourane, 8
Trade Tax, 85-9, 104
'Traitors', 99, 101-6
Tram Hoa newspaper, 236
Tran Dan, 233
Tran Duc Thao, Prof., 111
Tran Duy: The Giants, 235
Tran Huy Lieu, 146
Tran Le Van, 230n.
Tran Van Lai, Dr, 13
Travail, Le, 54, 55
Trieu Phong, 202
Trinh Van Yen, 24n.
Trotskyites, 53-5
Truong Chinh, 55, 113-17, 125, 127, 130, 133-4, 168, 172, 209, 214; Report on agrarian reform, 151-8
Truong Tu Anh, 61
Truong Tun, 235
T'sao T'sao, 110, 242
Tsin-tsi, 54n.
Tu Duc, Emperor, 8, 152n.
Tuong, Dr, 234

Union Inter-coloniale, 38
USA, 3-4, 10, 35, 59-60, 68, 102, 111, 119; aid from, 141, 201

Van Hoc, 113n., 180n., 230n., 235, 238-9
Varenne, Alexandre, 20
Viet-Bac, 67, 121, 130
Vietcong, 59n., 66n.
Vietminh, 24n., 30-1, 41, 54n., 56-68, 70, 84-100, 109-10, 125, 150; foundation of Vietminh Front, 59; full name of, 59; organised opposition to, 61; 'Revolution', 35, 56
Vietnam: administration under French, 11-13; administration now, 68-9; British in, 60; diplomatic relations of, 10; French conquest of, 9-14; history and culture, 3-8; Japanese occupation, 20, 56-60; partition of, 10-11; peasants' revolt (1930), 50;

people's behaviour, present day, 122; phases of communist control, 69-72, 241; republic set up, 31, 60; revolution, causes of, 35 (see also below, and Communist movement, Nationalist movements, Resistance war)
Viet Nam Hon, newspaper, 38-9
Vietnam, North (Democratic Republic of Vietnam), 31, 60, 67-8, 77, 106, 141, 143, 151, 173, 199, 201-2, 236, 241, 243; Chinese in (1950), 85; exodus from, 163; literary expression, 232-6; number of deaths in, 166; present food situation, 242-3; reaction in, 232-9; reign of terror in, 90-8; Sino-Soviet dispute, sympathies in, 243
Viet Nam Quang-Phuc Hoi, 17
Vietnam, South, viii, x, 11, 66n., 68, 84, 143, 244; present ruler in, 35; reign of terror in, 98-100
Voltaire, 15, 236
Vo Nguyen Giap, 54, 62, 67, 125, 196, 209, 214
Vo Quy Huan, 32
Vu Hong Khanh, 26, 61
Vu Van Tien, 221

Wang Ching-wei, 46
Wang Yang-min, 7-8
Waseda University, 17
Weeping techniques, 120-2
Whampoa Acedemy, 17-19, 42, 45, 124
Wilson, Woodrow, 38-9
Wu-han government, 46

Xa-Thon Viet Nam, 149n., 156n., 202n.
Xuan Dieu, 91

Yangtze River, 5
Yenan, 51-2, 54n., 58-9, 110, 122, 125-6, 242
Yen Bay, 25
Yen Lan, 238
Youth Movement, see Thanh-Nien